Barefoot

A Surfer's View of the Universe

Andrew Pacholyk MS, L.Ac

author of *Lead Us To A Place ~ your spiritual journey through life's season*

Forward by Surfing Legend Joey Cabell

Barefoot: A Surfer's View of the Universe

by Andrew Pacholyk MS L.Ac

Editor: Danny DeCillis

Cover design: Robert Collison

Back cover photo: Jeanne Atkin MS L.Ac

Cover artwork image: Polina Reed
polina.cheliadinova@gmail.com
@polinareedart

ISBN 978-1-7353199-0-2
Library of Congress Control Number: 2022903532
Wellness Press, New York, NY

About the Author

Andrew Pacholyk is an American dancer/choreographer, director, and producer. His transition to a second career with a Masters and Doctoral degree as a licensed acupuncturist and healer seemed like an unlikely path. But his love for surfing and the sea was the catalyst that helped with his transformation.

Through life lessons of courage, conviction, and dedication, learned through the joys of surfing, Andrew's ability to see beyond the horizon gave him the curiosity to seek out more.

Andrew is the author of Lead Us To A Place ~ your spiritual journey through life's seasons, and the International Best Selling author of The Crystal Light Crystal Therapy Course and his popular Chakracology Course.

As an educator, he has taught and certified over 100,000 students worldwide in these specific healing techniques. His articles on spirituality, health, and wellness have been published all over the world in 30 languages.

Peacefulmind.com is the culmination of his 25 years in the metaphysical and healing arena.

Surfing has been his life-long love and passion taking him all over the world in search of the perfect wave.

Foreword by Joey Cabell

Ho'omaika'i 'ana and congratulations to Andrew for writing a well-rounded and real tale about the life of a surfer and his view of the Universe.

As a surfer who has traveled around the world, discovered the incredible joys the ocean offers, and found peace in endless summers, I have relived these amazing recollections through this mesmerizing memoir.

Andrew conveys in this exciting book, the most important elements I personally live by in surfing that is dedication, commitment, and earning respect. Being prepared and ready for what's ahead is not only the mantra of a surfer, but are important life lessons we should embrace.

You can feel Andrew's sheer commitment to the ocean. From his exceptional descriptions of the sea and breathtaking sunsets, to how caring, clean-up, and community play a big role in how we love and respect our planet. The self-realizations and discoveries Andrew find on his journey are both awkward and wonderful as he captures just how every one of us stumbles through the processes of life until we find that road to self-confidence, self-love, and self-awareness.

This book is an ode to the love and art of surfing. It elevates the manner and style in which surfing is intertwined with life. Lessons learned in the soup can be taken anywhere. I have personally applied these lessons to my business practices, my relationship, and my overall outlook on life. Surfing has given me the various traits everyone can learn from and that is being faithful, honest, and committed to everything you love.

Mahalo, Joey

Joey Cabell is named one of the top twenty-five surfers whose innovative surfing style changed the sport. ~ **Surfer Magazine**

Dedication

This book is dedicated to all those who *dare to go beyond* the comfort of their front door and make their *dreams a reality*. For anyone who's looked up at the stars and wondered where their place in life lies… for anyone who has looked out over the horizon and wondered what's waiting for them over that line… or for anyone who's ever felt like there is something more waiting for them around the corner… I dedicate this journey to you!

Find your inner confidence and step forward. Discover the passion inside *your* heart. Use your *fortitude and raw guts.* This is what makes you ~ you.

We are all on a pilgrimage. We start from the birth of our unconscious beginnings. We gather experiences throughout our life span, no matter how short or how long that span may run and are finally reunified with the Divine.

As we travel the path, we are no longer polarized between unconsciousness and conscious, but if we pay attention, we may realize we've stepped forward with a better sense of who we've become.

This realization is surely illumination. In the process, we can fully gain a conscious understanding of who we are and if we're lucky, how we've become a more integral part of that Divine.

Take that journey. Take that chance. Remember, it's always best if you follow your heart.

Steen A Suarez
(Big Steena)
24 November 1949 – 30 June 2016

Acknowledgements

The sea is a collective group of microorganisms that all work in conjunction with one another. We are all interconnected.

~ **to Libby, Martha Jayne, and Billy Barrett**, we shared some of my most memorable childhood adventures. You are the greatest inspiration for this book. Never forget how special you are in my life. Many, many thanks.

~ **to Aunt Martha,** you were the "Yang" to Andrena's "Yin." Two amazing sisters. Two very powerful forces in my life. My Aunt Martha's free spirit and willingness to see life like no one else, offered me great inspiration and confidence.

~ **to Andrena Pacholyk,** your gift of that "little book of stars" and allowing me to go to LA were treasures that altered my life. I'm grateful to you Mom.

~ to **Steven Pacholyk**, brother, you always inspire me to do my best. Caring, concerned, loving. You set exceptional examples for me every day. I love you.

~ **to Tonito,** for your constant love and support through this lifetime and the next, I am eternally grateful.

~ **to Polina Reed**, I cannot thank you enough for the most inspiring artwork you allowed me to use for this book cover. You are a brilliant artist and even more so, a beautiful soul.

~ **to Joey Cabell**, you've influenced my life in ways you may never know. You are a surfing legend. You are an amazing business man and an inspiration to millions. Thank you for writing the forward to my book. I am eternally grateful.

~ **to Lori Helfand,** like each celestial body that occupies space, we orbit on our trajectory passing the furthest reaches not ever sensing one another. Yet, sometimes we move passed those who influence our every gesture or leave a lasting impression in a short amount of time. Your brief presence in my life changed me forever. This is for you.

~ **to Frank Alkyer,** one of the coolest, laid-back cats I know. Although our time working together was brief, we shared lasting adventures on the other side of the world. You and Lori will always be in my heart.

Live for the Sun

"Surf's up!

The board glides 'cross the water's edge with elegance and grace...

between the perfect wave that rolls us up and glides us down its face.

It shows how we should roll with life, just taking on each ride.

As resistance drags and pulls us down and slows the flow of ebb and tide.

From dawn patrol with breaks of light that slowly stretch 'cross morning seas,

to late day sun that glows with joy and peace and all the hope we need.

This sun it offers us great life and symbolizes conscious thought,

reminding us as day is done, the precious lessons we've been taught.

I'm grateful every day for what I've learned, perched out here on my board,

For these are gifts I'll take with me, as trophies and a just reward.

~ Andrew Pacholyk MS L.Ac

Table of Contents

Barefoot

I am the "every man." Every man (woman or child) that has ever been drawn to the sea and surf.

I represent the collective soul seeker who has been called to the sea. The person that finds solace at the water's edge.

I am a surfer.

I am not a world-class champion nor a kook, but a person who has mastered his board and has enjoyed countless days dangling his feet in the water, searching for the perfect wave.

I never set out to do anything more than be able to stand up on my plank and catch a wave.

What I ended up experiencing was how a small microcosm *of humankind has become regarded as the epitome of the Universe.*

I have engaged in some of my most life-altering moments, barefoot. I am most connected to the earth and sea through the hundreds of sensors at the bottom of my shoeless feet. When I'm barefoot, I am grounded, centered, and feel my best sense of balance. I am connected to my board. I'm more aware of who I am, when I indelibly dig my feet into the sand.

'Barefoot' is my journey through life on the waves. It is a cathartic and self-realizing journey of how surfing changed my life and helped me find self-esteem, courage, and self-confidence. These values I have learned in the "soup" have helped me in relationships, business, and being comfortable in my own skin.

This is a story for anyone who has searched for answers in their life. With *Barefoot* you will discover a connection to your own struggles and a "board buddy" to help you navigate your way across uncharted waters.

Surf's up!

Introduction

Dawn Patrol

The pungent taste of salt christened my tongue as I hit the sea running. I always liked to get this blessing over with so that my body could adapt more quickly. As I dove into the frigid water, I could feel the back of my neck react to the brisk attack. My back zip, although covering me from neck to ankle, did not seem to keep me from feeling the Arctic blast that consumed my soul in that moment. "God, I hate cold water," I thought. "What we do for love."

I dashed a little further through the soup and then hopped on my longboard for the appropriate paddle out. I loved to pushout past the wave breaks to a point in the sea, that I knew was "the spot."

My cousin Bill was close behind me, paddling out like a stealth fighter, seen but not heard. I looked back over my shoulder to see if he was with me. He reached up and gave me a Shaka, so I knew he was alright. This is where we stood dawn patrol.

The sun was just starting to stretch and exert himself over the Eastern horizon. His fingers slowly creeping over each wave awakening the lazy seals that were lying languid on the rocks along the Northern face of the jagged mount protruding from the sea.

On shore you could see colonies of seagulls, perched in the sand facing its morning Master as he rose with grandeur from horizon's lip. They meditatively consumed the rays of sun that exalted them before flying onward and upward to address their daily tasks.

We stopped paddling and straddled the rails of our boards. We turned the round nose of the sticks to the sun and simply took it all in. Each minute of the rising sun seemed to introduce itself to a new part of the ocean, just waiting for its power to blend with its own. I loved drinking in this morning energy. I could sense the grit of salty air, the warmth of the sun on my chilled face, and the promise of a day that offered a new hope.

As my body became more and more acclimated to the water's brisk temperature, I could equally feel the sun's power, recharging my battery like no other source. I could not wait to get out here. These moments of peace seemed to allow all other obstacles in life to melt away. Life's stressors were burned off by the warmth and commanding rise of his Majesty, the Sun. At one point, Bill and I simultaneously looked at each other. That was the sign. Time to find the perfect barrel.

We paddled further Southeast to catch the roll of the waves as they would rise and fall with a reverence you would not often see.

It was a good day to be on the water.

The remnants of some wicked gales the night before, now seemed to move the waves in a more uniformed and respectful approach towards the white sand, waiting to receive them.

Bill caught the first wave. He looked over his shoulder and found what he was looking for. He rolled with the water to its lip and popped up just in time to embrace his first morning venture. He glided down over its welcoming edge and took command as if it had his name on it. He simply rode it all the way into shore. A perfect 10. Showoff. I've always adored my cousin. He was a month older than I and a few minutes shorter. His strong upper body was fit for surfing while his ingrained Pennsylvania accent, wild, chestnut brown hair, and constant joking always made him the life of any party.

It was my turn. Time to prove myself. My cousin was expecting nothing less. Unfortunately, I was not expecting anything close. I waited (and waited) for what I was hoping was the wave with my name on it. Growing impatient, I decided to charge a roll. I looked with intent at my target, popped up, and went over the edge. I could feel the wall looming behind me, chasing me down the mount. I inched my bare feet closer to the nose of the board, all the time, trying to keep my balance between nature's fury and my own mind, naturally seeming to work against me.

From my right came another wave, melding into my own, forcing a double up. This humpback wave suddenly caught me off balance, tossing me from my board. As I took a header into the water, I could feel the leash tighten around my ankle as I seemed to thrash and roll under the double waves. While I was fighting for a breath, my board was tombstoning on the surface and all I could think about in that moment was, "what was Bill thinking?"

As I popped up to the surface, my first words to myself were, "smooth move, dude!" I looked up and saw Bill on shore. He was probably wondering, "when is it time for pancakes?"

I cleared the abrasive salt and stinging ice water from my eyes. My cousin, is now standing on the belly of his board, making an eating gesture. I knew it. "Man, we just got here. You hit one solid wave and you're ready to chow down," I thought. Bill was just a natural. I was not even sure he adored surfing the way I did, but it just came so easy to him. I suspected he was just bored and was ready to move on to the next task.

I needed to get my rhythm. Become one with the sea. Connect to Mother nature. I always seemed to have to work twice as hard at something to feel good about myself and my abilities. Of course, my surf buddy ends up being someone who exuded natural confidence, approached everything in life as if there was never an obstacle, and almost never seemed to have a care in the world. "Oh, lucky me."

As I bobbed up and down in the swells, I pulled my board back to me and slid on. I could see Bill applying a lap of wax to his board top, so I knew he was ready to hit the waves again.

We spent the better half of the morning trading off on rolls, finding our stride, and pacing the waves.

It truly was a great day to be on the water.

The swells were perfect, the sun was shining, and we had the whole beach to ourselves. Not counting the seals.

It was the perfect day.

Chapter 1

My Inner Beach Bum

I was a happy kid. I grew up in the landlocked farmlands of central New York. Isolated from the raging realities of the world outside the borders of the barbed wire fences that kept the cows from getting out and the culture from getting in. Although I was not an only child, I often played alone in the cornfields of summer or wandered through the hedgerows that lined the outskirts of the farm. During the brutal winters, when the snow drifts would cover the front door of our house and the pine trees lining the borders of our yard were heavy and laden with snow, I would crawl underneath them on my belly in my snow suit, pretending I was discovering new worlds hidden beneath.

My brother, Steven, who was two years younger than I, was more into his own creative expression. He was patient, reserved, and observant. He would sit for hours sketching or painting with my father while I would spend hours daydreaming and pretending that I was traveling on glorious adventures around the Universe.

Looking back, I seemed to use my imagination to create even more boundaries of self-reliance. The boundaries would only allow things in life that made me happy. I enjoyed keeping myself busy with my creative thoughts. Growing up on a farm afforded me isolation and gave me an amazing opportunity at living life amongst nature. This also showed me just how much I was in my own little world.

Everything my eyes could see was crafted by my father. He was a hardworking, learn-by-doing kind of guy, who never called a plumber or a roofer or an electrician. If something was broken, he would fix it. If he didn't quite know how, he would teach himself.

My father met my mother working in a beachside resort called The Breakers. Dad was a doorman and my mom a waitress who eventually transferred to working the elevators of this stunning hotel. In fact, dad opened the front door of the hotel, the first day my mom arrived off the train. Their beautiful love story was set along the beaches and intercoastal environment of one of America's richest and most decadent cities in the tropical paradise that is still Palm Beach, Florida.

My mom was a slender chestnut-haired beauty, with brains to match. She was the tough disciplinarian who always taught us that we could do anything we put our minds to, as long as there was passion behind it. She was not only a practical problem solver, but she looked great in a swimsuit as well. My mom idolized Ester Williams, the great Hollywood swimming star. Mom was an ace swimmer and loved the water as a fish loved the sea.

My father looked like he just stepped out of a 1960s beach movie. He was a 6-foot-tall, tanned, towhead specimen of a man. He was muscular and fit from his days working on his family's farm and spending time in the army. Dad was a lover of nature and life. He was the philosopher. He would randomly throw out phrases of wisdom that I only now seem to realize were earth-shifting lessons on life and how to see it.

My parents loved the beach and always seemed to be called to the water. We lived very close to Fair Haven Beach State Park. A 1,100-acre state park on the Southeastern shore of Lake Ontario in upstate New York. Almost every summer weekend we would be there. The lake had a narrow beach that my brother and I would love to play on. We would dart back and forth, barefoot on the pebble-laden sand, like firewalkers dancing on hot coals. We would spend hours splashing in the water and swimming in the cold lake. This was when I got my first boogie board at age 11. I would glide back and forth on this piece of fiberglass until my bare feet were blistered and my entire body sunburned from hours in the sun and surf.

After an exhausting morning in the water, my father would drive up a winding tree-lined lane to the breathtaking bluffs that overlooked this spectacular body of water. The intoxicating smell of burnt charcoal permeated the air. You could always smell the delicious scent of meat being grilled on the permanent outdoor iron grills. The mix of grilled hotdogs mingled with an aroma of pine that would be carried on the breeze over the bluffs.

My mom would open up the picnic basket pulling out a one pound can of Charles' potato chips which my brother and I would devour by the handfuls in minutes, craving the salt after a long morning of beaching around.

The next year, my parents put an in-ground pool in our back yard. We lived in that pool every summer from early May to Late October.

I was 14 years old when I first saw the ocean. My parents decided to take us on a family outing to Ocean City, Maryland. I remember walking up over castle-like sand dunes not knowing what to expect on the other side. Before my eyes lay a vast and breathtaking panorama that brought tears to my eyes. I wasn't even sure what I was looking at, as I had never seen such a huge body of water that seemed to have no borders. Only the Western skyline had a minuet separation between sea and air. If it were not for several boats on the horizon, I would have truly believed that the cloudless sky was pouring into the massive blue basin before me.

The warm July air kissed my face as a strong aroma of salt filled my nostrils. My mom took me by the hand and escorted me to the shoreline. The sandals wedged on my feet like shackles preventing me from running faster. I couldn't wait to get out of them and dip my digits into the surprisingly cool water. My brother and I were so excited! It was like Christmas and New Year's rolled into one. We spent hours swimming and building sand castles, sunbathing, and listening to the seagulls as they sounded the alarm every time the wind changed. It was a real beach, filled with treasures of colorful seashells popping their heads out of the off-white sand. The faint smell of coconut suntan oil and beach jasmine seemed to meld together in a sensory fusion of warmth and magic.

I would chase the receding water into the sea as the in-coming waves would chase me back on to the sand. I was in ecstasy. I would proceed to do this for what seemed like hours. It was as if I had found a new friend to play with. At one point, a wave caught me by surprise bowling me over into the sand, filling my mouth with water. As I stood up coughing out the sea, I could hear my father say, "ya gotta hold your breath." It wouldn't be the last time I got a mouthful of sea water.

It was then, that my brother Steven, pointed outward towards the horizon, "Look! Surfers!" he exclaimed. We all turned to see three guys straddling little boards that looked no bigger than the boogie board I got at age 11. They were all staring off into the distance seemingly waiting for the next wave to hop on. Unfortunately, the waves rolling into shore seemed no bigger than my waist. I thought to myself, "maybe they know something is coming." It was quite a conundrum to me. I was perplexed. What I did find so amazing was the incredible imagery it left in my mind. Three young, tanned, "surfer dudes" just hanging out on their boards, waiting to catch the next wave. I could glimpse their colorful board shorts and short sleeve wet suits. Their long, wet hair and confident postures inspired me as I yearned for that life style. I dreamt about it for years, making that the image of "cool" in my mind's eye.

I was an awkward, gawky kid by my teens. I hung out with the dreamers. Those were the kids with big ideas but had no idea how to execute them. Unexecuted dreams seemed more the reality, especially if your fate was growing up in a small, uncultured town. Although, somehow, I believed there was a way, thanks to the world my parents would show us whenever we got to go on a vacation or take a day trip.

I had the prerequisite acne most kids had, but mine was ten times worse than most. My mom took me to a dermatologist who gave me the most common topical drug for acne at that time, which did help the blemishes fade, but made my face bright red as if I were standing in the sun all day. I wore glasses from the age of six, had braces on my teeth, and suffered from deplorable anxiety and worry. I was always stressed about what people thought about me and what disaster would come next. I was constantly getting picked on or bullied for my acne or my glasses. I suffered with dyslexia and was extremely conscious about it. By the age of 15 my family doctor had me on Valium in order to quell the bouts of anxiety and teen angst I was suffering from.

I was a raging hormonal soup kitchen of anger, lust, and confusion. I had no idea who I was or why. On top of all this, I hated wearing shoes. My feet always seemed to be growing and it was really difficult for my mom to keep me in shoes that fit properly. I preferred being barefoot. I just felt "mentally" better when I was not restricted by some pair of clodhoppers.

My parents got me involved in everything. I ran track and cross-country, played baseball, and hockey. I was in the music department and played trumpet and piano. I sang in chorus and a local singing group. I think my parents didn't know what to do with me and were just trying to distract me from myself. I had low self-esteem and always felt as if I was taking up too much space in this world. I would even sit half way in a chair, because I remember thinking I didn't deserve to sit fully back and relax. I was a teenage mess.

I remember my mom gave me a book for my 15th birthday about astronomy. That book opened an entire Universe for me, literally. Several nights a week I would go outside, spread a large blanket on the grassy knoll along the side of our house, and lay back with my book identifying the constellations. I would shine my little flashlight on each page, eagerly drinking in the information about the planets and how they revolve around a massive sun that was at the heart of our solar system. That solar system, being one of many solar systems, was within one corner of our Milky Way Galaxy. That galaxy, was one of hundreds of galaxies stretched across a tiny fraction of space. The concept was hard to fathom. How insignificant it seemed to make me feel.

I would read stories about the constellations and how they represented Greek Gods, fearless animals, and symbols that honored ancient wisdom. I studied all about the moon and its phases and how it would affect our tides and some would even say, our mood. As I grew older, I would learn how the zodiac was intertwined within this narrative, along with the metaphysics of nature. These studies would often come together, blurring the lines between art and science, drawing me deeper and deeper into their powerful stories. I was hooked.

Spring break came and my parents wanted to take us to see Florida and share with us the wonderful memories they had created when they were young. We drove from New York to Florida, stopping in practically every state to see a little piece of history or at least a fun attraction. Besides Howe Caverns, dining at Stucky's, or buying 3-D post cards in South Carolina's South of the Border, most of the trip was a blur until we were in Florida.

The Sunshine State was aptly named. We stopped in Palm Beach to see the hotel where mom and dad met and fell in love. We swam at the beach and ate out every night. I remember never sleeping as well as I did in Florida. I was in paradise. I could run around in bare feet or flip flops. It was sun-filled days and breathtaking beaches, good food, and a carefree two-weeks of vacation.

Our last stop was Miami Beach. In the late 70s Miami was past its heyday and was now the "place you went to die." As we drove down along Collins Ave and turned on to Ocean Drive, I was traumatized by the hundreds of elderly people simply sitting on rocking chairs in the stifling summer heat. It was if Miami Beach had morphed into one giant old-folks home. We parked along Ocean Drive and walked across Lummus Park.

This sacred jewel situated between the mainland and the sea, was a strip of beach that was kissed by the warm Gulf Stream, which rose to meet the sand along Miami Beach. This part of the Gulf Stream, referred to as the Florida current, maintained an average water temperature at or above 77 °F during the winter. The East winds moved over this warm water and pushed balmy air from the Gulf Stream, inland. This kept temperatures milder across the coast than anywhere else throughout the Southeast, especially during the winter. When the Gulf Stream meandered up along this precious beach, it revealed the most beautiful blue green water that I'd ever seen.

My bare feet enjoyed the warm, gritty goodness as we plodded through the spikes of seagrass, over the dunes and down onto the palatial beach. There in front of us was a blue-green sea that reached as far as the eyes could see. The sun was behind us casting long shadows into the sand as the waves crashed upward to meet them. The water was as transparent as glass allowing us to see the shell and coral fragments at the bottom. Now, at low tide, the azure sea introduced large islands of sand that we would wade out to through the warm water. We'd stop to play on them, and then run through the ankle-deep liquid to the next one.

I was in my element. The unbelievable weather made every day an exceptional one. The cloudless, blue sky was constantly met by a turquoise sea. The warm, salty air seemed to be a natural remedy for my over active acne. The daily sun melted away my deep, obsessive anxiety, and constant worry. In fact, the entire two weeks had past and I never once asked for the Valium. I never felt stressed or thought once about school.

On our last day in Miami, we went down to the beach to see the sunrise and have one last swim in that magic blue water. The sun was just peeking above the horizon and I could tell it was high tide because the water was almost to the lifeguard stands. The waves were large swells that would break far out and roll into our feet. There they were. Surfers stretched out along the foreground of the rising sun. It looked like a gathering of birds migrating Eastward now, stopping to gather their resources and take flight again. Every now and then you would see a random surfer pick their wave, run their break, then paddle right back out to the flock. I was swimming along the shoreline, but couldn't take my eyes off of them. My dreams of surfing and being that "cool surfer dude," starting reoccurring once again.

My overwhelming emotions and anxiety returned after our trip to Florida. My only solace would be the two weeks of amazing memories left over from that trip. Thanks to our parents, they were able to show us a different view of the world, wherever we traveled. I knew they did not have a lot of money and were always struggling to pay the bills, but somehow, they managed to show my brother and me something other than the four corners of our farm. Because of them, we were encouraged to dream, even if they seemed to be a faraway illusion. Our parents encouraged it, nonetheless.

Now, back at school, the pressure of doing well and getting good grades was amplified by the stress of performing well in sports, in my music classes, and keeping up with every aspect of teenage life.

My parents thought it might be a good idea to expand my surroundings and perhaps make some new friends outside the school system that I so constantly dreaded. I started taking an extra-curriculum course at the local YMCA after school. It was free to the community and was a good way to keep kids out of trouble. By the second week, the astronomy class I signed up for was canceled, due to a personal issue the teacher was dealing with. Across the hall from that canceled class was a dance class. I remember being drawn to the glass window watching as the kids would bend and stretch their bodies in unbelievable ways. They would go through sequences of dance exercises and then put everything they had learned into a final routine. Their fluid bodies moved through space to a mesmerizing beat of drummers and musicians playing live music in one corner of the room.

When the instructor gave the dancers a 15-minute break, she walked over to me. "You should be in this class," she recommended.

"Oh, I have no dance training," I said sheepishly. I could feel my body sinking back into my shell.

"This is a beginner's class. Yes, there are a few dancers here who are at a different level, but the more experienced ones help the newer ones," she said proudly. "Your class was just cancelled. Come and take this class."

In my mind, I was working out every way I could possibly do this. I ended up not telling my parents that my other class was canceled and would come every week for this class.

I couldn't keep that secret too long, before my parents wondered why I was coming home sweaty and exhausted, limping my way into the shower, and pouring myself into bed. "I'm taking a dance class," I confessed to my parents after they drilled me with questions. The reaction was not what I imagined. My father simply walked away while my mother asked me more questions about the class. For them, I assumed they thought it was just another distraction to keep me engaged. What they didn't realize was that it went from a curiosity to an earth-moving passion.

It's as if my body and mind were made to dance. Each week, I would intently study the movements, learn to stretch further and deeper, as my body underwent a transformation. My athletic background allowed me the stamina to move freely and with strength, while my musical background gave me an edge on how I would hear the counts, cues, and rhythms that would bring me a better understanding of the movement. All the pieces were coming together. It was probably the defining moment of my existence! I knew it was all I ever wanted to do. I needed to dance more than anything else.

Along with this, I no longer seemed to depend on Valium to calm my nerves. My issues with dyslexia, seemed less, due to my strong ability to have to concentrate harder on how to move as a dancer. My mind was now distracted by trying to understand this obsession. It seemed as if dance took my mind out of my body. Dance gave me a reason to participate in life.

By the second month, my body started to change. I was losing my baby fat. My core strength not only gave me a better sense of my body, but a better sense of self. Much more than any gym class or run around the track could do. I worked hard and for that hard work, I was rewarded with confidence and a sense of pride I'd never known before.

Dance consumed my life. I could not get enough of watching dancers on television or in the movies. I bought books about famous dancers and read about different styles and techniques. A variety of teachers would teach us styles from all different genres of dance. After several weeks, they would change styles, moving from ballet to jazz, modern to tap. It's as if we would learn a new language every few weeks. By the end of the school year, I felt a metamorphosis overtaking me. This form of self-expression allowed me to feel as if I could emerge from my cocoon with unabashed permission.

Of course, this was a double-edged sword. I still had to go back home and face the same, small minded friends and close-minded individuals that seemed to want to hold me back, judge me, or felt I had to fit into their idea of what someone should be like. If not, then they considered me an outcast. So, I kept my dance life under wraps.

Chapter 2

LA, Here I Come

Summer vacation was here. It was my 16th birthday, June 21, 1978. First day of Summer. My aunt Martha always called me the Golden Boy because of this.

My mom's sister, my aunt Martha, had moved out to Los Angeles with my three cousins, Bill, Libby, and Martha Jayne, just a few years earlier. My uncle passed away several years before, and my aunt seemed lost in her old Pennsylvania surroundings. She was ready for a change. So, they packed up their 1973 two toned, Buick station wagon and made the trip cross-country to settle in Woodland Hills, Ca. This sleepy suburb in the San Fernando Valley was a subtle mix of city and country bordered by the Santa Susana Mountains.

For months, I had begged my mom to let me go out and visit her sister. I was so enamored by the lure of "Tinseltown", celebrities, and the laid-back lifestyle that LA had to offer. The fantasy was intoxicating. My 16th birthday present was a plane ticket to Los Angeles. This was the perfect "summer vacation" gift.

I arrived at LAX and walked out to the curb. I could see my aunt's Buick, half parked with the motor running. My cousin Bill was already outside the car jumping up and down trying to get my attention. I ran up to him and gave him a big hug. The driver's side door opened and out stepped my aunt Martha.

Aunt Martha was my mom's older sister. A pint size woman, with short brown hair that still looked like it hadn't met a comb that day. She was grinning from ear to ear with a Pall Mall cigarette hanging off the right corner of her lip. Her pale skin seemed as if it never met the sun. She was still in her colorful night gown and pale blue quilted house coat. She pulled the cigarette out of her mouth and gave me a big kiss on the cheek. "Well, it's about time," she said in a hoarse proclamation.

She was my favorite aunt. She was the exact opposite of my mom. She had an air of carefree bliss. She was the free spirited, pixie, that rolled with the punches of life. And she had a lot of punches thrown at her. She survived fire and flood, earthquake, death, and divorce. She just seemed to take it all on the chin. When in doubt, she would sit back, light up a cigarette and pour herself a hot, black cup of coffee. It would all get better from that point. I hopped in the car, threw my bag in the back, and off we went. I had arrived!

The drive from LAX airport to Woodland Hills was about 40 minutes. But when you got in a car with Aunt Martha, it could take you all day to get to your destination. She would always seek out the adventurous route. She couldn't wait to show me all the sights. Our first stop, Randy's Big Do-Nut Drive-In, just a couple miles east of LAX. A dozen donuts and 3 cups of coffee secured, we barreled down the 405 through Culver City and Westwood, until taking a right turn onto Santa Monica Blvd. Aunt Martha pointed out all the sights, she thought I would love to see…the Hollywood sign, Grumman's Chinese Theatre, the Hollywood Walk of Fame, Hollywood Bowl, and the Magic Castle.

She loved kitschy souvenir shops and we found several. We hit the drive thru at In and Out Burger for a bag full of hamburgers, fries, soda, and more coffee. Then, off we went again. The old Buick meandered up the steep South-facing slope of Mount Hollywood in Los Angeles' Griffith Park. We were met at the top by the Griffith Observatory. It was a breathtaking marvel of 1930s art deco design with Greek embellishments. It commanded a view of the Los Angeles Basin, including Downtown Los Angeles to the Southeast, Hollywood to the South, and the Pacific Ocean to the Southwest. Aunt Martha pulled into a sideways parking spot and jumped out of the car. "Bring the lunch," she suggested, coffee in hand. She found us a picnic table and there I was, on top of the world, so to speak. We laughed and shared family stories for hours.

The next day, Bill and I woke up really early. He couldn't wait to get me out of the house. He grabbed his old, dinged up surfboard and we jumped in the Buick station wagon. The inside of the car smelled like coffee and donuts from the day before. Because there were so many things in the back of the car, Bill's board could hardly fit. He closed the back door and jimmied his board so that it would just stick out the back window.

"You're gonna need two things," Bill said to me. He pulled a yellow sarong out of his bag.

"I can't wear that," I jumped.

“No, kook,” Bill laughed, “you don’t have to wear it. It makes a great towel and it takes up no space in your bag.”

“And what’s the other thing?” I squinted with anticipation. He held up a spray bottle. “Is that what I think it is?”

“Equal parts, water, baby oil, lemon juice,” Bill rattled off the ingredients. “The ultimate tanning formula.” We splashed it on.

As we got in the car, I said to Bill, “cool, you have your driver’s permit now?”

Bill turned to me, smiled, and raised his eyebrows. I’m not sure that was the answer I was looking for, but who cared, we were off to the beach. We drove Southeast toward Crespi St. Bill maneuvered down Topanga Canyon, Blvd and on to Mulholland Drive. We sang songs from our days back East and joked about the million memories we’d shared since we were five years old. Every summer, my Aunt Martha would let Bill come to the farm and spend the summer with my brother and me. So, we had accumulated a lot of good times. Now it was my turn to spend summers with him.

We made a left onto Malibu Canyon Rd. We wound our way through the early morning traffic as streaks of sun breached the canyon walls. Emerging from the canyon we could see the long blue horizon stretching North to South. The breeze coming off the ocean was warm and inviting. Bill looked at me. He gulped as if he swallowed a canary. I could always tell when my cousin was holding back a secret. But I knew he just loved having surprises up his sleeve and he wanted me to have an amazing summer, so I simply smiled back. No questions asked.

As we turned onto the Pacific Coast Highway, the radio was blasting *The Kinks - Live Life* over KROQ as we sang out at the top of our lungs. The windows were down with my bare feet sticking out absorbing the new-day sun. The tender, breaking wind blew our hair in every direction.

Along the PCH there were long stretches of beach. These sanctuaries were already dotted with heads of surfers bobbing up and down on long breaking waves as their early morning matins were being made at the Church of the Sea. It was both a place of physical healing and spiritual connecting.

We pulled into the parking lot of Malibu Surf Shack. We were greeted by a tall Mexican kid in his early 20s with an Elvis styled pompadour haircut and one arm completely tattooed from shoulder to wrist.

"Hey JackO, what's up?" Bill said as he shook his friend's hand. "We need to suit up my cuz."

His buddy JackO, sized me up as he gave me a big smile. "Dude, you ever surf before?" he asked in broken English.

"Never, I said as I admired his relaxed demeanor. He had bright blue board shorts and a tri-colored tank top that made the color of his dark hair and skin pop. I could just tell he was a surfer. Like my cousin, he had this particularly laid-back way of speaking and moving that I just didn't see in New York State, let alone in my high school in the middle of farm country.

“Let’s get you a real ripper!” JackO stated as he slowly strolled through a large quiver of boards, perched along one wall. I’d never seen so many surfboards in one place. Shortboards, longboards, paddleboards, kickboards all gleaming with creative expressions from a variety of artistic shapers. JackO browsed each board, contemplating its weight, shape, buoyancy, length, and even color. It’s as if he knew exactly what he was looking for after summing me up in minutes. He ran his hand across each board and suddenly stopped.

He pulled from the rack, a beautiful, natural brown colored board, with a single fin and diamond cut tail. It had electric blue trim and a striking blue lightning bolt down its center. The board was almost 7 feet long with a 3-inch bottom. “This is a cool Robert August,” JackO said, proudly.

I shook my head, pretending I made the connection. “This fits you,” JackO said with great approval. “Now all you need is a tan.” He turned to my cousin and asked, “Does he need a zip up?”

“Let’s see if he digs it first,” Bill responded referring to the wet suit that the surfers would wear in the water.

Bill rented the board for me for that day and I contributed to my re-invention by picking out a pair of Billabong board shorts. The long chocolate-colored shorts were trimmed with black on the sides and legs. There was a little strap for a fin key and Velcro pockets for board wax and a wax comb.

“Don’t forget your Sex Wax,” JackO said as he tossed a disk-shaped can into my hands. “It’s the best for your stick” he laughed, repeating the company’s provocative slogan.

Bill took me across the street to the Malibu Pier. The Malibu Pier was a Southern Cali icon. This historic landmark was located in the heart of California's surf culture. Surfers from around the world came to Surfrider Beach just adjacent to Malibu Pier. This strip of sea was considered a place of pilgrimage for young surfers who wanted a real slice of life on the waves. The area's reputation was cemented by the three-point breaks that rolled in giving surfers long sustainable waves that would collect an entire group of board walkers in one swell. It was the location for major surf movies such as *Gidget, Endless Summer, Big Wednesday*, and surfing legend, Miki Dora.

Here I was, a geeky farmhand, 16-years-old, with the first flush of youth, strolling on the beach of legends. Really? I felt as if I didn’t deserve to be there. Encouragement from my cousin was everything. He gave me the mental strength to look past all that and focus on today.

"Let's have some fun now,” he commanded as he ran through a bunch of exercises to get me accustomed to my brand-new appendage.

We stood at the waters' edge and watched surfers catch waves on the other side of the pier in the breaking water. As each guy mounted his board, Bill would explain the moves and give me an idea of what the parts of the waves were called. He would point out where the lineup for the wave started, like cars at a traffic stop, and how each guy would take turns catching a wave. Surfer etiquette, so to speak.

I spent several hours on the beach trying to mount my board and then practiced in the ice-cold Pacific water, applying the lessons Bill so patiently shared with me.

At points throughout the morning, JackO would run down from the surf shop, pick up my cousin, and paddle out to catch a few. I would stand there watching these two hotdogs slalom down some radical waves.

JackO was an impressive surfer. Unlike my cousin Bill, who was effortless and almost nonchalantly elegant, JackO was determined. This surfer had style and aggression. He liked the razor’s edge. He took chances, followed his own inner drummer, and went one way… JackO’s way.

In contrast, I always did everything by the rules out of fear of retribution from my parents. I never took chances or rocked the boat. Here was a guy who refused to play by society's rules. JackO was the epitome of the rebel surfer… cocky, arrogant, fearless. Him and Bill had complementary surfing styles. It was fascinating to watch.

My first several days did not go as I had planned. I thought my dance training would make me a shoe-in as a good surfer. I thought, on some level, my training could be helpful on my board or how I would move. What I came to understand was that surfing required an entirely different center of gravity.

As a dancer you are constantly taught to pull up. Lifting the energy of your body up and out through the top of your head, keeping your abs taut and lifting through the rib cage. As a surfer, it was just the opposite. The energy of a surfer was to stay rooted and move forward. You must stay grounded on a platform that was your only stability while an energy beneath you was traveling. Then, it was time to hit your target. Being one with the wave.

At the end of my first day, I was beat up and bruised from the repetitive motion of banging my knee on the rail of my board. My neck was sore from turning it constantly to find the right wave and the tops of my feet were rubbed raw from dragging them improperly along the board when trying to pop up.

Each day I became angrier with myself. I wanted to be a pro surfer, yesterday! Why is this taking so long? I'm paying attention to my cousin's instructions. I should be gliding in on waves by now. What's wrong with me? I was getting more and more frustrated and exceedingly embarrassed in front of Bill because I couldn't even catch a wave. I felt as if I was letting him down.

On top of that, I had a mean case of jock itch from the wet swim trunks harassing me all day. My shoulders and neck were fried to a crisp from the beating sun, and I couldn't keep my glasses on my face. Unfortunately, I needed them to see, so I bought a band to keep them somewhat in place as I drudged through the water.

Every day I would go through my routine. Body in the center of the board. Long paddle strokes with cupped hands. Look over your shoulder to see the swell you wanted, bring your hands to the deck of the board, directly under your shoulders. Arch up, then pop up. Keeping your weight centered underneath you, your feet on the midline, and lead with your front arm. Look in the direction you want to go. Rinse and repeat.

This routine was drilled into my head. I would repeat it over, and over, and over again. For the first few days, I was too afraid to pop up, I would just ride the white water into the shore, staying out of the way of the other surfers. I would then walk back out, hop back on my board, then paddle out again.

I could hear the voice of my dance teacher in my head. "Practice, practice, practice." I didn't seem to know why I couldn't get the hang of it. I would occasionally get to my feet and glide perpendicular to the beach only to fly off my board as if I were a house of cards in a hurricane.

"Hey cuz," someone shouted out to me. I turned to see JackO glide up behind me on his board. "You forget, the board has a relationship to the sea, just like you have a relationship with your board," JackO explained. "So, where are you running to? You're missing out on 'the right here.'"

I stopped. It took me a minute to come back to whatever part of the Universe my thoughts were in. I then realized, I was so busy assuming that I would fail, that I was rushing through the most important part of surfing - riding the wave. I just assumed I wasn't going to ride that wave, so in my mind I was thinking I had to get back out there on my board and try again. I didn't really visualize myself riding that wave.

I kept practicing connecting with my board, but when it came down to it, I was not letting my board connect with the sea. I was just too far ahead of myself.

"Let's go! We're gonna catch some soft waves to get your feet wet," JackO said. We paddled out to the shoulder of the wave. I could tell that he was really eager to show me what he meant.

"You need to visualize yourself past the break of the wave. You already know how to popup on your board. Now see yourself taking control of the wave. Don't overthink it. Just let it ride!"

He looked over his shoulder, then took four or five paddles forward allowing his timing to sync with the oncoming swell. He was up on his deck. He effortlessly glided upon the glassy surface commanding his ride. He rode for about 50 yards, then seamlessly got back down to one knee, transitioning to a straddling position alongside his rails. He turned his board back to the horizon to watch me.

I followed in his path. I found my swell and paddled towards shore. This time I was thinking ahead. I was now anticipating my next move. I felt the water come up to meet my board, as if it was cueing me to stand up. I popped up, rooted my feet to the deck, as the board came up beneath me. I saw myself on my wave, running like a bobsled down a slope. I rode that wave for about 30 yards and then, less gracefully, finished off on one knee. I couldn't believe it. It almost seemed as if I talked my way through the process. And it worked!

JackO paddled over to me. "Great job, dude."

"How did you learn this?" I asked excitedly.

"I had a great teacher," he replied.

“Do you like the board?” JackO asked nodding to the surfboard he picked out for me.

“It’s a great board,” I exclaimed.

“I’m gonna make sure you get to buy this one,” he said with confidence.

I thanked him profusely as he nodded and paddled off. I was in seventh heaven. I couldn't contain my joy. I kept breaking out in smiles while still shaking my head in disbelief. I just felt less awkward. The technique was not really about surfing, it was more about believing in myself. It was about visualizing my success. I had the basics down, but I could not seem to get passed that certain point until I believed I could do it and move forward. I worshipped JackO’s tenacity.

I paddled up to the shore. Bill walked over to me. "I saw that," he smiled. I was still shaking my head. " He's a good egg, that one," referring to JackO. "He may act like a hard ass, but his heart's in the right place. Well, I think it’s time to get you a wet suit.”

For the next couple weeks, Bill and I would show up at the Surf Shack and JackO would bring out the same surfboard I started on. With a pocket full of cash, I made from odd jobs back home, I bought my first wetsuit. The “back zip” covered me from neck to ankles and really helped me to brave the cold Pacific waters. It assisted with buoyancy and protected me from the constant abrasions I would get from the misuse of my board.

Bill, JackO, and I would head up and down the PCH between Malibu and Montecito searching for swells to ride. Some days we would find a great break and paddle out. We would seek out that long, rideable wave face that allowed a perfect dance between the lift of the wave and the length of the stay, gliding over the rolling water. I would often fall more than I would stay on my board, but the passion I had for dance seemed like an exciting extension that translated to my surfing. What I lacked in technique, I made up for in desire.

Most days, we would be at the mercy of the summer winds. If the onshore winds blew in from the sea, it ensured that the waves would have no shape, and basically be un-surfable. If a cross shore wind cut parallel to the shore, you would see choppy waves too messy to surf. But an offshore wind, blowing in from the land to the sea was the best wind for surfing. Some days we would be lucky, while others days, we would just paddle out and sit out back on our boards.

In the following weeks, I felt as if I had a crash course in surfing. Being coddled by two experts, made it seem as if I were in "surfer bootcamp." Bill and JackO made me work. When we found a new surf spot, they would help me to get the place "wired," or learn the landscape, as I called it. Knowing where the rocks, reef, and breaks where happening was important so that you didn't go blindly into a surf situation and get taken by surprise or even worse, get taken out.

They would teach me about the Magic Zone. This was the area you should catch the unbroken wave on the wave's face at a 45-degree angle in order to time your pop up. "You could never go wrong in the magic zone", they'd say. I am sure I proved them wrong many times. Each day, we would analyze the waves. Where is the best spot to catch it? Could I get to the best spot before it breaks? Is it a right or left wave? Or does the wave seem to break evenly across the whole surface, closing you out of the loop? It was incredible that these were the basics that every surfer must contend with in the beginning. It was learning a new language as well as observing how the water behaved.

The guys protected me the first few weeks by not having too many surfers around me, not even their posse of friends. They would just keep saying, "you'll meet the guys soon." They didn't want me to pick up any bad habits that would derail their training, so they kept me in this little bubble.

The athleticism required of a surfer was extraordinary. The physical demands of surfing were very similar to those of rollerskating, skateboarding, or dancing. Balance, grace, rhythm, flow. These sports required constant challenges of immense physical strength and intense endurance. Surfing required awareness, concentration, and control over varying surfaces and conditions, just like its counterparts.

I witnessed this first hand on the last day of our PCH road trip. We ended up back at Malibu pier because we heard there was a storm off Fiji and tremendous swells from the South-Southwest were coming to our shores, which I learned was a rarity.

"If the swells don't get too shredded from all the little islands on the way, we should have some great waves for ripping!" JackO was excited. His wish was granted. Huge barrels came rolling in, bringing, what seemed like hundreds of surfers to Malibu. Bill and I headed to the end of the pier to watch the pro do his thing. JackO delivered. He dominated the water. He would maneuver his stick through some incredible groundswells that reached 8 – 10 feet at its breaking point. His skills were amazing. He would stay right in front of the white water, advance into the curl, and "spray" out the other end. In order to adjust to the shape of the oncoming wave, JackO would "trim the wave", moving slightly lower or higher to surf along the shoulder varying his speed to stay in optimal position on the wave.

"Oh, oh, there he goes," Bill smiled, "He's gonna soul perch!" I looked at Bill with perplexity. "Watch", he said. As JackO rode over the current wave face, he would walk out to the nose of his board, then walk back to the center, then carefully back out to the nose, connecting with his spirit, embracing the energy of the sea. All this while balancing on a groundswell the size of the Hollywood Bowl. "It's yours, Antonio!" Bill yelled out from the pier.

"Is that his real name?" I asked as Bill laughed shaking his head. "How did JackO get his nickname?" I asked.

Bill paused and looked at me with a devilish smile. "Let's just say it has nothing to do with surfing," he smirked.

Chapter 3

Becoming Drew

Bill and I had been going to the beach every day for a month. It was the introduction to a whole new world. In a months' time, I had experienced so much that if I had to go home today, I felt I had lived another lifetime and that would have been fine with me.

This particular morning, at about 7 am I was awake and sitting in the sun-filled kitchen. The window was open and a soft warm breeze was gently batting the gauze curtains around. I could hear the cries of one of my aunt's three cats, in an attempt to wake her mother for a feeding. All of a sudden, my Aunt Martha stumbled into the kitchen and headed right for the coffee pot. She poured herself a cup of joe, lit a cigarette, took a big drag, and a long, loud sip of her steaming coffee. She turned around with great effort and realized I was sitting at the kitchen table. "Oh good morning" she managed.

She shuffled over to the kitchen table and sat down. We sat there in silence as I could clearly see her enjoying every single inhale of her cigarette. She chased every third puff with a swig of coffee. She pierced her lips as to really savor the combination of nicotine and caffeine. The pungent scent of the cigarette smoke in the air with the intoxicating aroma of the coffee wafting from her large mug would be a memory of her I would always cherish

"You're up early," I said.

She forced her eyes open and smacked her lips before saying, "Ya, I couldn't sleep. Too many wacky dreams!"

I raised my head as in agreement.

"Is Billy treating you right on that surfboard?" she asked. "He does love having you here. He has someone to go to the beach with."

"I'm loving every minute of it," I said.

She looked at me and took another long drag on her cigarette. She then looked back at me with hesitation on her lips. She took another swig of coffee. "It must be hard to surf in those big spectacles? Did your mudder get you those?" She was referring to my glasses which my mom had gotten me about six months before. "I'm blind as a bat, but the glasses help," I answered.

"You're a young, cute guy. Do you idolize Elton John?" she wise-cracked.

My glasses were a large pair of tortoise-shell style octagonal monstrosities that almost seemed too big for my face.

"I think, my mom thought they were hip," I shyly answered.

"We are going shopping today," she said nodding her head.

Bill and I hopped in the car as Aunt Martha commandeered the station wagon. She drove down Ventura Blvd. and pulled into an optical store. In an hour, I walked out of there with my first pair of contact lenses. "Oh, your mudder's gonna kill me, but you just can't look like a cool surfer dude in those binoculars," she said defending her decision. "Enough of this happy horseshit," she demanded. "Welcome to Los Angeles."

These new contacts boosted my self-esteem by 1,000 points. I felt almost normal now.

The next day, Bill had a special trip planned. We jumped on the afternoon Topanga Canyon beach bus that took us down through the winding canyon, with its vaulted hills, hanging houses, and lush vegetation. The ride took about 45 minutes and took us right to the corner of Main St and Beach Way. We got off the bus and walked in the direction of the beach. Every time we crossed another street, a faint noise could be heard coming from in front of us. A splash of color would catch my eye from above. A big cheer would sail in from my left. The smell of grilled hotdogs permeated my nostrils. I thought, "what's going on?" I started seeing throngs of people in a variety of outfits.

Suddenly, a herd of young skateboarders raced by us. Signs for cigarettes, suntan lotion, and surfboards were everywhere. Buildings with giant murals and eye-popping spray paint art seemed to draw your attention in every direction. Colorful kites dove down in a synchronized pattern close to the beach. A variety of different kinds of music could be heard from three different directions. We turned the corner and Bill said, "welcome to Dogtown!"

"Is this Venice Beach?" I screeched.

"Ya, this is infamous Venice," Bill exclaimed. As far as I could see, there were shops running along the edge of a long-paved road parallel to the beach. As we strolled down the ocean front walk, my eyes could not seem to take in all the action from a cacophony of street vendors hawking their wares and overstuffed souvenir shops spilling out onto the street. Cafes dotted the stretch of the street that seemed to double as a stage for every creative performer you could imagine, with the cafes providing front row seats. Bike rental, skate rental, and surfboard rental shops harkened you to their door by using cute girls in hot pants and boys flexing in muscle tees to draw in the unsuspecting passerby. Tattoo parlors were filled with everyone from young guys eager for their first ink to a grandmother eager for a follow up visit. I felt like I had just entered an amalgamation of Disneyland and Oz. The carnival atmosphere was intoxicating.

At that moment, a group of scantily clad girls on roller skates raced by us, as one tall blond, slapped me on the butt. "Nice caboose," she commented as she whizzed by. Her cut off t-shirt read, “Eat the rich.”

Bill looked at me, "I think you're gonna like it here."

There were roller skaters and skateboarders everywhere. The beach was filled with people just enjoying the sun. I noticed a group of surfers heading towards the water ready to find their waves. Artists had their goods piled high in the middle of the street with colorful paintings, miniature surfboards with spray painted murals, and rainbow-colored sarongs flapping in the warm breeze trying to garner attention.

Bill nodded over towards the beach. About 30 people were waving signs and protesting about the lack of attention being given to the Clean Air Act that was passed over eight years earlier.

“Andy, ya little shit, I heard you’s were in town,” My cousin Martha-Jayne came running up from the group of protestors. Her pale, cherub face was framed by fiery red hair and adorned with a wreath of daisies and colorful ribbons running down the back. She gave me a big hug. “Oh, your brudders not here?”

I shook my head no.

“I told her that, but my sister hears what she wants to hear,” Bill joked.

Martha-Jayne was three years older than Bill and I. She was a free-spirited, out-spoken, leader, who felt the world was too controlled by corporate America and that we had to standup for our rights. She was just the one to do it.

A young girl, about my age, ran over to me from the group of protesters. She was grinning with an award-winning smile, dragging her little sister behind her. Her sibling looked to be no older than five or six, with tousled blond ringlets.

"Our air quality is still deteriorating in this area," she announced, grabbing one of the flyers out of her little sister's hands. "We are all meeting in front of the Pan-Pacific Auditorium at 6pm to protest. You need to be there."

I took the flyer and smiled as she darted on to the next unsuspecting person. "Don't forget," she yelled, "Beverly and Fairfax!"

Martha-Jayne blew me a kiss as the three girls headed back to their cause. Bill raised his fist in the air, "Right On!" Then turned to me and said, "let's get lunch."

Pete's was a clapboard structure that seemed to be leaning in the direction of the ocean, weighted down by an old, hand painted sign, that had faded over time. You could just make out the words, *Pete's Grub. The best burgers in Venice.* The 1950s diner-style restaurant was filled with locals and tourists. The searing smell of hamburgers on the grill followed me in, as my mouth started to water from the golden-brown French fries piled high in a plastic basket, being served in front of my face. We grabbed a booth and looked around the crowded room for a waitress.

"Best beach burgers, ever," Bill said licking his lips as I reviewed the ketchup-stained menu.

"Zipper!" a waitress yelled, as she roller skated over to our table and gave Bill a big kiss on the cheek. "Been on the glass today? Where's your board?"

Bill introduced me. "Tally, this is my best cuz."

She smiled a big smile and extended her hand as if she wanted me to kiss it. I obliged and said, "Hi Tally, what's good here?"

"Oh the burgers, baby," she said in a sultry voice. I'll get you kids two and a split of fries. Hey Zip, I saw Canter and Sting waxin' on my way to work this morning. Thought you'd be with em?"

"Nah, I'm showing my cousin the ropes."

"Welcome to LA LA," she squeaked, as she skated up to the counter to announce our order.

I leaned across the table to Bill, "half the time I don't understand what people are saying here. And who's Zipper?"

Bill grinned, "you'll get used to the lingo around here. Just keep your ear to the ground. Oh ya, Zipper is my surfing nickname. Everybody gets a nickname."

"I want a nickname," I said pouting. I sat and thought a minute. Bill had twin cousins in Pennsylvania on his father's side who were both similar in age to us and their names were David and Drew.

"I always liked your cousin's name, Drew. I thought that was a much cooler name than, Andy," which was the name I grew up with. Short for Andrew. But at 16, I wasn't an "Andy" anymore. I was grown up now and I wanted a grown-up name.

"Cool," Bill announced raising a fork, "you are now, officially, Drew!"

As we finished our food, I could see two guys with surfboards pass the open-air window to our right. "Hey Canter," Bill stood up, calling his buddy. The tall, waif-like blond turned to see Bill waving at him.

"Zip, how's it hangin'?" he yelled through the crowd, pointing at Bill.

"Hey Zip," the second surfer said, holding up his fist, with his thumb and pinky sticking up. "Shaka-laka, brother."

"That's Sting Ray," Bill said. "He's short, but a powerhouse on the waves. He stings those babies, every time. These boys are my good pals. We always ride the waves together."

The two made their way into the restaurant, dragging their surfboards in with them. No one seemed to mind that they were half wet and their sandy, seaweed laden boards were tucked under their arms.

They both greeted me as if they'd known me forever.

"Boys, this is my cousin, Andy....ah, I mean, Drew" Billy corrected himself.

"Ah Drew. Cool name," Canter smiled. I felt a moment of acceptance as he said that. "Zip has told us so much about ya."

Canter was a year older than Bill and I. He was so tall, he had to duck to go through doors, yet so skinny you could see his rib cage. His long blond, straight hair just seemed to lay on his face with a part down the middle, while his gaunt cheeks and big blue eyes accentuated the symmetry of his face. His skin was bronzed from years spent following the sun and surf as a Venice beach lifeguard.

"We call him Canter, cause he always seems to cantilever over the nose of his board because he's so tall," Bill joked.

"Ya," he responded with an innocent drawl. "I'm so tall, I forget to squat down low enough sometimes."

"Hi, I'm Sting, Sting Ray," he said putting his hand out for me to shake. "We're gonna hit Muscle Beach later," he said with a forceful handshake. "I hope you're coming."

Sting Ray, was as wildly energetic as a live wire, standing about 5'4", with an overly muscular body for his height and weight. He would constantly push his messy brown hair to one side which would somehow balance his crooked smile, that seemed more prominent when he laughed.

"Sting Ray loves packing on the muscle at Muscle Beach down the block," Bill said.

"Then we're gonna hit the glass again," Sting Ray suggested. "That'd be cool."

The boys squeezed into the booth with us. They picked at the last strings of French fries and joked with Bill about the waitress, Tally, always giving him the eye.

“Dude, you’re like jailbait to her,” Canter surmised. “She’s old. Like 30.

Bill smiled. “It’s all just innocent flirting. Speaking of flirting, where’s JackO?”

Sting Ray winced. “Ohhh, too much of the hooch and beer bong at Big Steena’s party last night.”

“JackO is the other part of our wolf pack,” said Canter. “He’s 21, he can get away with that. Big Steena allows it. But then he pays the price for two days afterwards.”

“I met JackO. He picked out my board,” I said proudly.

“Ya, he’s like the board whisperer. He knows his stuff!” Sting Ray said shaking the ketchup off his fingers.

"Hey, why do they call this Dogtown?" I asked.

Canter jumped in. “Dogtown is a neighborhood between South Santa Monica and West LA that covers Venice and Ocean Park beaches. It's where our skateboard culture exploded! Thanks to the Z-boys."

Skateboarders, roller skaters, surfers...this bohemian beach life seemed to be the place I fit in the most, I thought.

Sting Ray tapped me on the shoulder. “Do you surf the asphalt waves?”

I looked at Bill.

“Skateboard,” Bill interpreted.

“Ahh no,” I confessed

“Well, we’re heading over to Windward Ave to see how the waves are acting at Breakwater.” Sting Ray confirmed.

The Venice Beach Breakwater was an outcropping of huge rocks jutting out into the ocean creating some great waves for surfing. It had become a mecca for locals and those wave riders who were attracted to the Venice beach allure.

We headed down the beach, walking along the sparkling sand, talking and laughing about the surf culture, the crazy Venice beach locals, and how I liked living in New York. Of course, the guys assumed I was from New York City. Just a city kid coming to the beach.

“Damn, it looks like the 405 at rush hour out there!” Bill scoffed, looking at all the guys lined up to catch, what looked like, halfway decent waves.

"Here comes Big Steena!" Canter interrupted, pointing out towards the sea. From a distance I could see a larger-than-life man, in his late 40s perusing the big swells in front of us. Surrounded by younger surfers, he took a beat, found his wave, and took control of the water's curl, barreling ahead of all his onlookers. He ripped across the wave, keeping ahead of the white water which chased him right up to the shore. He gallantly dismounted his board and strolled up to the group of us, as we stood there, clapping for his effortless ride.

"Caballeros," he greeted us, bowing his head.

I immediately felt an air of admiration towards this man from everyone around me. “Big Steena” was not tall in stature but had a commanding, knowing presence. His tanned body and white blond buzz cut added to his strong aura. At 5’10” about 200 something, this once physically fit man had a muscular frame that was now dressed with extra pounds, yet did not seem to slow down his wave riding skills. His hipster mannerism could not disguise the fatherly vibe he conveyed.

Sting Ray walked over and shook Big Steena's hand. "You left your students in the dust and rode in like John Wayne!" he exclaimed.

"I have to lead by example," Big Steena smiled, making light of his entrance. Turning to talk to Sting Ray, I caught sight of a larger-than-life tattoo of the Virgin of Guadalupe, blazing across his back. The details were mesmerizing.

My cousin tapped me on the shoulder, "Hey Andy, I mean ahh, Drew, I want you to meet my good buddy, the one and only Big Steena. Big Steena, this is my wayward cousin from back East," Bill introduced me.

Big Steena turned in my direction, seeming to notice me for the first time. "Why you're greener than the corn in June," he said, summing me up. "We'll get your surfing hours in."

I felt as if he looked right through to my soul. I quickly felt exposed. Was it that obvious, that I was right off the farm?

"Big Steena is our surfing guru," Bill explained. "A lot of those guys perched on their sticks out there are his students."

"Ahh, they're life's students. I'm just showing them the water," he said smiling at me. He motioned some type of sign language out towards the sea and one by one, I could see his students attempt to catch a wave and come into shore to meet him. "I'm finishing up with the guys and then we can go to Neptune's."

Bill, Canter, Sting Ray, and I meandered further along the beach. The ocean was glistening with the reflection of the sun. The hills were gently spilling into the sea and people were laid back, seemingly with no cares in the world. If guys and girls weren't squeezed into short-shorts or bikinis, then jeans, dark blue Vans, and white t shirts were "the look." I was the furthest from the confines of the farm that I could be.

"We're here," Sting Ray explained as he ran over to shake hands with three huge bodybuilders. As I glanced around, I could see weights and workout benches strewn around the beach. A group of bodybuilders were having a "pose off", while three gymnasts were working on parallel bars against a backdrop of palm trees and a wooden, hand-painted sign that read *Muscle Beach ~ birth place of the physical fitness movement.* Transfixed by the physicality of their bodies, I didn't know which way to look next. The ability to be able to grow muscle to that size from resistance seemed incredible.

Watching the powerful moves and gravity defying feats of the gymnasts was like watching the world turn upside down. Your body can do that? I realized just how intense the work must be to get to that point and just how much love and dedication was required to transform the flesh and sinews into an instrument of awe and wonder! I was now, all in. I could sense these "performers" confidence and manner of pride, as if I had entered a room of peacocks. Could I ever be that assured of myself? In a matter of minutes, Sting Ray had us all on weight benches doing bench press and shoulder presses. We'd move to pull downs and then bicep and tricep curls. I was the novice. Although I pushed weights around in my high school gym on the "all in one" machine, this was full on weight lifting. Queen's anthem, *"Don't Stop Me Now,"* was blaring over a tinny-sounding loud speaker, motiving everyone onward to the next rep. We'd spot each other as we did sets of weights and worked in between the "big boys." Everyone was extremely courteous and they would even throw out a pointer here and there. Sting Ray knew his way around the weights as if he'd grown up with them. Judging by his body, he had. His boy-like wonder shined in this arena and he was so eager to show us the ropes. Within the hour, we all had our workout in.

For the next several weeks, Bill, me, and the boys would meet up in spots between Venice and Malibu, depending on the swells and who had to be closest to one end of the beach or the other for work. Sting Ray helped me to master the duck dive.

"Sinking your surfboard to get under an oncoming wave helps you conserve energy and gets you outback faster and with less effort," Sting Ray explained. "You have the white water or the tall water. The more the mess (white water) the more momentum. The higher the tower, (tall unbroken wave) the less power." I sensed another Big Steena analogy.

"Waves that have already broken, have white water in your path, so you have to be at least the board's length, or about six feet away, to get enough momentum to dive under the white water that is already coming at you," Sting Ray animated the move.

"Tall, unbroken waves have a circular pattern they naturally move through. Like an iceberg, the tall wave you see on top of the water also has a circular motion moving underneath it," he smiled. "You can use this circular flow to get pulled into the wave and pushed out back with less effort."

Sting Ray's short, muscular power and smaller board made him a master at pushing the board with straight arms, nose first, deep under water. Pressing down with one knee in the center, he would get the board even deeper, submerging the tail with the other foot on the back end. Once he was parallel with the bottom, he would bend his arms and bring his body to his board. When the wave passed overhead, all he did was direct the nose to the surface and the natural buoyance of the board, along with the motion of the ocean would bring him to the surface. He did this effortlessly. It took me months to figure out the mechanics and years to really perfect it. Each wave seemed to present a different understanding of how to tackle its approach, but I found that if I stuck to Sting Ray's analogy of *"the more the mess the more momentum. The higher the tower, the less power"* it was the best lesson on duck diving.

Some weeks we would meet up with Big Steena and the six of us would paddle out and tackle waves off Huntington Beach, just north of the pier. We would hit the Sugar Shake for lunch and then head up to Newport Beach for more sandy bottom surf breaks. Nicknamed, Surf City USA, this was a great place to see surfers of all types and just immerse yourself in the "culture."

Each beach had its own cast of characters that would leave memorable impressions on me. They gave their home beach breaks "personality" and the locals always knew their stories.

There was the billion-dollar banana heiress who disowned her family in South America to come live and surf in LA. Nicknamed, Dolita, she was as beautiful as she was smart. She would dance back and forth on her long board teasing the boys who would fawn over her. She bought up the abandon, burned out houses on the corner block along the beach after a fire wiped them out. She had the homes reconstructed and then rented rooms to winter snowbirds and surfers who couldn't live anywhere else. She would collect rent each month and surf all day.

The bird man of Malibu would hang out at the end of Malibu pier and give the pigeons massages all the time. This colorful eccentric always sported his feather cape and silver surfer trunks.

The Skating Guitarist would serenade Venice beach onlookers naked, only wearing his 6-string in front and a thin guitar strap strategically running down his backside.

Taz, the Hot Dogger, was a bow-shaped thirty-something who was almost as tall as his longboard. On top of that, he would always ride tandem with Oscar, his little dachshund. Oscar would ride out on the nose of Taz's board and then dig his feet in and ride on the center line between Taz's feet, when he caught a wave. As Taz would adjust forward on his board, Oscar would do the same thing. If Taz adjusted back on his heels, Oscar would move to match him. It was amazing to see. Oscar always wore a little life jacket.

Ever since the day I saw those surfers in Ocean City, MD at age 14, I dreamt of owning this lifestyle. It represented the epitome of cool along with my unquenchable desire to be with the sea. It became a necessity to be at the beach. The smell of the salt air was intoxicating. The feel of the sand between my toes was invigorating. The heat of the sun on my face was essential. The climate possessed an alluring seduction that feed my passion for the ocean. It's the same passion that attracted every one of us.

I hated the thoughts of leaving LA and going back to that small minded, landlocked, hell hole, I called a school in the middle of farmland USA. What if I just don't go back? I knew, it was a pipe dream, but WOW, what a dream. I had just lived an alternate life all in one summer. It was the best summer of my life!

With a new name, a newer look, and the confidence to become a better surfer, California had captured my heart.

Chapter 4

Finding My Footing

By my junior year in high school, I hated being in that small town, especially after being in LA all summer. I had no problem expressing this to my parents either. I seemed to be a real handful for them. I disagreed with everything. I would have fits of anger, or cry silently in my room at night. I would be fearful one minute, then stubborn the next. Even though my tanned skin, thinner frame, and contacts made me feel like a new person, coming back to a school full of small minds seemed to negate everything I felt good about. My friends were a safety net, but I was still uncomfortable around them. I felt like I had less and less to talk about. It's as if I was living a dual life on the farm and Los Angeles was where my real life was. It was the life I felt more comfortable in.

My after-school dance class was my saving grace. I was devoted to it. I constantly felt my technique improving and my awareness as a dancer was changing the way I thought and looked at myself. I felt that the summer spent learning how to surf, now gave me an extra layer of strength and confidence. I was more daring and it seemed much easier for me to try new moves. I felt surfing had advanced me out of that shy space I was previously residing in.

Almost every evening, after going to bed, I would set my alarm for midnight. I would wake up and turn on the old radio receiver in my bedroom searching for a New York City radio station called WBLS. I could only pick it up at night, but the urban dance rhythms and dream of dancing at Studio 54 actually seemed like a possibility, even if I lived it vicariously. It became a source of happiness as I would listen to the sounds of the city, dancing around my bedroom until 3 or 4 am. I would sit by my bedroom window staring out at the stars wondering how I was going to find my way out of this insignificant, out-of-the-way, farm town.

The chill of November set in and I could feel myself crawling back into my shell. The shorter days and longer nights were something I dreaded every year. I just wanted to hibernate until June. Or I could just run away to sunny LA. and never come back.

In homeroom, there was a new name in roll call. "Tim McCreedy," the teacher announced. "Who's joining school this late in the year?" I thought.

"Aye," Everyone craned their necks towards the back of the room to see the guy who responded with a heavy Irish accent. Stretched out in a desk that seemed twice as small as his spindly body, McCreedy looked back at everyone's stare, raising one eyebrow, as if to defend his response. "When do we eat?" he barked back.

Who was this brash foreigner who stuck out like a sore thumb? Of course, at lunch, I had gotten the scoop. Adopted by one of the local farmers, McCreedy was a foster child who had moved in and out of the system year after year. Apparently, when he became too much trouble, he would be shuttered off to a new foster family.

He already had the eye of several of the girls at school and the coach of the basketball team seemed to have him pegged as the next star of the team. Throughout the weeks, he quickly found his stride among the jocks and the basketball team. Rowdy and an instigator, McCreedy quickly became in with the "in crowd." I didn't know then how often our paths would cross.

My brother, who was Mr. Popular in high school, moved seamlessly between different groups of kids and was well-liked by everyone. He was a good public speaker and could joke with the jocks and sing along with the musicians. I had my own little click of friends who were mostly in the music department and a few athletes who did both. My brother was two years younger than I and he already had the gift of schmoozing. Me? I wasn't a wallflower, but I wasn't Mr. Personality either. I could see my brother having great success as a salesman or business owner. Where did he get that personality? I was… awkward. I seemed to stick out like a sore thumb all the time. I was very blond, like my father. I had just experienced another growing spurt and again I felt like my clothes didn't fit and my feet always hurt in the shoes I had from last year. So, I would fidget.

Sometimes, I would feel good about myself, sporting my confidence on my sleeve. Other days I could sense my shadow trying to run the other way. This particular day, as I fidgeted in my wool sweater, that was now two inches shorter in the arms, my body was aching from a series of jumps my dance teacher had all the boys do the night before. We'd jump and jump and jump and then repeat that series over and over. My legs felt as if they were like rubber bands. Now, I wasn't watching where I was going. I turned the corner and ran right into what felt like a brick wall. It was McCreedy. As I felt my body slam into him, my books and papers went flying everywhere. Laid out on my back, I looked up from the floor, dazed and confused to see McCreedy standing there with his buddies. He didn't say anything, but just stared me down. I didn't know if he wanted to hit me or step over me. As I continued to apologize, he shook his head and walked off with his friends, who were happy to tell me to watch where I was going. I felt like a doormat.

Of course, the torture came in threes. After the Christmas holidays, our chemistry class was recreating the baking soda and vinegar volcano. When the teacher encouraged me to put a little baking soda into the mouth of our papier-mâché volcano, by accident, I sprinkled half the box into the vinegar, dish soap, and red dye concoction. This created a chemical reaction that exploded upward and outward, painting the ceiling with thick, red, soapy foam, and McCreedy happened to be face first in my mistake, silently fuming. He was either highly reserved or was conserving his outburst of anger for another time.

The third time was the charm. By late Spring, the weather was comfortable enough to have gym class outside. Mr. Allen, my gym teacher, picked two teams of four guys each to run a baton relay race. We would run the full length of the track once and hand the baton off to the next guy as we competed against the other team. I was to hand the baton off to McCreedy, who was on my team. On the baton pass, I accidently stepped on his heel, twisting his ankle. Writhing in pain, all he could do was curse me out repeatedly from his sprawled-out position in the gravel, as I kept apologizing and apologizing.

He was not able to participate with the basketball team for several weeks until he was able to put pressure on his ankle. McCreedy was one of the first-string players and someone who would score the majority of points each game. I became public enemy #1. Not only were he and his teammates angry with me, but once it got out that I was the one who injured the star basketball player, I was hated by classmates and fans alike. All I needed was the scarlet letter on my back. Everyone finds out everything in a small town.

Needless to say, when summer break came, my mom and dad thought it a good idea to go back to Los Angeles, spend time with my aunt, and perhaps, get a part time job.

Summer in LA and I was back to the familiar. I felt like I was coming home. I took an early morning flight from New York so that I could get into LA in the morning because of the three-hour time difference. Bill picked me up from the airport. It was great to see him. We had plenty of time to get caught up on what he and the guys were up to as we sat in heavy traffic on our way to Venice Beach. Bill had my surfboard and gear in the back seat, so I quickly changed. When we finally got to Abbot Kinney Boulevard, Bill informed me, he had to drop me off, and head to work. Typical cousin moves. He'd done that ever since we were kids. I assumed we'd spend the day surfing with the guys and hanging out, but I was wrong.

Venice was particularly quiet in the morning. A few roller skaters doing maneuvers down the street, danced between couples having coffee, and several artists setting up their works for sale. I passed by Pete's to see if any of the guys were hanging out having breakfast, but no one was around.

The waves were non-existent on this particular morning. I felt disappointed that I came so far for so little. I waxed the deck of my board and paddled out to "that spot." The entire process seemed so familiar. I imagined it would be like riding a bike. You never forget.

Sitting on my board, honoring the morning, I heard a huge splash next to me. I turned to see a spry pelican about the size of a small house who had come to join me for my morning constitution. "Well, hello," I said. "What brings you here this fine morning?"

He looked at me with hesitation, as if he were going to answer, and then slowly and silently turned to face the sun. His buoyant feathers glistened in the water as his long snout seemed to sense a possible food source below us.

He opened his enormous wing span and craned his neck, as if to scratch an itch. Then he returned to his resting position. There we were, two birds of a feather, so to speak… admiring the morning sun as we silently bonded on a sea of tranquility. In my mind, I immediately rephrased my previous thought. I came so far for so much. I didn't have perfect waves at my feet, it took over two hours to drive in heavy traffic from the airport, and none of my friends were around. What I did have was that overwhelming sense of ease and a calm I could find nowhere else.

All morning, I would observe the traffic of beach lovers come to their place of peace. As I looked around, I could see people exercising or doing yoga. Occasionally, someone would walk onto the beach, wiggle themselves out of their shorts and t-shirt. The last thing to come off were their flip flops in mid-stride, as they jumped into the surf. Some would swim in the white water or stroll along the sand while others would meander back out, pick up their clothes, and walk immediately back to their car. It was a ritual. A tribute to their mental health and well-being. It was if they were called to the sea by some unknown force that beaconed them. Then I remembered why I was here. I didn't want to be anywhere else in the world, but right where I was.

I saw Big Steena giving a private surf lesson to a shapely blond woman on the beach. I observed this scene for about 15 minutes. I then realized it was Tally, the waitress from Pete's. He was attempting to show her how to pop up on her board. She shyly committed to the action but seemed more worried about getting sand in her skimpy bikini, all the while keeping one eye on Big Steena. He seemed to be quite finished after showing her fifty versions of the pop up in order for her to understand the movement. She was more interested in him than her surfboard. She stood up, brushed off the sand, and provocatively picked up her beach bag. She then planted a big kiss on his unsuspecting lips. He seemed to resist at first, but then leaned into her advance. I guess he figured he would get some type of gratification after an hour of showing this woman how to stand up on a board firmly rooted in sand.

As she walked off, he turned and waved at me, seemingly knowing I was there all along, witnessing the show. He motioned for me to come over.

"I just wanted to say hi! I didn't want to interrupt your surf lesson."

"That's just an hour of foreplay," he smiled. Come on, let's paddle out!"

"But the waves are really bad today," I said, wondering how he expected to surf on nearly flat water.

"There are no bad waves, only bad decisions," he smiled as he grabbed his board and headed for the sea.

We paddled out together past the breakwater as we talked about how much I loved LA. We straddled our boards and watched the activity of the early afternoon unfold on Venice Beach. He was astutely metaphysical in his words and descriptions of life. He seemed like a man who had lived much longer than his physical years. I will never forget his explanation of how to choose a wave.

"Waves are like friends" he observed. "Some are big and bold, some not so much. Others come to greet you, while still there are those you have to chase. There are those which are deceiving, as they look good in the beginning, but will betray and crush you in the end," he grimaced. "It's truly hard to know the perfect wave. Only when you are within its folds do you realize it was either a good or bad decision on your part. By that point, it's either too late or just right."

He spoke with such eloquence and often seemed to see life in metaphors. I thought him the kind of person I could talk to for hours. Very much like my father. I could see now how he commanded attention. He was everyone's high priest. He was the Big Steena.

I told him about my experience I was going through in school with the new kid that came to town, explaining how I felt like the outsider.

"Life gets better," Big Steena reassured me. "We don't have to end up anywhere near where we started." We attempted a few waves and then he told me he had to head back for another surf lesson. I thanked him as he made a beeline for the boardwalk.

The following few weeks were like homecoming. Bill and I meet up with the whole gang, surfing different breaks that were known to the locals. Everyone's summer seemed busy. Bill had his weekly lawns to mow, Canter had lifeguard duty three days a week, while JackO had to work at the Surf Shack. Big Steena had his surfing lessons while Sting Ray worked part time at Gold's Gym. I told my folks I would try and find a part time job. Ugh. Regardless, we all seemed to manage to meet and pay homage to the sea.

The exploration of new surf spots, constantly pushed my physical limits. Every session would bring a new lesson for me to learn. The moving water always kept me on my toes. The water helped me to be more intuitive. Perched on my board, I could feel how the waves would work. Were they going to break right or left? Would I get closed out in a wave or make a quicker decision? The water would teach me how to react faster.

By observing others and practicing diligently, I discovered how to position myself in a line up. I learned where to sit on my board, understand when to move in because the tide was changing, or move to the outside because a set was coming. These instincts were developed responses.

Days of dangling my bare feet in the Pacific gave me further perspective on life from the sea's point of view. Those who sought it out, were its equivalent. Calm or angry as the sea could be, the same emotions were expressed by those who graced its shores, swam in its waters, or fought to stay alive. The mere fact that our bodies were made up of over 70% water, suggested the idea that our connection to it was inevitable. Nine months in the womb ruminating in a sack of fluid appeared to provide some metaphysical connection. Our allure to water seemed like a natural instinct.

"Hey daydreamer," Bill said, unrooting me from my drifting mind. "We need to work on your bottom turns."

I didn't yet know the terminology, but I knew that when you got to the bottom of a wave, you needed to generate more energy to keep moving forward. Bill was a master at this. So, it was time for me to pay attention to the master.

"This is your foundation of wave riding. I've noticed you instinctually attempting this without even realizing it, but now, I want you to understand mechanics," Bill said in a serious tone. "Two kinds. Forehand bottom turn, means you're facing the wave. Forehand = facing. Backhand bottom turn, means your back is to the wave. Backhand = behind."

"Everything seems like a formula," I responded.

"Big Steena's method of teaching," Bill smiled. "Your bottom turn is essentially how you transform the energy of your board to continue moving forward, because that's what we want in life, right? To keep moving forward?"

I could hear Big Steena's words coming from my cousin's mouth. It was amazing how a great mentor could change someone in a good way, without them even realizing it. This was the 2.0 version of the cousin I grew up with back East. It was incredible to see his growth.

"Based on the size of your wave and your position at the bottom, you can decide to cut back up the wave to the soft shoulder with a diagonal bottom turn. This is a minor progression. You can also cut back up to the face of the wave with a vertical bottom turn that gets you closer to the pocket. This is a major progression." Bill crouched down in the sand to show me the shifting of my weight.

“So, the vertical bottom turn is a much tighter turn to go back up to the top of the wave,” I translated back to Bill.

“Yes, that’s right. The more you surf, you will find yourself riding the steeper part of the wave and will progress to a more vertical bottom turn. Now that you’re aware of it, you have to get it into your body. You only discover that by doing.”

The following day, I got the opportunity to work on my bottom turns at El Porto in Manhattan Beach. Bill woke me up at 4am. "Roll out, bro. We have to beat the crowds," Bill nudged me awake. "Grab your board."

I was really hoping for a coffee run on the way. My body felt like it was pulled through a keyhole and needed a good caffeine fix to at least help me open my eyes.

Located in front of the El Porto neighborhood of Manhattan Beach, El Porto had been a favorite spot for locals for years. We drove north to the 45-street section of the beach. The day was cloudy and rumbling with thunder in the distance but by the time we got there the weather seemed to be moving out to sea. There was the dawn patrol sitting about 40 feet off shore. "The locals here are very protective of their waves," Bill said as if it were a warning. "Come on, I know a great hole we can hit up."

We walked along the wide beach past the local herd. The large oil refinery loomed behind us, as a testament to man encroaching on nature for profit.

"That's such an eyesore," I said, looking at the smoke pouring out of the stacks. Bill just looked at me shaking his head, as if there were no words, he could express about it.

"The winter swells here are amazing, but summer is more mellow. It's a good place to pull in some good technique," Bill said, pointing out towards the waves. As I looked out to the water, there was a lone surfer coming in on a waist high wave. "There's the man," Bill shouted.

Big Steena saw us and paddled into shore. "I was hoping you guys would find me."

"I knew where you would be," Bill laughed.

We paddled out and sat out back. The waves were changing. Big Steena pointed out the sandbar to our left and explained to me how the waves were being pushed past it on the right, creating good swells that broke into waist to shoulder size waves. I could see how the wind was pushing the water as it split around the sandbar then rolling up into waves being guided by the sandy bottom below.

We had a good morning set. We headed back to the beach for some coffee and some sandwiches Big Steena had packed for us. The beach was now starting to get crowded. Even "off season", the crowds at El Porto were notorious. "It's a good location and good waves for beginners here," Big Steena confirmed.

Lightning flashed in the far distance, North of us. We counted in seconds before we heard the rumble of the thunder. "That's about eight miles past us," Bill said to me.

"Why do you think the lightning is attracted to the sea?" Big Steena asked the rhetorical question. "The sea is a magnetic force that snares the attention of God's hand. She buoyantly floats below as he gracefully reigns above. But there is an unspoken attraction that pulls the fingers of God downward towards her just before the clouds rumble."

I looked at him, intently, trying to follow his analogy.

"Why do you think the prowess of the sea sneaks up regularly on the unwitting sand, massaging his grit and grain? It's the law of attraction. Yin. Yang. The inevitable push and pull of the Universe. The opposites that attract and release."

Bill smiled, as if he'd heard this story before.

"The moon pulls her magnetic carpet and pushes the resistant tides. The tide, in turn, rises and gives his energy towards her majesty, the sea, who then tickles the sand as he gives in to her advances. Yin and Yang."

I stood there with my mouth open, like a cod fish. "I can honestly say, I've never looked at nature this way," I managed to mumble.

"We are all just grains of sand," he retorted as he pickup his board and meandered into the water.

The waves were particularly choppy by the afternoon and the sea just felt as if she were disheveled. As I sat on my board waiting for the next swell, on the wind, I heard voices raised behind me. I turned over my left shoulder to see two guys and a girl waving their hands over their heads as if they were trying to get my attention.

One guy cupped his hands to his mouth and shouted, "grey suits." He paused, to see if I had heard him. I looked at him perplexed. He repeated himself, "grey suits!"

I thought, "ya, great soup," as I turned back to give him a thumbs up. At that same instance, my board hit something along the right rail. I thought, "damn, while these guys were distracting me, I hit a rock or some coral." I immediately looked back at the guys, confused. I then saw the girl, put her flat palm, turned sideways, up to her forehead.

My heart felt like it was squeezed up into my throat, as my body coiled. "Sharks," I stammered. My first instinct was to pull my bare feet out of the water on to my board. I froze. I looked back at the other three to see what they were doing. My body started to shiver as if I were cold, but it was the adrenaline coursing through my veins. On my left, about six feet away, my eye caught a fin pop up above the surface and then disappear. Then another fin appeared in front of me and then vanished again under the foamy water. I didn't know what to do. I was paralyzed. I couldn't move. I grabbed my knees and pulled my chest into them. My board would surge forward with each passing swell. I felt as if I was being feed to the sharks by the waves. "What if I fall off? What if they tip my board and start a feeding frenzy using me as bait?" My mind was thinking a hundred thoughts, but my body was stuck in the fetal position as if I were glued down by the sex wax.

Another fin popped up alongside my right rail. This time I could see the entire length of the shark. He was practically the length of my 7' board. His ominous grey-black sheen and pointed nose brought a shiver down my spine. "What the hell is a farm boy doing in the middle of the ocean," was the self-deprecating dialogue running across my lips.

I suddenly felt a swell raise my board upward leading me towards the wave's crest. I felt a looming presence over me as I looked to my left. Big Steena whizzed by me on his board yelling, "move it," as he departed over the lip of the wave.

I snapped back into flight mode. I looked behind me to see another wave surge upward. This one had my name on it. I waited to get the board right under the wave's momentum and popped up. Off I went, riding my gallant steed away from danger, my heart pumping a hundred miles an hour. With razor sharp intent, I dug my heels into the deck. I crouched further down to keep a lifesaving connection to this plank that was taking me to safety.

About two feet from the shore, I looked right and left to check if the coast was clear and then jumped off my board dashing up onto the sand. I collapsed on to home turf feeling a sense of relief. My head was pounding and my breath short and rapid as I tried keeping my heart from detaching from my rib cage.

I laid still staring at the moving clouds. Big Steena saved my life. It really was mind over matter. We both experienced the exact same frightening event, yet Big Steena somehow manage to get through it without falling apart. In my moment of fear, frozen on my board and wallowing in the possibly negative outcomes, Big Steena looked for a solution and did what needed to be done. That was to move and only pay attention to his useful, positive thoughts.

As I lay their sprawled out in the sand, a mental waste heap, words and phrases kept popping into my head...

"You have to be a problem solver," I could hear my mom lecture.

"You either do something or you don't," my dad always said.

"Just grains of sand!"

Chapter 5

Discovering My Resolve

I didn't go to the beach for weeks after "the event." I was too shaken up to even look at the water. It didn't seem to affect me as much that day, but it somehow made its way deep into my psyche, days later. I would constantly come up with some excuse as to why I wasn't going to the beach that day.

About two weeks into my funk, I was home, moping around the house. My aunt served me a big plate of spaghetti and meatballs for lunch. My cousin Bill was at the neighbor's house mowing their lawn, which he would do for many of the surrounding neighbors in order to make a buck. After lunch, my aunt served me a big cup of coffee as she poured one for herself. There was an awkward silence permeating the air and I knew something was coming. She sat down at the table and cleared her throat. "Did you and your cousin have a fight?" she asked, knowing all along what the real reason was.

"Oh no, aunt Martha," I said. "Bill and I are solid."

"Did you give up surfing?" she quickly spouted.

I felt like I was stabbed with a 10-inch dagger. It hurt me instantly to think that my favorite aunt considered me to be a quitter. She thought I gave up. After ruminating on her words, I quickly replied. "No, no, that's not it at all." As I was saying the words, I doubted them as they crossed my lips.

Another several minutes past. As she thumbed through the newspaper, she said to me, with the newspaper covering her face, "its ok to be scared."

I didn't speak. I felt she knew. I started to sweat. In that moment I was feeling that if I responded, it would become truth. It would make it all real. If I answered, it could spoil everything. Then my mom would find out. I wouldn't be allowed back to LA. My whole summer would be destroyed.

She lowered the paper. "The sharks have to live somewhere too," she said nonchalantly shrugging her shoulders.

I burst out with a response as if I couldn't hold my secret in any longer. "Please don't tell my mom. She won't understand and she will never let me come here again."

"Who?" she laughed and went back to her newspaper. At that very moment, my cousin walked in the door and came into the kitchen. He was sweaty and half covered in cut grass. He poured himself a tall glass of cool lemonade and stood at the sink drinking it down in one gulp. As he walked back to the front door, he casually said to me, "we hittin' the beach tomorrow?"

I responded instantly as if it were my subconscious reacting. "Definitely!"

I don't know if this was coincidental, but it just seemed as if I was set up. That was the last we ever talked about it.

The next day, Bill and I headed to Venice to surf. Big Steena was already on the beach. He was sitting in the sand with his eyes closed meditating to the sound of bells from the windchimes that were hanging on the metal swing sets situated in the sand not far away. Bill stuffed his surfboard into the sand and grabbed his bag. He ran up to Jeff Ho's Surf Shop to buy some more wax. Big Steena came out of his meditative state. He slowly lifted himself out of the sand and noticed I was there, standing guard over Bill's board.

"Hey Golden Boy" he called me. "Welcome back to the beach."

I thought, "how does he know I wasn't hanging out at another beach this past week?"

"If you knew the dangers that lurked outside your front door every day, you'd never leave your house. Tu sabes?" he added in Spanish. "Fear is important. It's a great motivator, if you use it as a learning tool. There will always be things in life that scare us. It shows you that you are alive. If you're smart, you will use it to become more aware. More aware of your surroundings. More aware of who you are."

I looked at him, with eager enthusiasm. He had become my "Happy Buddha" as what he said always seemed useful.

"Those sharks have to eat too. They were chasing the fish that were passing by us in the moment. They were just curious as to who we were. I'm sure they were more afraid of us than we were of them. We were hanging out in their home."

It was thoughtful of Big Steena to try and help me get past my fear. I knew it was coming from a place of love. I tried getting back in the water over the next week. Every shadow of seaweed floating just under the surface, any sudden movement of a fish jumping, or bird diving, would send me running back to shore.

Eventually I realized that we were invading the shark's habitat. It wasn't the other way around. Hopefully we didn't have to cross paths again any time soon. It took me awhile to finally feel comfortable surfing again. I took Big Steena's words to heart. I couldn't let fear control my life. I was going to be more aware of my surroundings and understand that we had to live in harmony with everything around us.

I was not there yet. Even on those days when my confidence was stoked and I was fired up ready to ride, the sea would make me aware of the fact that I was only a co-participant.

Respect for the water was a lesson I continued to learn. There was no place for "ego" in surfing. If I got too cocky and all knowing, the waves would pound me into submission. This was often a lesson in humility.

There were also two perspectives on trepidation. In one aspect, it offered up the reasoning that issues may not be as difficult as I perceived them to be. Perhaps I created too much drama around an issue or gave it too much power. The other aspect was that being too confident was just as bad as being paralyzed with fear.

Through my own learning process, I came to know myself and what I was capable of. This belief in myself was important for my emotional growth. The balance of humility and trusting in my abilities provided me with great clarity.

The summer was flying by and the thoughts of going back East hovered like a specter waiting to collect. I needed to stay focused and positive. All good things transition. These were transitions I needed to face head on and be ok with.

Big Steena wanted us to meet in Venice in the late afternoon on Friday.
I said to Bill, "Aunt Martha seems so easy about you going out and doing things on your own." Little did I realize she was in earshot of my words. She walked back into the room and smiled,

"I want you two to have many adventures." she said, "This way, you get to see how the world really works. I'll see ya when I see ya," she said with a wave. It was so different from my upbringing on the farm. I was envious of that.

We jumped in the station wagon and headed for the beach. The swell of tourists and summer weekend revelers jammed the highway and beaches to full capacity. Like all of us, they just wanted to have fun before their Monday doom and gloom settled back in. We meet Big Steena at Pete's. Pete had large bags of ice ready for us, so we helped Big Steena carry them through the crowds.

Venice Beach was a little hamlet by the sea. It represented a place where any outsider could feel welcomed. It was full of graffiti, plagued with drugs, and was often dirty and unkept, but Venice had a "spirit of community." Off this magical strip the evidence of urban decay was even more obvious. There was an apparent struggle between the old and the gentrification. "The flow of change," Big Steena would comment.

He must have seen the look change on my face as we walked further away from the ocean and Pacific Avenue.

"Dogtown was considered paradise. The ocean was the magnet that brought so many people here to Venice Beach, including me," Big Steena smiled proudly. "It seemed like the furthest point away from the confines of the establishment." We walked down Dell Avenue which led us to the Venice Beach Canals. "The canals were built in 1905 as a private real estate development. In their heyday, they were a gleaming tribute to the canals of Venice, Italy."

It seemed as if we were entering a secluded little beach community tucked away from the everyday world. Ducks meandered down the canal while tall egrets dined on tiny smelt rushing about in the water. Children played along the banks while locals strolled down the upheaved sidewalks, saying hello as if they knew you for years. I loved the bohemian vibe here.

Big Steena pointed down the long corridor of water. "The canals and the homes around them are now a neglected shell of their former selves."
Many of the houses were either in disrepair or uninhabited. The long canals reached outward reflecting the blight right back. "I've tried for years to make this place shine, but it seems to go through cycles of great and not-so-

great," he said sadly. "The problem is, most people go through life thinking they have everything to lose. When in truth, it's just the opposite."

"This is home," Big Steena announced.

The less than stellar clapboard house stood perched along the edge of the canal adjacent to a gentle sloping foot bridge. Its white weathered boards gave way to a sense of familiarity. He pressed the blue door open to reveal an orderly, overstuffed dwelling that seemed like an homage to the 1960s.

A pungent scent of patchouli introduced itself as he led us into the living room. Hanging on one wall was a large, white longboard with a black dolphin etched into the bottom left corner near the tail. Different colored sarongs hung over lamps like shades as a large wind chime gently gonged in the corner from the soft breeze blowing in from the open jalousie windows.

Against the back wall was a glass table half-draped with tassel-laden fabric. A black and white sugar skull stared outward from the table's top facing the door as if to stand guard. The scattered light from the late day sun gleamed off the towering points of milky white crystals that were strewn across the table. In the center of this makeshift altar was a statue of the Virgin Mary surrounded by half used candles and other much smaller religious figurines. A tall goblet of water and a burnt bundle of sage completed this sanctioned space.

On the opposing wall stood a large bookcase filled with volumes of law books, esoteric manuscripts, and books on art and philosophy. We dropped the melting ice bags into a little freezer. Big Steena poured Bill and me a glass of lemonade in the tiny little kitchen and took us down a short hallway past a large bedroom and out the back door of the house.

The exit opened out to an ample back yard bordered by the canal on one side and an old unpainted fence completing the boundaries. There were a few girls stretched out on a blanket in the grass next to a large statue of Buddha. Several guys stood around drinking beer and laughing. A couple were seated at a picnic table at the far end of the yard smoking a joint, engaged in what seemed like a serious conversation.

More locals started showing up to the afternoon soiree, bringing gifts of food, pot, and longwinded stories about the environment, the plight of the neighborhood, and how many waves they caught that day. Canter and JackO showed up with a keg of beer and I could see Sting Ray holding court, chatting with an array of typical California girls. "A real triple threat" Sting Ray would call them - blonde, tanned, and beautiful.

The master of ceremonies was also regaling a small crowd about how important it should be to do what makes you happy in life.

I was more of an observer than a participant. It's as if I was absorbing bits of information to utilize somewhere down the road to my budding experiences.

As the late day waned, the crowd, the music, and the laughter all seemed to stir, like the gas in a champagne bottle anticipating it's opening.

"The golden hour is approaching," Big Steena announced in a cryptic voice. It's as if that was the keyword. Before I knew it, the party was on the move. Several of the guys grabbed their surfboards while others gathered the blankets, food, and alcohol.

We all filed out of the back yard and made our way down the canal towards the beach. Luau torches were burning brightly. One, held by the leader of the pack and one held by the last one out of the house.

One of the party goers was coming around to people draping leis over their heads as she offered them a kiss on the cheek. Earth, Wind, and Fire's *Boogie Wonderland* was resounding from a large boom box behind me as a handful of roller skaters whizzed by dancing to the infectious tune. Canter and I grooved down the sidewalk taking turns twirling one of our new found friends, Maria, who was a dance teacher at a local studio.

The party train made its way past the board walk and down to the beach. Several of the guys jumped on their boards and hit the waves. I helped two guys set up a little tent that we put all the food and drink under. Bill, Big Steena, and a few other guys gathered dry beach wood and anything else they could burn and created a huge bonfire on the beach.

Sting Ray and Canter passed out beers as everyone then seemed to come together as if they were expecting something to happen. We were now all facing West as the setting sun began seeping into the watery horizon.

The Golden Hour was upon us. This time of day transformed daylight into a spectacular palette of red, orange, and yellow light splashing across the indigo sky. These golden tones reached upwards with fingers of fire while the sun waned into the twilight. I could hear the oohs and ahs as the sun's daily occurrence took your breath away.

"Amazing what you see if you pay attention," Bill said as he leaned on my shoulder. We watched the surfers in front of us sitting on their boards experiencing the phenomenon from a different perspective. As the final glint of sunlight disappeared beneath the water line, there was an unequivocal sense of peace before me.

"If you ponder the questions of the Universe and beyond, just stop and take a good look around you. You just might find the answers," Big Steena suggested.

Here I was, communing with my fellow surfers in nature. One year after becoming an Angeleno, I finally felt like I belonged somewhere and it made life that much sweeter.

Chapter 6

Rites of Passage

I began to feel a sense of rocking as my entire body shifted in the cool morning air. My eyes opened to the sight of seaweed staring back at me, as I realized half my face was planted in the sand. I slowly pushed myself up as my head began spinning from the immense volume of beer I consumed, evident by the number of bottles surrounding me.

"Hey Golden Boy, you still with us?"

I recognized the familiar voice, as I half-heartedly brushed the sand from my face and lips.

"She slipped away from you, dude."

I recognized the voice to be JackO's. "She who?" I managed, trying to get the words past the sand on my tongue. He just smiled.

I vaguely remembered a girl introducing herself as Sandra, totting a six pack of beer and an inviting smile.

"After a beer or two, your lips seemed as if they were sex waxed together. You two never came up for air."

"Except to down bottles of beer," I retorted, sensing my burning, chapped lips. I looked around in that moment. The bonfire was nothing but embers. Several couples were asleep on the beach and the smell of charred wood and seaweed introduced itself to my nostrils.

There was already a lineup of surfers in the water waiting to catch waves. As I slowly stood up, I could see my cousin catch a wave and roll in towards shore. He came running up to me, board over his head.

"Hey Drew, how ya feelin'?" Bill smiled.

"Don't worry Zip, I got my eye on him," JackO announced. "Big brother's looking out."

All I could do was muster up a half-smile that seemed tainted with both shame and uncertainty. My head was throbbing, but something inside me almost enjoyed the fact that I was part of a gang of friends that looked out for me and made me a part of their family. It was a nice affirmation of acceptance. A feeling that I did not seem to experience with my friends back at school.

Suddenly, we could hear the wailing of a whistle down the beach and a familiar voice yelling, "clear a path!" We could see Canter commanding the beach as we followed his gaze towards a small girl, thrashing in the white water about a hundred yards from shore. He immediately jumped up from his lifeguard stand, his eyes darting quickly back and forth, up and down the beach. He surmised that he was the closest to her and in a split second was in the water swimming towards this desperate soul. Bill went running towards the shoreline, with JackO and I trailing behind.

The girl had gone under the water and Canter dived in after her. There was a long, heavy pause in the air as everyone watched, anticipating the outcome. Suddenly, Canter surfaced without the girl. He took several deep breaths and dove under again. In a split second he reappeared again. The girl was nowhere to be seen. He took a huge gulp of air and dove back under the churning sea. My heart sank, anticipating the worst.

Suddenly, Canter broke the surface with the girl, unconscious. He flipped her on her back and swam, with impossible strength, back to dry land. He dragged her up on shore and laid her on the sand as his fellow lifeguard took over and started CPR.

Bill ran over to Canter patting him on the back. We watched as the grip between life and death teetered on the edge for this poor girl. She apparently just came out to catch some morning waves. It was a fierce reminder of just how thin the tight rope was that we walked between life and death. Big Steena would refer to death as the “lifting of the veil.” The idea that death was always over us, lingering behind a thin veil or shroud, in a space we couldn’t see or touch, was truly a frightening thought.

The crowd cheered on the diligent lifeguard as he methodically pressed life-giving thrusts to restart her heart. He would alternate with short bursts of mouth-to-mouth resuscitation. I glanced over to see an ambulance pulling up to the edge of the beach about 200 yards away, as two EMTs jumped out and darted towards the crowd.

In that instance, the young girl came to life, water spewing from her mouth as she contracted from the pain of someone pounding on her chest. The EMTs quickly took her vital signs, sensing she was stable, but thought it best that she be whisked off in the ambulance for further evaluation at the hospital.

As the crowd cleared, there stood Bill, JackO, Canter and I, in a perfect square formation, like guardians of the four corners of the earth! This was my first encounter with near death. I was not sure if it was because I was hungover or the trauma of the girl's fight for her life with me as a witness, but it struck a chord in me that made it difficult to comprehend. No matter what my reasoning, it was disturbing and humbling at the same time.

"Boy, did Sting Ray miss out on the morning drama," Bill said, breaking the silence. "I think our hero deserves a stack of pancakes. Let's go to Pete's."

"And some coffee for our party boy over here," JackO said, glancing my way.

The bravery Canter showed that day was impressive. It was a side of him I never saw before. He jumped into action, as if on auto-pilot. He did his job and rescued a life! That took a very special kind of person to be able to do that and it made me proud to be his friend. Was bravery a learned response or something that took over your body in a do or die situation?

Canter's bravery did not seem like there was an absence of fear, only the ability to manage it when the situation called for taking action. His Venice Beach lifeguard training kicked in. He wasn't afraid to expect more from himself. He was good at being patient. Mostly, he was not afraid to earn the right to lead. This is what I saw in my friend that day. All the qualities of a hero. Just another reason to look up to him and appreciate who he was.

The following day, after a good night's sleep in my own bed, JackO pulled up in front of Bill's house very early in the morning. There were West-Northwest swells rolling into Venice and the offshore winds were blowing down from the Northeast, making the conditions perfect for surfing Breakwater. "Wake up fellas, Breakwater is firing. There is already a line of traffic heading towards the beach," JackO said, in an authoritative tone. "Get your surfboards!"
I climbed into the backseat, wrapped up in my Venice Beach Lifeguard sweat shirt Canter had given me. It was warm and comfy and had a hood I quickly pulled over my head.

The water was powerful this morning. I could see how that young girl nearly lost her life the day before. The perfect conditions were not what I was used to. I attempted several pop ups, among the large group of surfers all trying to get a taste of today's exceptional conditions.

"Hey, locals only!" some guy yelled back at me after my failed attempt.

"Go back to Beverly Hills, princess," another guy yelled out, after my third failed attempt.

"Most people don't want to know your beliefs, but they often want to impose theirs on you," JackO assured me. "Don't listen to those clowns. They need to learn respect."

JackO was in a rare mood. He was encouraging, helpful, and even cordial. Maybe Canter's impressive actions inspired a different outlook in him.

JackO was the kind of guy who would normally intimidate me in high school, but there was an almost empathic side to him. He was always looking out as if he were my big brother. He also knew how close Bill and I were and he had so much respect for my cousin.

JackO had this ability to keep people off balance if he chose to. It was in his mannerisms. I would watch him intimidate a group of trouble makers who would come into the surf shop looking to steal something or cause a problem. It's as if he thought like they did. He would anticipate their actions. He had a "street smart" that gave him an edge.

Yet, there was an inherent sadness in his heart that I sensed through his eyes. Often hiding it behind that tough facade of his. He rarely let his guard down. I guess we all had some kind of armor on.

JackO had a funny habit of waxing his board and then using the wax like pomade for his thick, black hair. He drank as much coffee as I did, and had an intuitive sense about the water. He was fiercely competitive and seemed to have an unchecked temper, if provoked. He was a study in contradictions.

I was learning a lot in this environment.

Respect seemed to be the underlying glue that held the world together. Respect, of course for the sea, as the metamorphosis of the ocean was a constant. It was never the same on any given day. The sea commanded you pay attention and learn its lessons of order, humility, and … respect. Watching a life almost slip away was a sobering wake-up call.

As I'd learned, surfing was an inner struggle. Although you may be surfing with a pack of guys and gals who loved and adored the sport, ultimately, it was a competition within yourself. Just learning the basics could bring a whole new sense of awareness to your body and your mind.

The physical aspects of surfing were mastered through practice and awareness, but the mental relationship to the art of wave riding was so much more. It took persistence and passion. Both of which were a mental tug of war between how good you wanted to be and how good you could be. It offered traits of trust, believing in yourself, and ways to gain confidence.

Sure, it was about having fun, but as with anything you learned, the basics were essential to your foundation. The joy came when you felt more comfortable with your foundation and trusted yourself to understand where the enjoyment came from.

When I finally caught a great wave, I felt confident, assured, and then humiliated as I flew off the board, my body skipping across the waves until I flip-flopped face first. As I swam back up to the surface my board hit me on the head. I was done. It was either because of my hangover the day before, or the cat calls, or maybe the fact that I was surfing waves I wasn't ready for. I was psyched out. I did my walk of shame back onto the beach, dragging my surfboard behind me.

"Find the calm, not the chaos." I heard a voice from behind me as I sat, sulking on the sand. "Better yet, find the calm within the chaos." Big Steena had witnessed me getting berated by locals and beat up by waves.

"You're heads not in the game this morning." Big Steena was now standing over me, his shadow looming across my defeated spirit. "When there is distraction and turmoil all around you, you must go inward. Tune out the noise and pandemonium and focus on your breathing. The rise and fall of your chest. This mastering of your instincts will take over and you'll trust yourself again. You'll trust your training."

Every few weeks, JackO and Big Steena liked to check out the surf conditions further up the PCH. After surfing, we would always end up at Neptune's Net. Neptune's had been a Malibu staple in the Los Angeleno's community since the late 50s. Good food, close to the PCH, and right on the sea, made this place the perfect meeting spot. Fish tacos, onion rings, and burgers were their mainstay and had been the go-to menu for every hungry wave rider and biker from San Diego to Montecito.

As we pulled up to the diner, there was a large group of people parading around protesting the plight of the pelicans who were suffering from eating the garbage the diner would discard at the end of the day. I almost thought I'd see my cousin Martha-Jayne here. I guess she had other birds to save.

Paul, the current owner of Neptune's Net, was a good friend of Big Steena's. He greeted us and sat us down at a big table outside on the terrace overlooking the beach. "How's Dolly doing?" Big Steena asked.

"My wife is going crazy over the protestors," Paul confessed. "We lock our garbage bins up each night but somehow those birds manage to get in them and a disgruntled employee named Maxx has now led the charge of protestors here every night! It's perplexing. What do you think I should do?"

"Well, a person's right to express their grievances without fear, retribution, or censorship are fundamental to our democracy. It's a First Amendment right," Big Steena professed.

Paul shrugged his shoulders. “Well, guys, welcome to the Net." He passed out the menus and walked off.

"Wow, you sound like a lawyer," I said vaguely remembering the law books on his shelves. Big Steena just smiled back.

Later, I learned from the guys that Steen A. Suarez was not what he appeared. He was born from blended parents; his mother was Mexican and his father a white ranch owner from Texas. His fractured childhood was scarred by the fact that his parents let him know early on that he was a "mistake" so he spent his life trying to prove them wrong.

He graduated from Harvard law school, signed his diploma, and left it on his parent's kitchen table as a final FU! He hitchhiked to Los Angeles, moved to Venice, and spent the rest of his days in board shorts and t-shirts, never to practice law, but discovering a more spiritual life.

He became an activist for the community of Venice, righting the wrongs against the community and working to make Venice Beach a brilliant seaside resort, particularly the canals. I was amazed at all that he'd done and even more impressed with this gentle surfer who was teaching me so much about the ocean and life.

"How did he get his surf name?" I asked my cousin.

"Oddly enough," Bill laughed, "it wasn't from surfing. They were honoring him at a local community dinner for all the great work he was doing. The speaker called him "our great leader, the Big Steena" adding the A from his middle name, by mistake and that was it. The name stuck. It became as synonymous with him as the Big Kahuna."

There was another beach Big Steena was passionate about and it was Sunset Point Beach. "Take Sunset Boulevard West until you hit the ocean. You can't miss it," he would joke.

This is where Big Steena seemed the most comfortable on his board. It was more of a surf break for beginner and intermediate surfers, but I think he liked it because it was just easy. Long, smooth, soft waves that would break on the South, making for a gentle ride. Perhaps he didn't feel like he had to "perform" or play the exemplary teacher role, but he could just "be." It is where I would observe him at his happiest.

Big Steena had a foot work vocabulary and style all his own. Years of cruising the waters, navigating life's curve balls, and enduring adversity gave him a knowledge base to pick and choose from. He was a great mimicker, soaking up interesting techniques which he then seemed to improve upon. I think this is what made him such a great teacher. He would only take the steps necessary to get him from point A to point B, with no extras in between. He calculated every move on every wave, with no room for excess or showing off. He was an artful technician.

Often, after morning surfing at Sunset Point, Big Steena loved to drive back up along Sunset Blvd. He really seemed to enjoy having us along for the ride. He would show us places he loved to go and I think he enjoyed educating us on his adopted city. He loved LA and he always took advantage of what the amazing city had to offer. He would get so excited stopping at Tower Records. Like me, music was an important part of his life. We would pile out of his boat-like convertible and spend our hard-earned money on some of the hottest albums and 12" inch singles.

On Sunset Blvd between Hollywood and Beverly, the boulevard was called "The Strip." It was the love child of depravity and innovation and together this infamous part of Sunset Blvd made its own name for itself. I would gawk in awe at the larger than life, three-dimensional billboards touting the newest movie opening, Eddie Money's innovative album, or Cher's pounding disco anthem, *Take Me Home*. Home to Whisky a Go Go, Gazzarri's Dance Club, The Roxy, and the Rainbow Bar and Grill, these legendary haunts hosted musicians, and celebrities, gangsters and good guys, as well as the Glitter Girls and the Hollywood Vampires. All of them "staples" on the Sunset Strip.

We would finish the afternoon at 6360 Sunset Boulevard. The Cinerama Dome movie theater was a showplace, designed to show widescreen movies on its 86-foot screen. Its white pentagonal and hexagonal panels created a geodesic dome that could be seen from many parts of Hollywood and the surrounding Strip. Its one-of-a-kind cinematic environment indoors made the popcorn and movies seem extraordinary. The panoramic interior was a completely modern design that would rival the dome of the Griffith observatory and replicate the bow of the night sky. It was the only place to see a movie.

Big Steena's love for the City of Los Angeles was transmissible. He wanted us to be well-educated and informed. Not necessarily book smart, but conscious and aware of the life around us. He saw music and movies, water and nature, and community and history to be great teaching tools, which we could participate in freely. All we had to do was pay attention.

Chapter 7

Surfing Lessons

Surfing in Malibu and Venice, as well as along the coast of Southern California, was once an intimate experience done by a handful of guys on long wooden boards. In the summer of 1959, the surfer's life changed in ways no one could predict with the release of the movie, *Gidget*. The movie popularized surfing like never before. After what was called "The Big Bang" surfing exploded across the world! Southern California beaches were never the same. Along with the movie came thousands of kids who now wanted to be a part of the hip surfer scene, flocking in droves to Malibu, Venice, and Huntington Beach. In many ways, it was the best exposure for the sport. It brought commerce, money, and notoriety to the world of surfing. It changed how the industry designed boards. It altered the way we would surf, and it opened up a billion-dollar industry in accessories, clothing, and products every surfer "must have." In other ways, it was the worst for so many others. Especially the pioneers of this once ancient art of board riding.

Bill relayed to me Big Steena's story of how he saw this paramount movement in the industry. "So how do you maneuver from here? Change was not always easy to handle. For some, it's much harder, especially when there is an emotional attachment to a situation. Big Steena saw it as an opportunity."

I had no idea how surfing became popularized in the states.

Bill continued. "Big Steena invested money in many of the local surf shops and through those shops offered surf lessons to the eager new comers to the sport. When shoppers would come into the surf shops to buy equipment, the next natural question was, 'who is a reputable surf instructor?' Big Steena built an empire off the 'Big Bang' of surfing."

On this day, Big Steena and JackO were going to San Clemente to give surfing lessons to a group of guys who were in town for a convention. So Big Steena had JackO get the guys together so we could all make a day of it and cruise down to San Onofre beach for some waves.

"There is only one place that's best for surfing in San Clemente and that's "Lowers at Trestles," Bill explained.

"What is Trestle?" I asked.

"Trestles is a group of surf spots at San Onofre Beach that were along the train trestles. It's the sacred jewel of surf spots!"

Big Steena and Bill drove two cars loaded with eager wave riders and their boards protruding out in every direction. With coffee in one hand and Pete's famous apple crullers in the other, we sang songs blaring from KMET radio at the top of our lungs, as we cruised down the coast.

"I'm on the run
No time to sleep
I've got to ride
ride like the wind
to be free again" **

As Christopher Cross wailed his anthem of freedom, we felt his words as if he was reading our minds. At least my mind. We rode like the wind down Interstate 5.

We found a parking spot near the intersection of S El Camino Real and Cristianitos Road. A dirt path led us down over the dunes, and along the train tracks. This 15-minute walk allowed us to take in the salty morning air, sun breaching the horizon, as we came upon the wide expanse of the beach. This magical landscape was filled with signs of nature putting her best foot forward. The June morning granted us the perfect balance of balmy air and cool sea. The call of seagulls welcomed us while the glistening dew sparkled on the seashells strewn in path-like patterns on the golden sand. Surfing dawn patrol at Lowers, as it was so fondly known by the local surf culture, had been sought out by nearly every kind of surfer for over 30 years.

"Perfect Southwest swells, boys," Big Steena smiled.

"And East winds," JackO chimed in. "The best combo."

I stared at the surf as each wave rolled up and broke left in a perfect cookie cutter formation. One after the other. It's as if the waves were man-made.

We paddled out together just past the break. We sat on our sticks for a moment taking in the breathtaking sunrise.

"You're up," Big Steena gestured to me.

I looked for my wave, and there it was. Three quick paddles and I popped up. The wave peaked perfectly as I rode the glassy face for at least 75 yards. Then Canter went and Bill breezed in. Sting Ray hit a smooth ride, followed by JackO and then Big Steena. Each of us experiencing a mostly perfect set, one right after the other. It's as if we were machines on a conveyor belt. It was an extraordinary feeling. I took a few spills from either improper footing or being too far over the front of my board at times. But I chose not to be over critical of my actions. After about a 45-minute set, it was time for food and more coffee.

Canter and I paddled into shore. “You did really well out there,” Canter commented. I felt a sense of accomplishment. I was proud of how I chose to treat myself. Even though it was insignificant to the rest of the world, I did something right and I gave myself a true stamp of approval. I guess it was then that I realized just how hard I tended to be on myself.

“You have a great surfing style,” I commented. Canter’s tall, lanky body seemed strangely awkward in his transition from flat to pop up. Yet, he surfed the water with a certain buoyancy which seemed to keep him slightly above and beyond the wave at all times. I would sometimes see him walk forward on his board with child-like wonder, testing the limits of just how far he could alter the laws of physics.

We laughed and joked around as we discussed our surfing technique and Maria, his latest crush from the party. "The dancer?" I recalled.

"Ya, that little cutie," Canter beamed. "She said you should come by the studio and take some dance classes."

"Wow," I thought to myself, "I should really experience the LA dance scene."

We were interrupted by a loud group of guys coming over the dunes, yelling and howling at the tops of their lungs. A tall gnarly dude with the face of a boxer, dragged a longboard behind him barking orders to his buddies. "Set up over there," he yelled to one crony. "We can wax up over there," he told another. "Maybe these kooks will get out of our way so the pros can surf," he grunted as he walked by Canter and I.

"So much for surfer etiquette," Canter mugged.

"There's always someone willing to disrupt your peace, if you let them," Big Steena whispered as he walked up behind us. "They are usually the ones short on talent."

Surfers had an unspoken code. Respect the locals. They were the foundation of any surf spot and they set the rhythm. Follow their lead. This was a lesson you could apply to life. New at your job, just starting out in a new field, or learning the ropes in a new profession? Hang back. You will always benefit if you observe. Learn from others. Learn what to do and NOT to do.

Most guys stayed organized and in order. Surfers took turns riding and sharing waves. You just didn't nuzzle your way onto a great swell that you thought you could drop in on and cut off your fellow surfer. There was a line. Take your turn. This was done by being aware of your surroundings and getting into the groove of an on-going flow you would become privy to if you paid attention.

I could see JackO pacing the beach. He was not as forgiving as Big Steena and I could sense his blood beginning to boil as we continued to watch this new group of surfers disrupt every group of wave-worshippers on the beach who were trying to have a zen-like morning. Instead of respecting the breathtaking gift nature was sharing with us, this group of marauders were only interested in disrupting it.

After a rest and some nourishment, Big Steena and JackO headed for the waves. Bill, Sting Ray, Canter and I were having an intense conversation about the East Coast surfer verses the West Coast surfer. As if like shadows, the "gnarly dude" and his cohorts followed Big Steena and JackO out. So, now they were all in the line up together, with the tension so tight you could feel the electricity on the beach.

Big Steena was now first in the lineup. He rode a wave as if he were running a long knife through soft butter. Smooth and easy, without effort. There was not just skill at play here. It was his attitude. It was his approach to looking at the action that gave his surfing style that "eeeease."

I saw JackO about to catch his wave. As he popped up on his board he was quickly cut off by the "gnarly dude" with the loud booming voice and long board. "Gnarly" snaked in front of JackO in order to be closer to the peak and dropped in on JackO's wave. Furious by his actions, JackO rode in behind him yanking on his leash causing "gnarly" to falter and crash, head first, into the sea.

"Never drop in on another dude's wave," JackO howled, "or suffer the consequences," he yelled as he rode the wave into the beach.

Once on shore, "gnarly" faced off with JackO. The two looked like pit bulls ready to attack. JackO didn't hesitate, letting his fist connect with the side of "gnarly's" smug cheek.

As I watched the trail of blood expel from his mouth, I thought, "how did I get caught in this?" Three of "gnarly's" buddies inched up on JackO as I saw Bill and Canter advance towards the mayhem. They were ready to step in and fight with JackO. Never being in a physical fight before, I could feel my entire body tense up. "What do I do?" I asked myself. I'm not ready for this."

JackO quickly reacted kicking sand in one of his perpetrator's eyes then turned and kicked his other attacker in the solar plexus causing the guy to double over in pain. "Learn surf etiquette or stay off the beach!" JackO growled. In that moment, it was over. JackO picked up his board and walked away.

At this point "gnarly" and his crew of misfits dragged their boards further down the beach scoffing off in embarrassment.

Canter and Bill walked over to me, patting me on the back. "Just another day at the beach," Bill joked.

"That was the first time I had seen real aggression over a wave!" I exclaimed.

"That's nothing," Canter said shaking his head. "That was just a little misunderstanding." It opened my eyes to the fact that not everyone played by the rules… as in life.

By 11 am, Big Steena and JackO met their executive clients who wanted to learn how to surf. It was a lucrative day for them both. Sting Ray, Canter, Bill and I surfed the perfect waves off Lowers for the rest of the day.

The day was filled with some deep conversations between us. It just seemed as if we were all getting closer. Perhaps we were now at an age where life was starting to move in different directions or maybe we were just growing up. Between sets, we would visualize the vast sky as an open invitation to choose the way our lives could go.

"My parents want me to go to dental school," Canter confessed.

"My parents want me to go into business school," I said.

My grandmother has high hopes for me," Sting Ray laughed. "She thinks I'm gonna be a doctor or something."

"More like, 'or something,' Canter laughed.

The possibilities seemed as endless as the horizon. Sitting on our planks, observing the way the clouds would drift or the direction the birds would choose to fly, seemed so random.

But in reality, there was a reason and a purpose for their journey. The clouds would be pushed by the prevailing winds while the birds would follow their desire to find food or move away from danger. Were we, as humans, doing the same thing? Were we being pushed into decisions or directions by our family or peers or following the crowd by choosing what was practical and safe? I would often ask myself, *if I could do anything I wanted in life, what would I absolutely desire to do?* It seemed like an impossible question to answer. The answers seemed so random.

We drifted on our boards watching the sunset from the sea. We were enamored by the breathtaking colors splashing upwards from the setting sun onto the sky's blue palette. As we shared our stories, it proved to be everyone's unanswered question.

I got a job washing dishes at Pete's three days a week. This was good in several ways. It got me down to Venice every other day, I was making some pocket change, and the job also came with free food. Pete knew it was only for the summer and that I would be heading back to New York, but because of Bill, I had good references. I could juggle shifts with the other two dishwashers so that sometimes I would work mornings or I could come in during the late afternoon shift after surfing the Breakwater.

Finally, with a little money in my pocket, I went to visit Maria, the now on-again, off-again girlfriend of Canter. She remembered me from Big Steena's party. She taught Luigi's style of jazz at the Dance and Skate Studio in Venice and she insisted I come take a class when she found out I was studying dance.

"How did you hear that I was studying dance?" I asked her, curiously.

"Oh, everyone has a big mouth around here. Especially your cousin," she reminded me.

I explained to her that it was a class I was taking at the YMCA back home, but that I wanted to pursue it professionally.

Maria was a tall brunette with beautiful flowing hair and a long neck. You could tell she was a dancer just by her posture. "My mom had me in ballet class since I was six years old. I love dance, but I really love teaching dance technique instead of performing," she confided in me.

She was a great teacher. She was probably two years older than I, but her comprehension of the movement, especially this jazz technique, was incredible.

She had the owners comp me the class. "He's a dancer from New York," she told the owner. "We need to take care of him."

And they did. The family who owned the school insisted I come back whenever I wished to take class, "on the house," they said. Maria gave me a wink.

As we walked through the canals back to the beach, Maria asked me how Canter was doing. "He's doing great," I smiled. "You should call him. I need to catch this bus," I told Maria. I thanked her and we parted ways.

It felt good to take class again. I was there three times a week, after work. Getting my body back into a disciplined movement was an important step forward. This LA style, expanded my dance vocabulary, sparking a new desire to want to study dance further.

"Big Steena called this morning," Bill came into the kitchen, prying the sleep out of his half-shut eyes. "He said Malibu is already firing, and he said he'd meet us at the pier."

"That sounds amazing," I responded with half a piece of toast hanging out of my mouth, "let's go!"

The word was out, probably because they were touting the swells on KROQ all morning. There was a traffic jam along the PCH. Guys were abandoning their cars on the sides of the road and dashing for the beach, board in hand. It was a frenzied crowd as we made our way to the pier. We finally found Big Steena with ten of his students. The waves were double overhead and there was a longboard traffic jam on the backside of the pier. These waves were unusually large for Malibu this day.

Canter and Sting Ray paddled out. There was a robust gang of locals that they hooked up with who were happy to see them join in. The off shore winds were making for some pushy, ropey rights off the pier. The regulars peeled off mounting the face of a huge breaking wave.

Sting Ray was a pumper. His muscle-bound body and short stature seemed to put him at a disadvantage. It was more mass and density he appeared to have to initiate movement. It almost looked like he was using brute strength to paddle and pop up, but once he was up, he had the speed of a bullet shooting through a barrel. He had a technique of squatting and pumping his legs downward, as if he were peddling. This kept the nose of his board a little higher than most of us, with his weight centered and back.

Canter was eager to catch any wave and that impatience got him caught on the inside. Not catching the wave at the proper location or speed, he started a chain reaction of chaos. Canter's mistake suddenly had him hitting the wave head on, as the white water buried him under its fold. He would pop up for air then quickly disappear again beneath the surface, churning and churning in nature's washing machine.

Bill pointed to a spot about 40 yards from where we last saw him go under. Canter popped up for air in one spot, his board in the other direction. Bill jumped in to fetch his board, as Canter made his way back to the shore.

Exhausted from his struggles, he collapsed on the beach. Bill came ashore with only three-quarters of a board in hand. "That was a powerhouse," Bill yelled out.

We ran over to Canter as he sat up to catch his breath. "That wave came in two directions," JackO said pointing East. "It caught a lot of guys off guard." He tried reassuring Canter that he wasn't the only one.

"How can I avoid that next time?" Canter asked, staring up at Big Steena.

In his usual manner, Big Steena answered, "Don't surf."

"But I have to surf. Sometimes it's just so challenging" Canter retorted.

Big Steena smiled. "Then do something else."

Canter was speechless. I think he expected some kinder words of advice. Instead, he got tough love. Yet, he knew what he had done wrong and he wasn't owning up to his impatience.

I thought a lot that night about what Big Steena said to Canter. I think what he was trying to convey to Canter was that you're going to take hits in life. So, you either have a choice. Take the hit, learn from it, and move forward or change your path entirely. I got the message loud and clear. I think Canter did too, only I felt Canter's underlying anger in the moment. I rarely saw him angry, but it could also be the fact that he nearly drowned. He was looking for more sympathy than wisdom, in that moment. It was just Big Steena's matter of fact way of teaching us another one of life's lessons.

By late August, I was already dreading the thoughts of going back home. I was looking forward to showing my friends in dance class, my new "LA moves" but the rest of my life that came with it, was nothing to look forward to.

Libby came running out of her bedroom, switching on the tv. "Look it's MJ on the news!"

Bill and I were at the table having coffee. There was my cousin Martha Jayne with a huge group of protestors at Neptune's Net.

A reporter covering the massive protest happened to single out Martha Jayne. "This restaurant is killing the pelicans along with other natural wildlife! They have to be held responsible," she proclaimed.

"What a crock," Bill exclaimed. "My sister has to jump on every band wagon."

"Well, it's his responsibility to maintain all aspects of his business. He seems to be neglecting the environment," Libby smirked, referring to Paul, the owner of Neptune's.

"The situation had gotten out of hand. We were there and talked with the owner about it. He seemed as unclear as the rest of the public as to how this was happening," I said.

"Sure, that's what he says. Just like I say I am going to wash the dishes," Libby said as she tossed her blond locks over her shoulder, grabbing her car keys and making a mad dash for the door. "Ya comin' Andy," she gestured. She couldn't get used to calling me Drew. "You're gonna be late for work."

"I gotta go cuz," I looked at Bill.

"I know, work. Well, I got work too," Bill said walking to the sink. "Libby's dishes."

Libby laughed as she flew through the front door.

Libby and Martha Jayne were on two ends of the spectrum. Libby followed the laws, while MJ protested over them. These two polar opposite points of view were often the unraveling between sisters.

Bill met me at Pete's after work. At this hour, Breakwater was so crowded, Bill wanted me to get a sense of the waves along the Santa Monica Pier. Further down the beach at the end of Colorado Avenue, The Santa Monica Pier stretched far out into the sea. This double pier was a fun-filled spectacle of amusements, concessions, and a discord of color, light and sound.

We stayed South of the pier to try on some waist high surf. The growing South-Southeast swells didn't help conditions much, but we surfed a few sets before we met a pod of dolphins who'd come to play with us.

Paddling out back, I was suddenly greeted by three fins gliding by me. In a panic, my first instinct was sharks. I quickly noticed the bottlenose snout of the dolphin as he lifted his head out of the water. I breathed a sigh of relief; grateful they weren't the same sharks seeking me out from our last encounter. As we'd catch and ride on a wave, the dolphins would jump and dive just ahead of the nose of the board seeming to compete with us along the water. They would leap from the encroaching wave in staggered formation three, then four, or five dolphins at a time.

“Duck dive,” Bill yelled out. Diving under, I could see eight or nine dolphins traveling at high speed beneath the waves, close to the ocean floor. They would burst out of the crest of the wave at a velocity that was hard to believe. They jumped and played with us for over 30 minutes until they disappeared.

Bill and I sat out back straddling the rails of our boards, breathing heavy as we tried to recover from the competitive round with Mother Nature’s high-spirited mammals.

We couldn’t go home after that. Feeling completely energized, we headed for shore and walked up the beach to the Pier. We spent hours cruising the girls, eating, and playing skill games long after sunset. The summer nights in LA were incredible. After the sun would go down the overheated days would cool down to a temperate evening. Perfect for hanging out and people watching.

“Sting Ray,” Bill called out. Chatting up some pretty tourist, he looked our way and yelled, “JackO’s lookin for ya!” He smoothed back his wet hair and put his arm around the unsuspecting girl from Iowa. “He wants to meet you at Pete’s at 11pm.”

We strolled back down the pier and walked the long stretch between Santa Monica and Venice.

JackO pulled up in his Firebird. "Come on, get in."

"What's up?" Bill asked.

"A favor for Big Steena," JackO said in a serious tone.

Bill and I looked at each other. We drove up the PCH. It was a beautiful night. The windows were down and the cool night air felt good on my sun-fried skin. The new moon was just a dark shadow in the star-speckled sky. I could hear the waves crashing on the sand as we traveled along the pitch-black road. I loved this drive, no matter what time of day or night. It was freeing. It always seemed like the highway to dreams.

We pulled up along the side of the road. "Come on, let's go," JackO jumped out of the car with determination.

I looked around to see if I recognized anything familiar. In the distance I could make out the silhouette of Neptune's Net.

"Aren't they closed?" I asked.

"Come on, Einstein. Big Steena asked us to look into something," JackO retorted.

We crawled down along the side of the cliff, slipping and sliding on the steep hill. We reached the side of the restaurant and hunched down behind a massive rock hanging precariously onto the side of the sandy terrain. My eyes caught sight of a van parked on the other side of the restaurant.

"Nancy Drew over here, thinks there's something fishy going on." Bill whispered.

"There is! Big Steena asked me to scope things out. And I prefer the Hardy Boys!" JackO said with a half-smile.

"He's been sleuthing around here for days," Bill said.

"He's been what? And who's in the van?"

"Shhh, you chatter boxes, look."

Maxx, the disgruntled employee, was sneaking up to the garbage bins with a crowbar. He slowly jimmied the insufficient locks and flung the garbage bins open. Now the pelicans could have free reign of everything they shouldn't be eating.

Little did this trouble maker realize, the guys in the van were tv reporters with the local news station, filming his actions.

"Smile, you're on candid camera," the reporter yelled, switching on his headlights. There was Maxx, caught, red-handed with crowbar in hand.

He quickly reacted like a deer in headlights, running back up the hill to his car, parked on the side of the road. He sped off down the PCH in the direction of Malibu.

"You can run, but you can't hide," the reporter yelled after him.

We stepped out into the light and walked over to the reporter and his cameraman. They shook JackO's hand. "Tell Big Steena, this will be on the evening news tomorrow," the reporter assured us.

The guy leading the protests against the restaurant, was the same guy who was creating the problem, not the owner of the restaurant. Bill and I looked at each other, not quite believing what just happened. "So, does this officially make us the Hardy Boys?" Bill laughed.

"There's only two Hardy Boys and that's me and Golden Boy," JackO smiled. "But you can be Nancy Drew!"

Sure enough, the next night on KTLA, the story ran about the vandalizing and sabotage at Neptune's Net. The news piece made Paul, Neptune's owner, look good in the public's eye, especially when he chose not to press charges against his former employee, Maxx.

That was about as much mystery and excitement that I was ever a part of. I somehow felt as if we had a small part in vindicating the restaurant's reputation and finding closure to the situation. Of course, it was really Big Steena pulling the strings, behind the scenes. But, nonetheless, it was cool.

By the end of the summer, I had to head back to New York earlier than usual. As an upcoming senior, I had meetings to attend to in order to prep for the final year of my teenage life! Although I had several weeks before school started in September, I came back from LA in late August.

It was a blessing for me that dance lessons were still happening at the YMCA. Although my regular dance teacher was not there, they allowed me to take class with the end of the summer group that was studying currently. After a week of dance with this new teacher, I was impressed by the level and intensity in which she worked. They weren't kidding when they called the course a "Summer Intensive" as it was new technique every day and the group currently dancing seemed older and more competitive.

At the end of class, I sat on the floor, my body collapsed over itself, with puddles of sweat dripping through the hardwood floor boards. It was then that I had a real "A-ha moment." Dance was a discipline I chose for myself. Unlike my activities in school that I was either encouraged to join or was cleverly persuaded by my parents to get involved with, dance, like surfing, was something I chose. I was now extremely conscious of what both disciplines gave me. I no longer felt like a clueless live wire flapping in the air trying to connect. I found my path. I realized then, that I was driven by passion. Yes, singing in choir and playing an instrument gave me another language to learn, which helped me, rhythmically in dance, while sports gave me the stamina. But it was the physical discipline of dance and the demanding rigors of surfing that ignited me in a way I could not explain. I felt like a kettle of hot water boiling over, steam escaping in every direction.

Before this, it's as if my "ideal self" could not match up with my "actual self." In dance class or when surfing, I had less inhibitions, anxiety, or stress. At home and at school, I felt judged, as if I didn't belong, or was completely misunderstood.

While dancing or surfing, for those brief moments, I felt like my actual self. I had permission to be free to express myself through movement, explore my own courage, and embrace the sheer joy of doing something that made me feel connected to my body.

I then realized it was actually me standing in my way. At home and at school I was adhering to what I thought people expected me to be. I would look around and assume I had to be "like this" to fit in or conduct myself "like that" so I wouldn't call too much attention to myself.

I had a new sense of life outside the farm. I was studying dance in a room full of kids that would be shocking to my peers at school. I was surfing with kids who were delinquents, and worldly, and fun.

That stepping out of bounds felt good. It felt rebellious and I was starting to learn how to turn my anger at the world around me into a statement of defiance and self-worth.

By my senior year things were going to be different. I was going to stick to my goals and values, no matter what.

Chapter 8

The Winds of Change

Over the next several months, I seemed to have less classes as a senior, yet I had more meetings to go to. Prom committee, band practice, track, All-state choir rehearsals, French club. I was still going to the YMCA three nights a week for dance.

The pressure was on. I applied to two colleges. The State University of New York system of colleges were a more affordable option for my parents, so we looked at two schools which had a major dance program, as well as a good business school. It was SUNY New Paltz and SUNY Purchase. New Paltz University was in the foothills of the Catskill Mountains, about 90 minutes from New York City. Purchase University was in Westchester County, about 30 minutes from New York. I knew the only way out was through my dancing. It was what I had passion for and I was going to follow it. If it was under the guise of a "business degree" it would give me a foot in the door and a way off the farm.

I was a straight "B" student so I wasn't too worried about my grades not being good enough to get into college. I was more concerned about the dance audition. The schools both asked for a video of the applicant, either in a performance or in class. The video had to focus on the auditioner and had to demonstrate the level the student was at. For a nominal fee the YMCA offered to videotape me in class one day and that's what I sent both colleges as an audition tape. Now I had to wait. Wait for them to decide my fate.

Waiting and observing. The older I got, the more it seemed to come down to those two actions. Both my father and my brother were great observers, which is why they were both great painters. I happened to fall in love with an art form that was fleeting and intangible. I could live and give my art to the public in a visual sense but I could never hang it on a wall. Both dance and surfing were forms of self-expression, which were there one moment - gone the next.

Yet, from the sea, I discovered the fine art of observation in different ways. I'd learned to be more in tune with my surroundings and it came from a simple shift in awareness.

For me, it happened while surfing. Poised in the line-up with other wave worshippers, I could take a moment to witness the colors on the horizon or the dance of the sun splaying across the water. Observing these natural interactions of the elements at play, offered up a feeling that was unparalleled.

In dance, the observation of a combination of dance steps in a routine were crucial in order to quickly learn and repeat it back during class or in an audition. Dance was a series of observations which lead to execution in a matter of minutes. How quickly could you observe something and then repeat each detail back?

Surfers were great observers. Sitting in a line up, waiting to catch a wave, a disturbance far in the distance could be seen. Sitting in the sea on a surf board often gave you a different perspective on things. You could see storms coming or feel their presence before they arrived. You could sense the wind changing or feel the air get heavier. Sometimes you could “smell” the presence of change. To those savvy enough to pay attention, the turmoil of life could also be preceded by a warning before a storm advanced. But every once in a while, an unsuspecting deluge would come out of nowhere and catch you off guard. These were the storms you needed to be mentally ready for. Life could be a "catch and release" or "catch and devour" situation that you needed to try and anticipate - contemplate, in order to have a better outcome. Storms would always come, but it was up to you to learn how to deal with them.

Saturday’s dance class always featured a guest teacher. Madame Taralova had a Russian ballet background and was a strict disciplinarian. She had the ability to drive you harder, push you further, and worked at a pace that forced you to think on your feet every minute. She would be much harder on the girls, especially those working on point. When the boys were up, she expected perfection. My head was in the game. I was focused. I was sweating profusely, struggling through a difficult routine when my eyes caught three guys from my high school staring through the window. McCreedy and two of his new found cronies were pointing and laughing at me through the glass. I broke out into a cold sweat. I crossed the floor and put my back up against the wall. My heart was racing. My secret was out. Oh my God. They saw me. My first thought was *what were they doing at the YMCA?* Secondly, *what were these troublemakers going to do with this new found information I had tried so desperately to keep secret?* I was now caught off guard in the middle of a what was to become a hurricane. My unsuspecting storm had arrived.

In less than a week, the rumors started to fly. I couldn't walk down the hall without getting some side eye or downright sneer. I got to my locker and I had the word "homo" scratched across it. I could feel myself retreat into my book bag. My inner torture was amplified by what I thought people were thinking about me and it was unbearable. "They don't even know me," I cried to myself.

I couldn't go to school for the next few days. I told my mom I felt sick and didn't want to get my friends sick. "What friends?" I thought to myself. Not the cowards who would try to avoid me because they didn't want to become targets too. But staying out of school for a few days was not the right move. It only created more room for speculation and other rumors to spread.

4th period gym found me sitting in the coach's office. He asked me if I needed to talk to him about something? I slumped in my chair with embarrassment. "No sir, I'm just the butt end of a practical joke."

For some reason, he didn't seem to console me or support me in any way. He simply nodded his head and told me I was dismissed. I half felt he believed the rumors. I went to my gym locker and found a note shoved through the grating. "Communist."

The following day, our foreign exchange student came up to me after class. "Are you really a belly dancer?" She asked innocently.

"No," I answered.

"I heard some kids in class say you were a belly dancer. I studied too."

"Oh, that's great. But, no, I'm a ballet dancer," I smiled.

"That is good too," she laughed.

I took Thursday and Friday off from school. It would give me more time to console the tattered fringes of my nerves over the weekend. According to these rumors I was a homosexual, communist, belly dancer! How could people I grew up and knew for years, see me this way? How could I become such a target in this stranger's crosshairs? I had to start thinking logically. Why was I under attack?

I was under attack, because I was following my dream. It was a desire that was not common to others, or often ever seen, where I came from. Yet, only miles away from school, there was a class filled with different kinds of people. Boys and girls who were devoted and committed to a discipline of dance that was only understood by a few. In LA, I had real friends who surfed, loved the sea, and walked a fine line between rebel and go-getter.

Big Steena would say to us, "ride with the flow of the winds. Do not slow or resist them. If you successfully sail the waves of impermanence, you'll never go under."

Ok, well let's see... I liked girls so I wasn't homosexual. I believed in the US Constitution so I wasn't a communist, and I couldn't belly dance. I knew this, but unfortunately, people did not. It was just easier for them to believe the rumors. Including my friends.

I didn't know how to handle this.

It was weeks later, and my mom talked me into going to dance class on a Saturday. It was the last thing I wanted to do, but she saw in my face that I was distraught. I wouldn't tell her what was bothering me, but somehow, I think she knew.

"Why the long face? What's wrong with this?" my dance teacher, Madame Taralova asked as I walked into class. I gave her a quick synopsis of my problem.

"So, you want me, feel sorry?" she poised.

"You asked me," I thought to myself.

"You need Russian resolve," she said pounding her chest. "Especially being boy, in girl's world. You need thick skin."

"You love what you do?" she asked as she crushed the resin under her toe shoes.

"I love to dance," I exclaimed.

"I see this, by expression change on your face." She raised her arms to fifth position over head. "You remember boy, you have no control over what others think or say. You do have control over how you handle it."

I thought about her words the entire class.

I became infuriated. How could some stranger come into my life and turn it upside down? I grew up here and in less than a year, some person I barely knew, had made me the laughing stock of my whole world.

In a few months, some other scandal in school broke and the focus seemed no longer on me. One of the cheerleaders got pregnant from a member of the visiting football team and that was all anyone could talk about. I had sympathy for her. I would still get dirty looks by some people in the hallways, but the environment didn't seem as insufferable. Regardless, the damage was done.

I kept thinking about what my dance teacher said. I needed a thick skin. I was in control of my life. It was up to me to learn how to deal with problems that would come up. I needed to take charge of my life and how I chose to handle a situation. I had to stop caring about what others thought. Now, how would I do this? How do I do this when everyone expects me to be who they want me to be?

I ruminated about this for weeks. Then, I thought about my cousin Bill, my new friends JackO, Canter, and Sting Ray. They all seemed so confident in themselves. When I was with them, I almost felt the same confidence. They each had a sense of who they were. Even though they came from widely different backgrounds, they were so much more mature than those I went to school with. It was just perplexing to me.

It was time I stood up for me, because keeping myself uncomfortable, quiet, and small for the sake of someone else's comfort wasn't worth it. This was my life. Ok, so I knew that time was on my side. I would never have to walk these halls again or see these same small-minded people in my life after graduation, if I didn't want to. That alone gave me strength.

But this could happen again. Somewhere else. How would I handle this again?

It was Memorial Day weekend and my father wanted to take a nostalgic drive up to the bluffs of Fair Haven State Park to embrace the unofficial start of summer. Just like when we were kids, we spent the morning on the lake along the pebble-laden sand on that narrow beach where my brother and I zipped around on that boogie board we loved so much. I took a solitary walk down the beach to sit along a large stone jetty where the incoming waves would break. My mind wandered back to a day in Venice, sitting along the Venice Beach Breakwater, listening to Big Steena talking to a group of his surf students.

"It's our moments of struggle that define us," he would say. "How you perceive something, how you approach something, is what defines your actions. How much energy you give to something will determine its value. What are you paddling away from? What are you paddling towards?" he questioned.

Thinking back, I remembered how those words resonated with me. He was talking about surfing, right? Or was he referring to something else? The more I contemplated his words, the more I started to apply it to my current situation. The more energy I gave to McCreedy and to everyone who wasn't on my side, the more I would let that define me. It would define me as a victim.

"How much you allow something, good or bad, will define your choices." Big Steena lectured.

I was no longer going to be that victim. That decision is what would define me. I was no longer going to give it any power, by letting it be the center of my Universe.

"Summing up a situation, especially one that is constantly changing, and then making that decision, is what makes you a better surfer," he reminded his students.

"...and a better person," I thought to myself.

The following four weekends in June, the YMCA offered graduates one day at their summer camp on Owasco Lake. As a graduate in the program, I was able to go and take one guest with me. I took my brother, Steven. That day, we chose sailing as our activity.

My brother, now a sophomore in high school, was excited to go on the water, as it reminded us both of our adolescent years by the many lakes and oceans we had experienced together.

The small little sailboat was manageable for two, so we set sail on Owasco Lake being pulled by the breath of the wind as that billowing cloud of a sail whisked us gently across the lake. It was the perfect day as the sun was hanging low in the late afternoon sky, the loons escorting us along the soft breaking waves.

Steven had come into his own and possessed such courage by this time in his life. My brother, of course, was very aware of the calamitous year I had just gone through, but instead of comforting me or offering me words of advice, he was a rock for me to look to, even if it was unexpressed. This afternoon was our coming-of-age event, that we could share together. We leaned back in that sailboat, allowing the Westerly zephyr to carry our worries away with its momentous push. We laughed about the days behind us, sharing anecdotal gifts we had each forgotten about. "I wish Bill was here," Steven grinned.

We meandered across the lake for hours, laughing, sharing serious memories, and even crying together, for we knew, life would never be the same for us again.

I was accepted at New Paltz State University the following week. I graduated with my classmates two weeks later. The Universe had granted me the opportunity to move in the direction I so desperately hoped for. I was now gone from that small town and insufferable community that held me back. I was on a plane back to Los Angeles.

Chapter 9

The Aloha State

It was so great to see Bill again. We shared our graduation stories and caught up with each other's progress. I didn't have the nerve to tell him about the horrors of my senior year. I told him about college and how I was going for a dance and business track.

"Well, you'll have all the bases covered," he joked.

Bill had big dreams of expanding his "lawn-scaping business" to include the 90210-area code. "All you need is one or two good clients to get the word out," he surmised. "We are going to Venice today. Big Steena has a surprise for us."

"Well, this is initiation year," Big Steena proclaimed once we met with him in the late afternoon. "We have two graduating into the arms of adulthood. You are both legally considered adults now." He handed Bill and me two plane tickets to Hawaii. "Adulthood is about relationships and how you relate to the world. You have a golden opportunity to make the best out of your lives. You don't realize that your life has just begun." Big Steena looked at us with a soft melancholy expression on his face. I immediately thought of the story Bill told me about Big Steena leaving his law degree on his mother's kitchen table and walking out of her life.

Pan Am airlines would run summer specials to Honolulu from LAX. And every summer, Big Steena would introduce his students who did well or his close friends to experience surfing in Hawaii. He knew that most of us would probably never be able to afford to go there or would be too intimidated to surf in those waters, so he felt it part of his "duty" to enlighten us. Last year was Sting Ray and Canter's graduation, since they were a year older than Bill and I.

Later that week, I called my folks to tell them Bill and I would be going to Hawaii for our graduation celebration. "A gift we gave ourselves," I told my mom. "Does your aunt Martha know?" my mom asked with trepidation in her voice.

"Of course. She might even go," I lied.

“Pack light,” Big Steena recommended. “We will be traveling around Hawaii a bit and I want you to be comfortable.” Bill and I showed up at LAX with backpack and surfboard in hand. The almost six-hour flight was surprising to me. I assumed it was an hour or so from LA. So much for high school geography.

"Welcome to Hawaii," JackO beamed as we deplaned in O’ahu. We were met by beautiful girls draping fragrant floral leis around our necks. Big Steena pointed out the lush, jagged mountains as our taxi made its way to a little hotel in Honolulu near Waikīkī beach.

The island of O‘ahu, nicknamed “the gathering place” was truly that. It was a place where most tourists, the largest portion of the Hawaiian population, and yes, surfers would gather. It was the crossroads between the mainland United States and Asia.

We found our way to the center of Waikiki, unpacked our boards, and took in the local flavor. "We are going to get our feet wet in Waikiki today and then head to Maui in the morning," Big Steena directed.

I honestly couldn’t believe I was here. Hawaii was some place I dreamt about but never thought I would actually see. I was brimming with excitement as Bill and I made our way through every surf shop, gift emporium, and t-shirt hut we could discover.

Waikiki in the summer was every surfer's paradise. JackO told us it was a different kind of wave energy than in the popular winter months, but it is a unique time all its own. “In the summer, South swells roll into Honolulu, making for a great ride all season,” JackO assured us.

This white stretch of sandy beach was meet with light blue shimmering surf. It was the land of the longboard. We watched guys hit the waves with 9 – 9.5-foot sticks that were even brighter and more colorful than the tourists who gathered to watch the spectacle.

“So where are we surfing today?” JackO asked Big Steena. “Pops, Queens, Canoes?”

“Ala Moana Bowls,” Big Steena informed us.

“Ala Mo, it is,” JackO concurred.

"We would like to go over to reef #5 for the best long waves near Waikiki," Big Steena suggested.

"I couldn't agree more," said the taxi driver, who fit five surf boards on his roof, including his own.

“Where is your home break?” JackO asked the taxi driver.

“Jamaica,” he smiled. “But I have a secret sweet spot I love to go to here.”

Ala Moana Bowls was the premiere surf spot on Waikiki. With Diamond Head standing guard in the distance, this deep channel was forged due to a man-made phenomenon that created these fast and furious waves. Restructuring of the Ala Wai harbor along with an adjacent jetty at Ala Moana, helped form the perfect left-hand wave.

“A fresh South-Southwest swell that made its way into the Bowl last night continues to provide some nice size waves,” JackO commentated as if he was describing the scene over the radio. “It’s a bit inconsistent surf on the South Shore, but nonetheless, a picture-perfect Saturday afternoon.”

“Wave heights are hovering in the waist to chest high range,” he continued, two fingers to one ear, “with sets hitting the shoulder to near head high range at the better exposed locations.”

“Look over there,” Big Steena pointed.

The water was a mass with surfers, all trying to get one wave in a set of five that would roll in. There seemed to be some extended wait times between the bigger sets as we watched herds of surfers bob up and down on the swells.

“If we are patient and know where to look, then we will score some fun waves today.” Big Steena added.

It was intimidating to see so many boards in the water. Just getting out to the shoulder could be a challenge. Surfers were rippin’ doing tricks left and right. Air turns, reverse air turns, closeout re-entries. These surfers were crazy and chaotic. There did not seem to be any line-up or pecking order.
“It is high summer and the waves are spillin’,” JackO laughed.

We entered the water crossing over a rocky reef and jumped onto our boards from the far left. It was even difficult for me to paddle out, but I kept up with Bill, JackO, and Big Steena as we made our way out to the shoulder, dodging every kook and trickster on the journey. The water rose and fell in large swells that would almost make me feel nauseous. Bill was itching to catch a wave and didn't hesitate. He saw the wave he wanted and paddled, anticipating its breaking point. He was up… then he was down. My cousin loved a challenge. It rarely seemed like anything was difficult for him. He was already paddling back to find his next one. "You're gonna grow moss on that board if you sit there any longer," Bill joked as he paddled up to me.

"Here comes a beauty, I'll take this one," I said as I started paddling. I popped up. I was moving at a turbo-velocity that was manic. I looked off the nose of my board. There were surfers flying everywhere. I crouched down further to keep the board and the sea as one entity. At the same moment, my head seemed to push me too far forward. I could feel my feet start to separate from the board as I plunged sideways into the white wash. I tumbled and tumbled under the heavy surf, holding my breath for what seemed like minutes. I had to come up for air or I was going to choke to death. I opened my eyes underwater to see a large wave pass over me. It was my time to move. I headed up at an angle, hoping to catch some air at any second. I could feel my board tugging behind me on the leash tethered to my ankle. I met the surface and took a quick gulp of air, before I was bowled over by another wave pushing me back down.

The leash suddenly caught on something and then released. I needed air. I felt a lull in movement above me and now could feel my feet touch the bottom. I had to be closer to shore. I pushed off the sea floor to garner enough speed to hit the surface once again. I was right off the reef. I swam to the rocks with my board in tow behind me. I sat on the rocky jetty, catching my breath as I pulled my board in to me. After sitting for several minutes, hyperventilating, the rhythm of my breathing seemed to return to normal. I took a closer look at my board which now had a new dent near the tail. "Where did that come from?" I thought. "Better my board than my head."

I was now psyched out. I stood on the rocks watching the action unfold before me. I was happy I was done. Not my finest hour and it was my first day in Hawaii. I was hoping that this was not a premonition of things to come. I got the courage to go back in the water, but basically straddled the rails and played spectator. The guys were catching a few. Nobody seemed to have a spectacular run. Not even Big Steena. I don't know why I was comparing. Maybe to make myself feel better. It worked for the moment.

The Hawaiian sunset had a reputation of being one of the best in the world. I would imagine every tourist beach town would want to hold that title. The guys made sure to join me at the water's edge for a glimpse of one of the most awe-inspiring sunsets, Ala Moana could offer. Arching domes of red and orange seemed to pulsate upward as the sun set far in the distance. There were probably 40 surfers in front of us, sitting about 50 yards out in the water, straddling their boards, honoring nature's twilight eventide.

The next morning, we boarded a little puddle jumper to the island of Maui. We were met at the airport by Big Steena's friend and caretaker, Kai. "Hop in gentleman." He drove us in his jeep across the island's valley-like topography as we marveled at the incredibly lush, green landscape that would be occasionally interrupted by the hardened black lava flows that scarred the island over the years. "It is how the island rebuilds herself. Nature is quite ingenious," Kai smiled, almost proud that he could share such a feat. The jeep turned a corner as we barreled down a long stretch of road, with the ocean rolling in from our left.

"You're in the land of the relentless sun, boys," Big Steena exclaimed opening his arms out wide to great the sun. Lahaina was a beautiful, historic town situated between the ocean and the towering westerly mountains. Once Hawaii's capital in the early nineteenth century, Lahaina was also a famous fishing village and old whaling port.

But the real attraction in Lahaina was not breathtaking sunsets or its precious town square, but its enormous banyan tree. This gorgeous triumph of nature, spanning almost two acres across, and towering more than sixty feet high was "the most auspicious and adulated tree, the world over," Kai beamed. "The banyan tree symbolizes the fulfillment of wishes and enlightenment in Hinduism and Buddhism, respectively."

Big Steena was smiling. I could tell he was so honored to have Kai in his life. They were on the same wave length. Two men of a certain age, who loved and respected nature and saw the world as a force of living energy. His admiration was palpable.

Kai pulled the jeep over by the side of the road. We walked the length of the park and reached the huge tree that spanned a quarter of a mile in circumference and possessed 16 trunks reaching down to the earth. These trunks then became a supportive pillar for the next generation of growth from its iron-like roots. We walked up and touched the massive tree limbs. Its bark felt more like a metal pipe. You could sense the weight of its life span hanging heavy in its limbs. JackO hugged one of the downturned roots, all the while Big Steena had two hands on its massive trunk, head bowed, saying a prayer.

Big Steena had a little house just to the West of town, a few yards from the ocean. The white clapboard structure seemed oddly similar to his little house in the Venice Canals. With a porch that spanned the length of the front of the house, its only color was from the weathered blue shutters on the front windows. Inside were four small bedrooms in the back with a kitchen and living room dividing the front. It was the perfect beach house.

I feel asleep right after sunset and woke up at about 6am with the smell of coffee tempting me to rise. There was a stream of syncopated tunes coming from the songbirds outside my window. I slept like a baby. I couldn't remember when I had such uninterrupted sleep. It must have been the beach air. I walked out to the kitchen to find everyone already up and enjoying coffee in the big rocking chairs on the front porch.

"Golden boy, you have returned to this world," Big Steena joked. "I'll grab your coffee." I had to thank him for the amazing experience he so generously provided. "Wait," he said, "this is just the beginning."

"Does surfing have its origins in Hawaii?" Bill asked Kai.

"The surfing we know in Hawaii today, is pretty much a gift from the Polynesians. My ancestors brought surfing to Hawaii and the Hawaiian people integrated surfing into their culture. At that time, surfing was only reserved for the privileged Royals and the upper class, along with chiefs and warriors. It was considered more of an art form than anything else. Surfing was a sacred act that honored the mysteries of the ocean and was done to appease the Gods.

The local kahuna or priest would first pray to the Gods for protection, abundance, and strength. "*He'e nalu*" or wave sliding was then performed to honor the Gods and compete for place or stature in front of the king."

"So, surfing was a natural progression from the elite to every man?" I inquisitively asked.

“Not really,” Kai frowned. “The Western world infiltrated the islands, bringing disease and colonization. The suppression of the Hawaiian culture occurred through mixed breeding and religious conversion, desecrating the rich and wonderful traditions of the island's people. The art of surfing a carved piece of tree in the middle of the ocean was almost lost as well. Considered a primitive act, it was pushed aside like many of the other rituals and beliefs of the Hawaiian heritage.”

“Tell them about your grandfather,” Big Steena chimed in.

“Well, in 1911, my great great grandfather was one of the original members of the surf club called "Hui Nalu," meaning "Club of the Waves." It was created to reintroduce surfing back into the minds and hearts of the Hawaiian people. It was pretty much just for the locals. About 10 years later, the haoles started their own, elitist surf and canoe club, that was basically for the rich white man only. But the seed was re-planted again in the hearts of man.

Thanks to our own Duke Kahanamoku and George Freeth, surfing reached worldwide recognition and brought back this art for all the world to enjoy!"

Bill and I were so grateful for the history lesson.

“It’s always good to know where our traditions come from. Especially the ones we embrace,” Big Steena smiled. “Grab your gear, we’re goin surfin’ JackO and Zip are going to the Breakwall Reefs. Golden boy, you’re with me.”

The sun breeched the horizon spilling liquid gold across the early morning canopy of palms. I was made aware of the symphony of paraquats hidden away in the banyan trees screeching their discord over who was to eat first.

I could hear the repetitive rolling of the waves just beyond the trees. The brisk breeze brought the relaxing sound to my ears telling me that the waves were going to be great this morning.

We stopped to wax our boards under a brooding mango tree. Big Steena bent down and picked up a large juicy mango. "Oh look," he said, "breakfast!" He quickly whipped out a pocket knife and proceeded to separate the beautiful yellow-orange skin from its meat. He handed me the sweet golden fruit. "Chupa," he said. "Chupa, chupa."

I looked at him, half asleep.

He picked up another mango, peeled off the skin, and put one end into his mouth. He made a slurping noise as he pulled the dense meat off the pit with his teeth. "Awwww, chupa," I said. I quickly followed suit enjoying every bit of the mango's pulpy goodness.

We walked to a spot that Big Steena thought would be good for my skill set and there they were. An entire pod of wave worshippers perched off the coast on dawn patrol. You could hear the laughs and the ribbing going on between them as the air carried their howls to the shore. A couple heads turned to notice us. Probably wondering where we were going to park. Big Steena leaned into me and said, "come on, let's wander." Which meant, let's go down the beach a little further to find our own waves.

I suddenly felt an uncomfortable feeling under my heel. I bent down and picked up a very small, smooth stone that had a little barnacle protruding from its face.

"Let me see that?" Big Steena gestured. I tossed him the stone as he carefully observed it. He rolled it over in his hand several times. "It's a gratitude stone," he said tossing it back to me. "Keep it in your pocket. When you reach in there to get some change, you will always remember to be grateful."

"A gratitude stone?" I smiled. "I will remember that."

"Whenever you touch the stone, tell the stone and essentially the Universe something you are grateful for. It's a powerful and affective way to bring gratitude, humility, and positive thought into your life."

On the South end of town was Kammies, one of Lahaina's reef breaks. We paddled out to the soft shoulder. The waves were coming in at a strong, but even pace with the off shore reef adding to their size. It took me a couple of waves to get my bearings as I felt more and more comfortable with the right-handed waves that were pushing in. "Keep in that Magic Zone and you can't go wrong," Big Steena would remind me.

We surfed with a few of the locals who came over to greet Big Steena. "I knew these guys since they were little delinquents. Their parents turned them over to me as a path to rehabilitation after they got out of juvey," Big Steena confided.

These guys were a little older than me. They cautiously looked me up and down to deduce if I was worthy of a nod. Even though we were surfing together, they kept that silent courtesy wall up between us, nodding occasionally when they seemed to approve of something I did.

"Me *hoa* says the harbor is really firing today," I overheard one of the local guys telling Big Steena. He answered as if he understood.

"Well Golden Boy, Taavi says his friend thinks that the harbor has good waves today," Big Steena translated for me, once he saw the confusion on my face. "Come on, let's hit the harbor."

He was right.

Kahului harbor was Maui's premier surf spot on the island's North central coast. Known for its deep-water channel and reef break, this wide-open surf spot was full of locals and one of the most popular for tourist as well.

After half a day in the harbor, we moved over to the West side. It is here that large swells crossed through the wide harbor entrance and often combined with swells bouncing of the jetty. We were joined by Bill and JackO. The wind had shifted and was now coming in from the South. The waves started increasing in size exponentially with swells coming in from the Northeast. "Just in time for the big ones," Steena gestured to the boys joining us.

We sat out back, experiencing the increasing size of the ground swells. The waves were now towering and plunging into the sea. Because of the swell size combined with the steeper sloping shore, the waves were now cresting and creating perfect curls. The crowd of surfers in the water had increased. The water had changed. You always remember your first big ride. It was my turn. I was up.

This was not a wave. It was the power of chaos. It was a meticulous balance of beauty and temptation coercing you into its majestic folds, all the while testing you to see just how familiar you wished to become.

This was not a wave, but a bone breaking, board crushing steam roller that only gave up its power once sea collided with land.

This was not a wave, but a fine crafted sculpture of liquid mass, magnetically pulled towards you and you to it.

"Take the risk," I told myself! "Even if I fail, I can get back up and try again." I was too far into my comfort zone and it was time to make a move. If I didn't put myself out there, I'd still be standing in the same place.
Here it was, the right wave. Can't think about it, "go, go, go". I swallowed the big ball of saliva amassing in my throat. Three strokes and I was up. "Just relax," I told myself, "It's only water."

In a split second as, the water continued to roll over me, I would catch glimpses of sun spraying through the barrel, illuminating the curl with a prism of color. My heart was pumping with the possibility that I was actually doing this. My laser focus was steady, staring directly over the nose of my board with the beach to my left and the towering wall of water to my right.

I felt confident in my actions, as if I had done this a hundred times before. I sensed the water escorting me through the tunnel as I reached the end of the curl. The wave would christen me with one final spray as it closed down behind me. I stepped off my board into the now shallow water, grinning from ear to ear. I suddenly remembered the little stone in my pocket. I reached in and touched my gratitude stone. I offered a quiet thank you. Exhilarated, I could only try to calm my rampant breathing as I recognized the accomplishment of a surfer's ultimate dream!

I woke up very early the next morning. I imagined the adrenaline was still coursing through my veins on some level after my incredible experience in the water. I put the coffee on. The smell of the fresh, hot liquid was my favorite scent in the world. I walked out onto the old wooden porch and looked out over the vast sea in front of me. I couldn't imagine waking up to this beauty every morning of my life. What a blessing to be able to choose this as an option.

Here I was, on a rock, in the middle of the Pacific Ocean! The vast seascape only seemed to represent uncertainty. As far and wide as the sea stretched, its unbounding energy seemed, unrestrained and uncontrolled. It conveyed a sense of mystery and unknowing. "So much like life," I contemplated. It almost appeared that this ambiguity was the norm and that change was not only certain but expected. So, I wondered, was life like the island, taking whatever comes its way, adapting as it goes? Or was life the untethered raft, following the sea's currents? Was life as uncertain as the murky depths beyond what our eyes could see from the surface? Or did we have a say in all of this?

"I think it's time for coffee."

We headed to the Breakwall Reef in the morning to get a quick surfing session in together. Big Steena had additional plans for us today. We loaded into the jeep and took the scenic route to the top of Haleakalā, the East facing mountain volcano that formed more than 70% of the island of Maui.

"Haleakalā at sunrise, is a sight to behold but since we missed that, I still wanted you to get the feel of a real volcano," Big Steena smiled.

The jeep veered up and around the winding red gravel road. We could feel the temperature slowly dropping the higher we got to the summit. Long wisps of morning clouds were now crossing the road and obstructing the view, only to clear from the prevailing winds. The sun was already 45 degrees in the sky casting a short shadow across the ancient lava flows and decreasing tree line as we ascended. We pulled up in front of a series of cabins just below the summit. The visitor's center was a rather make-shift construct put together to hold basic information and some weather gadgets for visitors to view. We hiked to the peak and then down over the edge to the crater floor, some 2,000 ft below. The terrain was red and almost Martian like. You could hear nothing but the wind howling over the top of the caldera. The clarity and dryness of the air was crystal clear. The stillness was almost foreign to us. We each seemed to venture off in our own directions. I automatically connected to the massive energy vortex that seemed to circle around us. This immense vista was literally breathtaking. We hiked back up to the summit and got back into the jeep.

"All aboard?" Kai asked. "Well, we've seen the 'house of the rising sun' and tonight we are going to witness the *poepoe* moon."

"The full moon celebration," Big Steena added.

"This was my astronomy book coming to life," I thought. The book my mom gave me at age 15 was something I could not forget. Its influences got me out of a dark time in my adolescent years. It was now bringing back those happy memories.

We did a sunset surf at Puamana Park, located just south of Lahaina. It was high tide, so less of the sharp reef was exposed, making it easier to maneuver the beautiful rolling waves. Big Steena signaled us to come together for a front row seat to one of nature's fiery spectacles. We straddled the rails of our boards and commented on how much red and orange there was glowing in the Golden Hour moments as the sun slowly approached the horizon. Explosive frays of pink, indigo, and violet light seemed to illuminate the surrounding clouds as we watch the sun slowly slip beneath the arch of the earth. We were speechless.

The Royal Lahaina Resort always held lunar celebrations for their hotel patrons and invited guest at their incredible accommodations on Kaanapali Beach. Kai drove us to the event, explaining the traditions that were woven into Hawaiian culture.

"The Hawaiian *malama* or monthly moon cycle is separated into three periods of 10 days each. These three *anahulu* start when the moon increases in size or waxing and is called *ho'onui*. The second cycle is when the moon becomes full. We call it *poepoe*. Thirdly, when the moon is decreasing or waning in size, it's named *ho'ēmi.* The Hawaiian people love and worship the moon and her Goddess, *Hina 'aikamalama.* The ancient people would behave according to *Hina's* phases - planting certain crops, gathering food, fishing for certain fish or seafood, observing reflective times, or even proposing marriage. They would observe the ebb and flow of the island's environment and act according to her changing moods."

Kai was truly knowledgeable about the island's traditions and local history. I found out later that he was a part-time tour guide for the very hotel we were enjoying this evening. He had the perfect disposition for it.

She didn't disappoint. Rising from the East, the moon's full luminous orb filled the night sky. It was the moon I remembered as a kid. Awe inspiring, mysterious, and almost impossible to take your eyes off of. The hotel served delicious roast pork on a spit with traditional Hawaiian side dishes, complete with a Polynesian dance show explaining the exact history Kai had explained to us. It was so interesting to see the traditional use of movement from an ancient culture, expressing their heritage and beliefs through dance.

Our final day in Hawaii had come. It was the last cup of morning coffee enjoyed in the rocking chairs on the front porch of Big Steena's magical beach house.

"We are in luck, gentleman." Kai said hanging up the phone. "Pele is smiling down on us. Jaws is going off," Kai exclaimed with child-like excitement.

Big Steena explained to us that "Jaws" was the nickname for Pe'ahi, Maui's biggest surf break off the North Shore. It was known for its monstrous and unpredictable waves. The fact that this was happening so late in the Spring was another anomaly.

"Waves must be at least 20 – 30 feet" Kai exclaimed. "Only large swells can wake up this spot."

"It must have been that magical moon last night," I thought. We jumped in the jeep and headed for Pe'ahi AKA "Jaws."

The Pe'ahi Lookout was about an hour's drive from Lahaina on the North Shore. It was the best vantage point on the cliffs above the break. It was the perfect view of these monster barrels roaring in from the distance.

We watched as the waves would swell, then break right, catching many hopefuls in its wake as it ate up and spit out more surfers than could actually ride its face. Occasionally, some brazen professional would crest the huge peaks and ride its powerful expression, moving parallel to the beach. But those guys who happened to get up on their feet, but did not turn to ride parallel, would be swallowed up in the raging white water that spilled over its top.

Was anyone keeping track of these lost souls who would tumble into the sea and churn on the bottom below? Surfing Jaws was truly the ultimate rush and thrill ride for anyone wanting to conquer the thunderous power of God's fury.

We walked up to the low hanging cliffs. The rocky reef bed was jutting up out of the sea, disseminating the water into different directions.

The waves crashed along the rocks as if they were cymbals in a synchronized symphony. The water sprayed upward dispersing droplets that mingled with fragments of light and air, emerging as a great mist. It christened our faces as we watched this natural, rhythmic dance. At last, I'd seen the spirit of the sea.

Chapter 10
Spiritual Awakenings

Going to college in New Paltz afforded me many opportunities. Although landlocked and 90 minutes away from the closest ocean, this bohemian village had a vibe from the 1960s with a typical small-town college feel. Situated in the foothills of the Catskills, it offered a less formal setting than a larger University, but had a strong New York City influence from its staff to its teaching curriculum.

Sixty percent of the school's population were made up of kids from New York City and its surrounding areas. Most of the friends I made had some connection to inner city neighborhoods in New York. It quickly gave me an education as to how savvy these kids were growing up in the "City" as opposed to my upbringing.

The Bachelor of Arts program was a rigorous schedule that was headed up by two competing departments. Theatre and Dance. Ballet and modern dance were the major curriculum, and you were expected to be proficient in both, as well as dance theory, history, musical theatre, and tap. Theatre arts expected you to take acting and voice. The faculty was made up of working actors, dancers, and performers from Broadway, TV, film, and every major theatrical hub in the country.

My schedule was divided into arts and academics. In order to go to this school, I had promised my parents that I would double major. In order to study dance and receive a Bachelor of Art degree, I needed to also get a Bachelor of Science in business. I would have promised anything in order to come as close to New York City as I could to study dance. I found that perfect blend with New Paltz.

Being a male in any dance program was a privilege and it was also easier than what the female dancer had to endure. The boys of the dance world were basically the frame and the girls were the picture. So, the boys were required to be there to hold them, catch them, support them, and make them look good. If a boy was to get a brief 8 or 16 count solo, you'd better make it count because that was about all you would see in the ballet world.

Once I got over the shock of really leaving home and separating from my parents, I was off and running. It was different than going to LA to live with my aunt and hang out with my cousins. With college, I was all on my own.

The safety net was gone. Thank God for dance, as it took my mind to a place where I could endure, compete, and thrive in my new found surroundings.

I lived in a dorm across campus and close to the Quad, which was a beautiful, treelined circular park in the center of four dorms. The Quad was a meeting place for everyone who wanted to get together in between classes, hangout on a nice day, or just get some reading done under a tree.

The Quad was the barometer. It would show me the seasons as they changed, if it was a good day to go out and get some sun, or see if friends were out studying. The Quad registered the anger of a community through the many protests it would host or share the best of humanity when the school needed to come together and heal. It was a spiritual center of communing and gathering. It gave solace to those seeking comfort or familiarity and a place for those to just connect with nature.

The largest dance studio was just across the way, with its floor to ceiling windows, displaying its contents for all the world to see. Perhaps it was designed like this for the dancers to be on display. This worked in two ways, as it pushed the dancers to work harder, especially while being watched. It was also an inspiration for the non-dancer, looking in and observing just what impossible feats of human strength and endurance the body could achieve.

Diana Banks would come firing into the dance studio on all eight cylinders. She was an energetic woman who stood just shy of five feet, but had the absolute stamina of a sparkler that resisted going out. She smiled with great sincerity and taught with utter diligence. She was the master of her 70-something body and knew how to mold young dancers to picture perfect images. She was a ballet master and Broadway/jazz star who taught us both styles and showed us how to go between them proficiently. "Ok my dears, right hand on the barre..." she would always start the class. She would teach three classes of ballet in the morning and three classes of jazz in the afternoon. She became a mentor who encouraged my talents and helped with the mental endurance needed to handle the excruciating pain, angst, and suffering your physical body must undergo to become a professional.

The preparation for dance classes during the winter months was different than Spring and Summer. I would get to class at least 45 minutes before in order to change and warm up. It seemed to take me twice as long to get my muscles pliable for the strenuous routines. It was here that I learned how to be disciplined. The professional dancer needed to master better control of foot positions and the way your feet would strike the ground. Your stance would help improve balance, proprioception, and body awareness, which would give you strength. Repetition of movement would lead to sounder foot mechanics, which would lead to improved muscle memory of the hips, knees, and core. Jumps and kicks would give you stronger leg muscles, which helped to support the lower back region.

Each day, I would work harder and sweat more profusely, to not only please the teachers, but to show myself that I could do it. I wanted to be the best I could possibly be and I was determined to prove that.

Spring offered a beautiful campus filled with flowers and budding trees in the Quad. The mountains were bursting with green, a stark contrast from their hibernated state all winter. Spring also introduced new classes to my curriculum. Economics, Business Forecasting, and Accounting were added to my schedule, while Tap Dance, Modern Expressions, and Duets were new on my dance schedule. My friends could not understand my duality. But I had a long-term plan.

Brenda Bufalino was a tap dance impresario. She had gotten her start performing with her mother and sister touring in shows. When she got to New York at 17, she trained as a protégé with Honi Coles, America's tap dance wunderkind. Now, finding her way to New Paltz she joined the dance faculty. Her teachings were a combination of Afro-Cuban, rhythm tap, jazz, and vaudeville styles, which were unique. It was not just tap dancing from the ankle down. Brenda's style forced your ear to hear long rhythms and expressive tempo changes that could be mimicked, not only through the body, but by the time it met your tap shoes it was complete body language. With Brenda, you tap danced with your entire soul. On very rare occasions she would bring Honi Coles to class and we would work on routines from their traveling group, The Copasetics.

Dr. Gloria Bonali was the head of the Modern Dance department as well as my teacher for Choreography and Dance History. She was a no-nonsense woman, in her mid-60's, short cropped salt and pepper hair, and an astute ability to determine your talent by summing you up in two minutes. She was very neutral and lacked the passion Diana would present, but Dr Bonali was very invested in us, in measured doses.

With the turn of the season came a new group of students who would filter into our classes. From the corner of my eye, I noticed this beautiful brunette with shoulder length hair and pale white skin. She moved more like a gymnast than a dancer, but was capable and very flirty. It did not take long to learn her name and Donna and I started going out on a few dates.

A Southern girl from Alabama, she transferred to New Paltz after moving around the country with her Army enlisted parents. She seemed like an innocent yet vivacious girl with a propensity for thrills. By our third date she had me hang gliding across the beautiful Shawangunk Mountains, which was a long stony ridge west of New Paltz. Each date seemed to be a test of my resolve. She was testing and I was resolving. I felt like she was subjecting me to an obstacle course just to see what I was made of. Perhaps it was a trait she learned from her Army parents or maybe she just wanted to see if I was the right guy for her.

Each weekend we would blow off homework and hike the magnificent trails, climb up the sides of cliffs, or swim naked in the many swimming holes that graced the breathtaking landscape around the University.

We would sneak into the Mohonk Mountain house, have high tea on the rustic porch, and then quickly bolt out through the kitchen before any one was the wiser. The towering hotel sat alongside Lake Mohonk situated high on a mountain cliff. Somedays, we would walk along the lake admiring the foliage or the mirrored facade of the grand hotel reflecting back at us.

I was falling for this girl. It seemed to be my first relationship outside of my puppy love crushes in high school or my flirting/make out sessions in LA. After several weeks of exploring, she lured me back to her off-campus apartment. Although it was mid-afternoon on a school day, I couldn't resist her saucer-like doe eyes and vibrant smile. She offered me a drink. At two in the afternoon, I thought it a bit early for a beer. I politely declined and she poured a scotch and soda over ice. "That's quite an adult drink," I thought to myself.

"Bottoms up, " she cooed as she belted half a glass down without hesitation. One sip and I could feel the scotch burning my throat on the way down. "I like to chase the scotch with soda," she whispered, "it's much more subtle."

"As a freight train," I thought smiling back at her. Her whispering lips moved from my ear to my lips. She was the first to introduce me to French kissing before I knew what a tongue down your throat meant. That's all it took.

She mounted and rode the surfboard with the gusto of a pro. Not her first time on a board, she seemed to know how to maneuver her way through every obstacle and pitfall. Pumping and encouraging her new found stick, she advanced ever closer to the breaking point, using the wax to her advantage! Through her skillful pull back and then rushing tactics she rode the wave to a complete release of energy! Even though it was quick and premature, she came off that with gusto and assurance.

I walked out of there as if I was caught in the washing machine of a turbulent wave that did not allow me to come up for air. I was half relieved and half dumbfounded at how tactical this girl was. I guess your first time with an experienced driver is always better than the other way around. I was no longer a virgin.

We continued seeing each other for several months until one day I went to her apartment to pick up some homework and found her in bed, test driving another surfboard. We drifted apart after that. I was devastated. I thought we were in love and it felt like my heart was just ripped out of my chest. I was now dealing with the side effects of betrayal.

For weeks, I searched for something to drag my heart out of the gutter. If only I had my actual surfboard. If only I had an ocean. Neither was close by and I knew they were the only two things that would make me happy again. The fact that this girl was not sincere seemed unfathomable to me. We were having such a good time together too. Maybe I missed the signs. Did I do something wrong? Was it me? I was not only feeling devastated, but I felt lost.

Trust. How could you come back to that security? That belief that your safety net would always be there? Naïve? Maybe I was. But it still felt like I was bludgeoned to death. I actually felt like I was her "plaything." As the time passed, I did realize that maybe I was looking at the entire relationship too seriously. She was just out to have a good time and I (apparently) was ready for marriage. God, I had a lot to learn.

I was walking through the quad on the other side of campus, lost in thought, feeling sorry for myself, when I passed the music building and a flyer caught my eye.

Voices of Unity - gospel choir auditions. This Friday 7 pm.

I looked at my watch. It was 7pm on Friday. In the distance, I heard a soprano hit some high notes and an alto harmonize beneath her. I followed the lilt of their voices down a long corridor deep into the music building. The entire building was dark, except for some secondary lights left on for the custodial staff. I always loved the joy in gospel music and now I was following these echoes like temptresses enticing me down the rabbit hole. I was more willing to follow, than I had realized. I discovered these angelic souls gathered in a music room at the end of the hall. The basses and tenors joined the harmony.

"Tenor or bass?" the music director asked as I walked in.

"Tenor," I quickly responded.

Daryl Ware, the tall, slim, well-dressed choir director pointed to the tenors singing at the far end of the group. "Just follow along," he said. I went over and stood next to George, the only other white guy in the room. He handed me sheet music and I followed along, getting into rhythm, following the sway of the 15 other singers.

Consuelo Hill was the adult in the room. Faculty member in the music department, she was our sponsor and guardian, who allowed the official creation of the group to be sanctioned by the University. She was a short, robust woman, who loved gospel music and had a lot of faith in Daryl and what he was going to do with this group. Consuelo was very supportive of all the members as if we were her own children. She sat in the back of the room tapping her foot, clapping along, and mouthing all the words to the songs.

Something transformed my spirit within that hour. The music, the smiling participants, the praising of God through song. I fast become one of the original members of the Voices of Unity (VOU).

In the weeks to follow, Daryl took us through our paces. We learned 8 – 10 songs and perfected their harmony. Daryl would add choreography, pick soloists, and fine tune our style. He had a very unique way of blending voices and the methodology of constructing a song. Often singing classic gospel spirituals or church hymns arranged for choir, Daryl had us performing in every local Baptist church, special event, or ice cream social from New Paltz to New York City. About every third week, we would go into New York, sing at a church event or Sunday service and then the grateful participants would feed us a banquet of home cooking and invite us back for another performance. Needless to say, I forgot all about, what's her name.

Because of the choir, I felt it was the closest to God I had ever felt up to this point in my life. Growing up as a staunch Catholic, we would go to church every week. We would stand and repeat the same dry prayers and responses, singing the same puritan-esque songs with about as much enthusiasm as a wet bagel. Singing with the gospel choir, I felt God in the room. The synchronized movement, the calling of his name, and the heartfelt expression through rousing music gave power to the Universe.

Of course, my presence there was not without controversy. On some rare occasions, I would be snubbed or treated rudely, by a few of the same people or church folk who hosted us. There were those who did not think I belonged there or should not be in a gospel choir. On every level, Consuelo was quick to defend me, stand up for me, and diplomatically deescalate any prejudice. I had to say, that so much of my ignorance or not realizing what was happening in the moment, was a gift from my upbringing. Even at almost 19 years of age, I was very much a sheltered guy. Growing up on the farm, I didn't experience racism, let alone being treated with prejudice because I was white.

Consuelo would always encourage me to take command of my voice. She would make an open palmed gesture leading from her throat, signaling me to sing out and not hold back. "The way you express your feelings and emotions can move you towards your greater goals in life," Consuelo would remind me after class. "You know this, you're a dancer. You express yourself through movement. I've seen you dance. You don't hold back. The same goes for your vocal expression. Don't be afraid to sing out. It's the same as speaking out. How do you think others will learn about your intentions, if you don't let them know?"

Consuelo had found that balance between biting her tongue when she knew her words could hurt someone and speaking her truth when she needed a situation "defined." She was a true diplomat. "Expressing what you want builds a foundation on which your life can grow. Some paint, write, sing, dance, others speak, play sports, collect objects, or express themselves through their work. Expressing to the world who you are, is your right and privilege. Don't ever be afraid to do this."

I learned more about standing my ground, believing in God's plan, and the resilience of my spirit, from the words within those gospel songs we'd sing each week. It gave me another way to commune with God in a manner I never experienced before.

.

"The world's fierce winds are blowing temptations sharp and keen.
I felt a peace in knowing
My Savior stands between.
He stands to shield me from danger when earthly friends are gone.
He promised never to leave me,
No, never alone" **

The performing classes, along with the music and art classes, had a lot of fans that would gravitate to the numerous art shows, music concerts, theatre, and dance shows the college would sponsor.

The Voices of Unity would perform in the Quad and would draw large groups of fans and onlookers. I befriended a group of three students who loved to come to see VOU perform. Vanessa, Damon, and Richard were an interesting trifecta, all childhood friends from the same neighborhood in Brooklyn and now going to New Paltz.

After realizing that both Damon and Vanessa were interested in me, sexually, I had to break the news that I had just come out of a relationship and was not looking for anything but some good friends to hang out with. We all become great friends after that. We would hang out in Richard's dorm room listening and dancing to the latest 12" singles of the hottest house music coming up from the New York City club scene. Richard was a dance music aficionado and knew everything about the DJ's, new groups, and their record companies.

"We need to go to the Garage," Richard huffed, as he struggled to sit his extra-large frame into a chair half his size.

"Yesssss, child," Damon drawled, his tall, skinny body swung out as he and Vanessa hustled to MFSB's classic *"Love is the Message"*

"The Garage?" I asked.

"The Paradise Garage. The only dance club in Manhattan," Richard slurred, rolling his eyes.

"The only?"

"The only one that matters," was the retort.

Friday after classes, we took the train to New York. I wanted to stay in my first Manhattan hotel, somehow thinking I would relive my childhood nights glued to that Manhattan radio station listening to dance music and fulfilling the dream of "living" in New York City. Vanessa, Damon, and Richard went home to their apartments.

Damon and Richard were neighbors in Brooklyn and lived off Nostrand Ave. They insisted we meet at Richard's apartment before going out to the City to dance. So, I hopped the train to Brooklyn and found myself in a very different neighborhood than the one I'd left 20 minutes ago. After a few cat calls and one or two solicitations for drugs, I found Richard's three-story walkup.

The room smelled like reefer, clouds of smoke meandering through the room! "Golden Child," Richard exclaimed as I walked in the room. "You has got to try this weed, it's mind-altering." He passed me the blunt. I took a quick toke and started coughing out the warm smoke.

"That's a kicker," I appeased him.

Damon stepped into the door frame of the bedroom, "Ta-da," he posed. He was dressed head to toe in red nylon stretch pants and a revealing short cropped t-shirt with vertical lines cut in strategic places. "Daaaaaarling," he cooed. Did you make it through the neighborhood without all those banjee boys taunting you?"

I had to give Damon credit for completely being himself. It took a real man to find himself and be comfortable with who he was. "I managed my way through," I answered. "Where's Vanessa? Running late?"

"OH, she's surfing the crimson wave and will not be attending this evening," Damon said throwing his hands in the air, as if he had enough of her already.

Disappointed she wasn't going, I understood how that could be a problem. I was now the white filling between two Oreo cookies. It was time to make a scene.

Back in Manhattan, we got off the number 1 train at Houston. A few blocks south was 84 King St. In the bowels of an old parking garage was the famous Paradise Garage. This private invitation-only club was home to the famous

"Garage Sound," a house beat blend of driving rhythms, melodic overtones, and different genres stylishly crafted into the structure of songs that would build and build. The Garage had become a beacon for the most savvy, urban mix of gay, straight, and everything in between!

We waited on the ramp going up into the club. Richard pulled out his membership card. "I have a guest," he said to the girl at the door. She smiled at me, and we were in. The Garage was a palace of debauchery and love, of escapism and pride, of fantasy and magic. The warehouse-like dance floor was packed with writhing bodies moving to the deep, driving beat coming from the two-story speakers strategically placed around the floor. The faint smell of poppers and weed caught my attention as Damon and Richard dragged me through the half-naked crowd, bodies pulsing to the sound of Grace Jones's *"Pull Up to The Bumper."* It was a dancer's paradise.

"With the love I have inside of me
We can turn this world around
We can live through all eternity
And we'll never touch the ground" **

Yewohhhhh! Damon screeched as he darted for the dance floor! Larry Levan, the famous DJ who ruled the Garage, mixed D Train's song, *"You're the One for Me"* over Grace Jones' mystical anthem. The crowd erupted! I wasn't quite sure what just happened, but a mass of revelers pushed forward to the dance floor and we were off.

I was in my element. The middle of a dance floor filled with people who understood. They understood the absolute power of music. It was the life-altering beat of the Universe with ramifications of pure joy! I was ecstatic, as we danced, and danced, and danced. The stamina and drive of the crowd never faltered. I wasn't sure if it was their drugs or their desire. For me, it was just a feeling of absolute freedom. No labels, no judgment, no prejudice.

Music had never let me down. It was a comfort when I needed a pick me up or a trip down memory lane when I needed to feel good. Larry Levan understood this. He had an ability, like no other DJ, to blend spellbinding musical genres together from 115 to 130 heart-pulsing beats per minute. He would spin anthems of house and soul, rock and disco tracks together that would take his followers to a mystical plain. He was the "Pied Piper of House Music."

I could hear the silvery metallic brilliance of Richard's tambourine over the crowd. He wasn't much of a dancer but he swayed right in front of the enormous speakers, playing and singing his heart out.

"These hard times we've all had to share
There's a new horizon waiting for me and you
Tell you what we're gonna do
Leave everything, leave it behind
You need nothing
All you got to do is make up your mind to dance forever..."

Ashford and Simpson's call to mobilize, rose the energy of the crowd even higher than you could possibly imagine. Wringing wet from head to toe, all I could do was gyrate and look up at the amazing light show above my head that seemed to accompany the music in perfect synchronicity.

Hours past. We would take short breaks and discover the non-alcoholic punch bowl or trays of fruit in the back room. We would sit for a few minutes to catch our breath and view one of the movies they had playing in the small theatre room. But we couldn't stay away from the dance floor for long. Our feet wouldn't allow it and Larry kept enticing us to dance his way.

"Come on, it's almost time," Damon grabbed my hand as Richard and some of his new found friends followed us up to the roof. The roof was an incredible tree lined paradise amongst the big bad city. With circular benches rounding huge trees and greenery all along the border of the roof, it was a great place to meet the Manhattan sunrise. The rays reached upward breeching the pinnacles of the smaller buildings in the lower portion of Greenwich Village. We laughed and found ourselves finally winding down from the absolute throes of musical heaven. We made a pact to come to the Garage every other Saturday night.

"The sweat is drenching my whole body as I writhe, and pulse, and press, my half nude body against the two who've sandwiched me between their chests.

I look up and the room is spinning, keeping time to Larry's beats, the bass is driving bodies forward as we move in sync, in heat.

For me I cannot think of any other place I'd rather be, then in the center of a dance floor, expressing everything that's me.

It's like my church, a place to be, communing with my fellow men, as music lifts us higher, faster, deeper ~ even more than life itself.

Between the downbeats, we can breathe and stroll throughout these hallowed halls, where sound transforms the lives of everyone within these Sacred walls.

We laugh and sing and dance once more on top the famous roof, as rising sun again reveals there's magic – here's the proof.

The world can be so hard sometimes, so take a little advice, put on your dancing shoes and make your way to Paradise."

Chapter 11

LA, Together

Libby picked me up at LAX after my long flight from New York. "You always take the early morning flight," she said, rolling her eyes.

"I love leaving New York really early, and gaining three hours when I get to LA. It's like a start over to the day," I laughed.

Libby drove a 1979 baby blue Volkswagen beetle convertible, very befitting of her personality. Working as a legal assistant to a large law firm downtown, she was my self-reliant cousin who came and went as she pleased, because she had the money to do so. It was her independence. "Are you lovin' college?" she asked tapping her long, high glossed nails on the steering wheel.

The year was such a shift in my life," I smiled, as I thought more about her question.

"It's like, a wakeup call to life, isn't it? I totally couldn't do any more school, oh my God, it's not for me," she exclaimed.

"You're like, such a Valley Girl now," I joked.

"I am not," she huffed. "I never go to the mall."

It was my first summer out of high school and with a year of college under my belt, I felt the growing pains of being an adult and now having to really support myself. My folks wanted me to come home after college, but I needed to come back to LA. There was a constant pull that kept me coming back. I needed to be here.

I was asked by some of my dancer friends if I wanted to do a college dance retreat in NYC during the summer break, but I was not ready. The intense program at school had me worn down and in need of rejuvenation. I needed the sea again and there was no way I could handle anything else.

That's where I went. The following day, I got up early, carted my board on the bus and headed to Venice Beach. The early morning skateboarders were up running jumps and practicing maneuvers on the cement barricade that sat in front of Canter's favorite smoke shop.

Jamal, Hector, and Jose were up from the night before, after a night of debauchery. As the sun breached the horizon, they were now back at their usual spot on Ocean Front Walk, working together on their break dancing moves. They gave me a high five as a dragged my board past them.

From the corner swing set, I walked to the Breakwater and just followed the beach South, listening to the screech of the early morning seagulls fighting for food, while the thunderous sea accosted the shoreline, repeatedly.

"I'm stoked about these waves," a familiar voice whispered in my ear.

"Cuz!" Bill came up from behind me. We gave each other a big bear hug, our boards clashing into each other. "Ok," I said, "what's she like?"

"A Barbie," Bill laughed.

Bill had started dating a "Malibu Barbie." She was a blond haired, blue eyed beauty who had a panache for surfers and loved spending her days in the nail salon. Bill liked her enough to stay at her apartment on the beach a few nights a week. For my cousin, love and romance seemed like a past time. He liked the challenge and enjoyed the chase, but after he got that, his interests seemed to wane. This became a summer romance that fizzle out by September.

Sting Ray was a chic magnet. What he lacked in height and "Don Juan" looks, he made up for in brawn and balls. Sting Ray was a manipulator. He always seemed to have "two on the line" at the same time, without the other one knowing. His feeling loved, validated his efforts and helped to make him feel important. He swore he was incapable of being monogamous. He just felt there were too many beautiful women in the world to be devoted to just one.

Canter had an ideal image of what type of girl he liked. That was Maria. Good-looking, tall, clever, and funny, he liked to nurture this imagine in his mind. Unfortunately, it kept him from seeing other girls. Canter's tall stature and odd-like look, was never a deterrent. On the contrary, this lean, tanned lifeguard had a career path that girls were incredibly drawn to. He was flirtatious, so Maria would get jealous. Maria's natural charisma and dancer's body was always turning heads, which made Canter jealous. This on again, off again relationship was like a wave pulling them back and forth, constantly.

JackO was a world traveler. Phillysha was an African princess who had long legs and looked great in a bikini, but hated the water. So that relationship was short-lived. In another few weeks, he had Wai Chin on his arm. A Chinese beauty from Beverly Hills who was half his height and drove a BMW. The next month, Tara, a Mexican lovely, was on the beach with him. Although their cultural backgrounds were the same, that's where the similarities ended. Jacko was a player. He had a knack for falling in love, weekly.

I realized I was more of a traditionalist. I wanted my girl and I to live in the house with the white picket fence, dinner at six, a sweet devotion to one another, and someone I could share my interests with. I came to understand, I modeled my desires after my parent's life. My mom seemed to be super-woman and did everything, while my super dad worked 60 hours a week. Even when my mom started working in my school, years later, she still had dinner ready at 6 pm, cleaned the house, and did everything in the kitchen. She canned all the fruits and vegetables from the garden, made everything from scratch, while mastering the laundry for the four of us. I had high expectations from my incredible role model. I just thought all girls were like that. I was so naive.

It seemed we all had our own ideas about love. We may not have been going about it in all the right ways, but I discovered that there was a learning curve to love. I also learned that whenever I didn't understand someone because we didn't see eye to eye, I needed to remind myself that just like me, they wanted to be loved and accepted. Respect for each other, was the greatest lesson in a relationship, and that communication was essential for growth. None of us may have been going about it in the right way, but there was no manual in life for dealing with relationships. It was trial and lots of error.

It was the first week we could all finally get together to actually go surfing. We decided on Malibu because the waves were firing and it was also the closest central point for all of us to meet.

The air was heavy and muggy with the rolling of thunder in the distance. The clouds lay so low, seemingly weighted down by the oversaturation of water. There was a sense that rain could burst forth from them at any moment. The summer rain came...and went.

After the downpour, the clouds began to pull back as if they were curtains opening to a new day. The warm California sun began to beam through the parting wisps, glistening on the waves below.

"Mira, un arcoiris!" JackO was so excited, he couldn't express it in English fast enough.

"The sun's cousin," Big Steena added pointing upward. A beautiful rainbow stretched from one end of the beach to the other, aglow in a perfect prism of color. It was as if the arch of light had its own energy source, punctuating the grey sky with intense layers of pure brilliance. We stared at it for what seemed like minutes, admiring the gracious gift of nature. "Our day's blessing," Big Steena smiled.

It was great to be surfing in Malibu with all my buddies again. It seemed like such a longtime that I had seen them. Exactly a year, yet it also appeared as if we'd never left each other. We now seemed to have more attachments around us… jobs, girlfriends, college, bills, more responsibilities, yet when we surfed together, there was nothing else to distract us.

Without a doubt, our surfboards were a magnet for girls on the beach. I wasn't sure what it was, but they held a power that gave a guy or girl…. status. Maybe it was because surfing was a metaphor for life. Surfing through life gave the impression that everything was easy and that everything was ok. If you were a surfer, it would appear that you subscribed to that belief. Maybe that was the attraction.

"So, is that your surf tribe?" a girl asked me as she passed by tossing her hair over her shoulder. I looked over to see Bill, Sting Ray, Canter JackO, and Big Steena all standing, board tips down in the sand staring at the blazing sunset. Managing the words in my head that she used to describe my friends, gave me a new perspective of who these five guys really were to me.

"Yes, yes they are," I returned with pride.

Big Steena had organized a Venice Beach Clean Up, the following week. It was a quarterly event that would focus on cleaning up the beaches and water ways. The event would raise awareness in regards to the tons of garbage and waste that was continually dumped on the beaches. I liked to call it, my lesson in humility.

Big Steena would get all of his students involved. The week before they would fan out and let all the locals and businesses know that they needed volunteers for the event. The surfer community and the Canals would get together, recruiting skateboarders, street performers, and anyone who loved their beaches, to come help us collect trash. The event had turned into a who's who of celebrity supporters and corporations who wanted to make a difference and Big Steena made sure the press was all over it.

It brought awareness to the public and showed people just how much garbage was left behind during an average stay at the beach. Armed with gloves, garbage bags, and sunscreen, we would meet at the Santa Monica Pier and work our way South. Groups of people would work together in teams, picking up everything from plastic cups and soda bottles to fishing gear, drug paraphernalia, shoes, sandals, and towels. People would leave boogie boards, suitcases, glasses, and food littered everywhere. We would pick up shopping carts, automobile parts, wedding rings, as well as, weapons such as knives, shives, and even guns. The Venice Beach police were always on hand to take these articles into possession. It was incredible what people would discard.

This was constantly a "feel good" event that made you realize just how neglectful we could become. It also made you feel like you were making a difference in the community, in nature, and in the world, in general. There had to be some karmic reward for these actions, because it just made you feel bigger than yourself. That, together, we could achieve anything.

For someone who defined themselves as a loner, it was more and more evident how being together with others enhanced my life. That being with others could give you a sense of pride, comradery, and a realization that despite our differences, we all had a lot in common.

Since leaving home and going to college, this was becoming more apparent. Even though, as a dancer or a surfer, your internal struggles and challenges were your own to conquer, it was nice to know that at the end of the day, you could be with others who understood. In leaving home, I was now more aware of the fact that I was searching for a nuclear family to fit into. It suddenly seemed like my new friends at college, my surf buddies from LA, and my communities were much more important to me. They were becoming a valuable aspect in my life. I didn't realize, that all this time, I was laying a foundation for love and support.

Because of college, I hadn't worked and the little savings I had in the bank was not going to cut it, so I needed a part time "something" to have some pocket cash.

Sting Ray knew one of the managers of the Sports Connection. This was a big gym in West Hollywood that was an absolute scene. Nicknamed, the "Sports Erection", it was LA's hottest pick-up joint! The gym was in need of an aerobics instructor. Because of my dance training, I was offered the job and taught three classes a day. I worked three days a week and was paid under the table, which made the offer even sweeter. I would commute on the bus or get a lift from my cousin, teach my classes, and then head to Venice or Santa Monica to surf.

My classes were high-powered, high-energy, full body blasts that would work out every muscle. I called a DJ I knew who was a part-time dancer, and worked part-time at one of the local nightclubs called Rage. He knew how to make an amazing aerobics tape for my classes. Laced with night club anthems and kick-ass cardio beats, Kevin could fuse songs seamlessly into a masterful mix of dance music, no one could keep still to.

My classes grew in size, as word got out. I was now commanding 40 eager guys and girls per class who were serious, die-hard aerobic fans. These LA cardio-addicts lived for their aerobic classes. Together, we would create the best daytime party on Santa Monica Boulevard. I loved the commitment, the intensity, and the love people would show me through these classes.

"If you touch me with your smile
I'll get you to paradise
I can make it worth your while
I'll get you to paradise.

Reach for the sky
I want you; I want you more
I'll be nearby
Come with me, I'll take you there
I'll take you to paradise" **

Each class would start out with Change's dance anthem, *Paradise.* It was a foreshadowing of where I would take my devoted students each session. The crowd was vocal. They would scream, when their favorite songs came on, exploding into cheers with each musical motivation, pushing them beyond what they thought their limits were. The music and the moves inspired them to be even more physically fit and mentally strong.

As I got to know my regulars, those who were constantly in my classes, I worked into the routines, exercises that would help them in life. I had quite a few surfers in my class, so I made sure I did several balancing and strengthening exercises. Those who were dancers, I made sure to do choreography that was challenging enough for them, and the very muscular body builders, got great cool down stretches to help lengthen their bulky muscle fibers in order to move easier.

This temporary career move was fulfilling because I could use my talent as a dancer and choreographer, apply my passion for music, and help other athletes stay fit at the same time. We did it together. It was difficult to go back East to school. I was leaving my extended family behind, again.

** Lyrics reprinted by permission: "PARADISE" WC Music Corp. On behalf of Little Macho Music Co. Inc. (Tanyayette Willoughby, Mauro Malavasi and Davide Romani)

Chapter 12

She Changed My Life

I was offered a summer scholarship to dance at the Martha Graham School in New York City. This was a bittersweet honor as it was the greatest privilege to be chosen for this, but it also meant that I could not go to LA for the summer to surf.

Graham's technique worked with the opposition between contraction and release. A concept based on our breathing cycles. Its other dominant principle was the "spiraling" of the torso around the axis of the spine.

The incredible thing I liked about her technique was that you danced in bare feet. I've always felt that my body would receive feedback from the ground when walking barefoot. As children this peripatetic process improved awareness of the body within its space and environment. When we were toddlers, we learn to walk barefoot. It was a natural process that occurred without shoes. For me, it had always helped me stay particularly grounded. I thought this would be amazing. I wasn't able to head to the beach to surf, but at least I would still be without shoes all summer.

Come summer, I rented a room with a fellow dancer in the East Village and took the subway uptown to classes each morning. The classes were held in Graham's beautiful brick townhouse on East 63rd street. I was in one of the last classes she would teach and the experience changed my life as a dancer and, little did I know, as a surfer.

Martha Graham was one of the most magnetic and commanding people I have ever met. She had a long face with a prominent forehead and a defined chin, balanced with large angular cheekbones. She wore her salt and pepper hair in a particularly large chignon all the time. At 5' 3" tall, she would walk into a room and her mere presence commanded attention. Even now at 88 years old, bent over from age and hands gnarled from arthritis, she was electrifying.

The summer proved to be brutal. Eight hours of classes each day, six days a week. Early morning class set the pace for the day. There was an underlying competition that I rarely felt in the confines of my college dance classes. This rivalry was constantly felt with every dance sequence learned and executed.

Martha Graham was by far the toughest teacher I ever had. She gave very little encouragement and had a strict teaching style. She often made an example out of students' weaknesses. One day we were doing an exercise where we were seated on the floor with our legs bent, one in front and one behind. The exercise was a series of contractions from your center, which would slightly turn your body so that you were free to lift either the front or back leg off the floor. As I was going through the routine, Martha was not happy with the lack of distance I was unable to achieve with my knee coming off the floor. So, she proceeded to place a lighter under my knee so that the flame would allow my front knee to lift off the floor higher. As I struggled to contract and lift my knee higher, I could smell the hairs burning on my leg as she continued to hold the flame there and lecture as to how the knee should be lifted off the floor in the contraction.

Although this was one of the most memorable incidents, I took with me, it truly allowed me to 'turn a corner' in my dancing and made me even stronger and more accomplished.

She had taught me how to use my body as an instrument. She would always say to us, "great dancers are not great because of their technique, they are great because of their passion."

By the end of the summer, I felt like I had been through a war. My feet were now bloodied and bruised from the constant repetition of jumping, sliding, and turning on wooden floors. My body, wracked with pain daily, had now obtained a new language hidden somewhere within my muscle memory. It was one of the most difficult challenges I had ever been through. It was hard for me to handle at the time. The overall experience made me doubt myself as a performer. But on the other side of that long and painful journey I emerged a new dancer.

The following year I was given rave reviews by dance critics, my teachers, and fellow students as I blossomed into a stronger performer and innovative choreographer.

When I got to LA again the next summer, my surfing style had changed. I was now a more grounded, confident surfer. Because of Graham, I was now more aware of my center of gravity. I could move more freely from a place of balance. In a stance, I was closer to the board and could easily shift the weight of my body between my heels and my toes. This gave me incredible turning power on a wave. The "Graham spiral" seemed to help me understand how to turn my board by leading with the head. I was now a master of the bottom turn. I could ride vertically up the wave face and maneuver better. I was able to zig zag the line, ride back up to its crest, and re-enter the wave just by shifting my weight and spiraling in the direction I needed to go. I could now "feel" the concept that Bill talked about when he first taught it to me. My passion had multiplied and I owed this all to Martha Graham. She changed my life.

Just like a dancer, the fine-tuned surfer reached deep into the core of their training to find the ultimate image of how they wished to be, in order to achieve this ultimate goal. They would discover a resolve they had on tap, that they may not have realized they had. This could be accessed at a moment's notice. A surfer used their auto-pilot and trusted their bodies to react, determine, engage, and perform.

I was on track to graduate by my third year of college. I crammed enough credits from both majors to get my diplomas and get me out the door. New Paltz gave me such an education. Sure, the book learning was great, but the variety of dance training, the social interactions, and knowledge I gained about myself were even more enlightening. I was also walking away with a degree in business and administration. Somewhere in my head I had obtained the information to understand how the inner workings of managing a company, creating a business model, and comprehending supply and demand could play out. Perhaps I would be able to use that knowledge someday.

I had a knack for choreographing and loved the process of interpreting music with movement. I was now efficient at so many techniques, it gave my choreography variety. My forte was moving large groups around a stage in an intricate and circuitous way. I could see the “big picture” very well.

I owed this to Dr. Bonali. She encouraged my love for choreography before I even knew I could do it. She nurtured and encouraged me through little pearls of praise. Not too much, but just enough to string me along and let me believe I was capable. She changed my life.

Diana Banks had pushed me and encouraged me in different ways. She was motherly and endearing in her praise and generous in her love for her students. I would rarely see her serious, but when she was, they were moments that you would pay full attention to. In her own life, she had beat all the odds, being a very short dancer in a world of amazons. She went on to have a successful and fruitful career as a dancer and then teacher. She made sure to teach us that the odds were never in our favor in this business. It had to be a combined effort of passion and persistence to carry you through. She changed my life.

Brenda Bufalino, my tap teacher, was a drill sergeant, who never had a compliment for any individual in class. She seemed more attached to the moves and less concerned about her student's personal progress. I think that was probably why I worked so much harder to impress her. I wanted to master this art and I would go through great lengths to win her approval. All though, she would shoot me a smile now and then, it was all I ever got. It was then I realized, I didn't need her approval, I needed to know what I was doing. That would be my reward. She changed my life.

I even had to thank Donna, my first "girlfriend" for teaching me that, although I was young and naive, not everyone's intentions should be taken for granted or were in line with your own. I learned how to be with a girl, how to separate my attachment issues, and how not to take myself so seriously. She changed my life.

The Voices of Unity maintained a full performance schedule, mainly singing at churches in the Hudson Valley and New York City. By my last year in college, the Voices of Unity had grown in membership exponentially, performing with various distinguished college gospel choirs, including Howard University, University of Virginia, West Point, and today we were going to Syracuse University. What made this so extra special, was the fact that it was about 15 miles from the farm I grew up on and my parents were coming to see the show.

The show was a rousing success and my parents insisted on hosting the choir for lunch. There we were, 30 members of VOU enjoying lunch in my kitchen and living room and basement and patio. We were everywhere, laughing and remembering the highlights from the show. I don't think my parents ever had 30 people in the house at one time, let alone so many black folks. Consuelo filled my parent's ear with praise for raising such a strong-willed son.

Daryl sat down at my mom's upright piano and started singing the show stopper from the concert. In minutes, the sopranos chimed in. Then the tenors and altos joined. The basses hit the low notes and in seconds, the house was a blaze with gospel music!

Here we were, kids from all different upbringings, socio-economic, racially diverse, and such extreme backgrounds, yet we were all bound by one common thread. Music. My mother grabbed a tambourine, while my father beat the nearby stack of books to the uplifting melody. It's amazing how one familiar strain of music could give solace for hope and bring individuals and generations together.

It was already late into the night and my parents wouldn't hear of us driving back to New Paltz, so my dad passed out some blankets and pillows, mom found some night gowns for the girls and all 30 of us slept on the farm that night. I woke in the morning to see my friends strewn all over the house. Sleeping on every sofa, every inch of living room floor, and even on top of the pool table.

Dad was up before dawn, brewing coffee and cutting potatoes for hash browns. Mom was frying eggs and browning sausages so by the time we woke, we had breakfast on the table.

As we were leaving, the choir thanked my parents profusely. Each girl and guy gave my mom a kiss on the cheek and all the guys shook my dad's hand. I couldn't remember a greater sense of pride and joy on my parent's faces than on that day.

It was a musical adventure I'd never forget, until we all met again at my college graduation. Consuelo made it possible for the choir to perform that day and Consuelo made my parents honorary members of VOU. She changed my life.

Chapter 13

Whirlwind Manhattan

Now a graduate of New Paltz University, New York was calling. If I was going to put this training to work, I had to end up in a place where the opportunities abound.

With surfboard and tights in tow, I hit the New York streets running. It was essential to have 3 things:

- A place to live.
- A place to dance.
- A place to surf.

At last, I had made it to New York City. My dream of coming here was finally realized. I was almost anxious to leave Los Angeles and get my professional life started.

New York had a rhythm all its own. The driving force felt like an unstoppable wave. Manhattan had two high tides a day. The morning rush hour washed in like a tidal wave while the after-work rush, had even more intensity. Avoiding the highest concentration of whirlpools including Grand Central, Penn Station, and the bus station at Port Authority were essential if you could do it. If you could maneuver around those crowds, you were better off.

Manhattan would swell to eight million during the day, then release its flock into the evening hours. The nightlife would flow into the darkest hours and ebb into the wee hours. It was a constant inhale and deep exhale.

Everyone had their pace and if you observed it long enough, a pattern would emerge. The blue-collar workers or the working class who performed manual labor, were on the trains by 4 am heading to work. They were mostly from the outer boroughs and were heading home by 3pm.

The white-collar workers, typically the salaried professionals, general office workers, garmentos, and managers would be on the train by 8:30 am and headed home at the 6pm rush hour.

Then you'd have people like me, the no collar workers, students, artists, and "free spirits" who tended towards passion and personal growth over financial gain. We'd be on the train at all hours of the day and night observing the other tribes.

But, when you looked closely, there was a connectiveness between all of us and that common denominator was the human spirit. We all seemed to have the need, the drive, and the courage to be right where we were supposed to be. Those who hated New York, wouldn't make it for the long haul. But for those who had New York in their veins, we would live, love, and endure all that New York would dish out.

Within the year, I lived in four out of the five boroughs of New York including Queens, Brooklyn, The Bronx, and finally Manhattan.

I waited tables in a dumpy Italian restaurant on Restaurant Row in the theatre district for rent money. Never waiting on a table before, I had no clue what I was doing and I resented the fact that I had to do it. The rent needed to be paid, I had to pay for dance classes, and I was not going back to the farm with my tail between my legs. I had to make this new life work. So, I waited tables. After spilling water in a patron's lap and dropping two trays of food within the week, the owner was probably tired of yelling at me. "You don't know what you do!" Giuseppe yammered at me shaking his hand, five fingers touching each other in an almost fist-like motion. "You need training. I'm no trainer. I'm just the boss," he sniffed. "Here…"

He jotted a name down on a piece of paper and tossed it at me. I picked it off the floor and read it.

"That's my second cousin. He works downtown. Go see him. And leave your apron with cook!" Giuseppe continued, "and work until the end of your shift tonight, huh?"

The address was One World Trade Center. I met Giuseppe's cousin, Bracco, on the 106th floor. "My cousin thinks you need help," he said, looking me up and down as if I were a commodity. "They train people here. If you want to be an excellent waiter, you train here."

"I don't want to be an excellent waiter, I need to pay the rent," I thought to myself. "I need to work at night," I told Bracco.

"What for? You an actor, musician? What?"

"A dancer," I said proudly.

"Oh," he smirked. "You and half of New York. That's no living."
I gave him a polite smile at the same time biting my tongue in an attempt to tell him off. I subdued my inner anger, as I still had to make the rent.

"Windows on the World will train you. You will be busboy and follow a waiter. You will be trained in proper service, wines, and proper restaurant etiquette. We will feed you before your shift and clean your uniform at the end of the day. Does this sound agreeable?" he asked.

Within days I was showing up for morning breakfast three days a week, sitting in wine and service classes from 8 am to 9 am and trailing my waiter, Michael.

Michael was a tall, sweet black guy with wire rimmed glasses and a very effeminate walk. He was very helpful and constantly guiding me and showing me how to serve and take away plates, decanting wine, and short cuts every waiter at "Windows" needed to know.

He was accompanied by his good friend and fellow waitress, Kimberly. She worked the other side of the restaurant, but was always meeting up with Michael to share gossip, eat left over Truffle cake that would come back into the kitchen, or finishing off bottles of wine that were left untouched.

The three of us soon became inseparable. Kimberly was a night club singer, and I was a dancer. Michael - was a waiter. "I never got the showbiz bug," he proclaimed. "Everybody in New York has two careers. I'm exhausted with just the one," he said, faking a faint and falling into the large leather booths that faced North.

Windows on the World was at the top of the North Tower on the 107th floor. The large floor to ceiling windows offered a breathtaking view of all of Manhattan, looking North, past the Empire State building to the Bronx and East, looking towards Brooklyn and Queens. In the daytime, you would have an unprecedented view of the "World." In the evening, the dimly lit restaurant would showcase the millions of diamond-like lights that would twinkle in the Manhattan skyline below. It was, by far, one of the most exciting places to work.

All of this was under the command of one woman, Mrs. Lee. Mrs. Lee was an elegant Eurasian mix of tall with chic, and a two-faced task master. She was angelic to every guest and a tyrant to those serving under her. She ruled the roost. She was exquisitely dressed in tight calf-length dresses and matching jackets. Her jet-black hair was always tightly pulled back and swept up with some decorative piece holding it all together.

Mrs. Lee would tell you something once and not repeat herself. She was precise and to the point, never saying too much or understating what needed to be said. She was a study in self-discipline and I admired her for that.

Now, I needed a place to dance for free, because dance classes were expensive. I needed to get a scholarship at one of the major schools who would hold auditions for new students.

I stood at the barre, erect as the Chrysler building. Head on top of the spine, hips over the legs, knees turned out over the toes. I was wrapped up in layers of sweaters and tights. A thin scarf hung around my neck, keeping my cervical muscles warm with long leg warmers stretched from my knee caps to my ankles.

The studio door swung open and a parade of “suits” walked in followed by two obvious dancers in rehearsal clothes. The ballet master followed behind his assistant using a cane to help him along. The suits sat behind a long table in front of the room while the ballet master sat in a chair in the corner, as his assistant took center space.

"First position. Slow demi plie," she commanded. The piano player who was situated next to the ballet master, started playing a slow composition by Mozart as we bent our knees out to the side without lifting the heels off the floor.

"Second position, grande plie. Fourth position, grande plie. Close fifth," she instructed. "Passe into attitude, four counts, arabesque four counts. Back to passe, close fifth position. Don't forget to work through your feet," she punctuated.

The assistant led us through a series of exercises to demonstrate our proficiency, timing, and foot work. "Girls center stage," she pointed.
The females in the class quickly removed their leg warmers, sweaters, and coverings. "We'd prefer point shoes. Move fast now," she pushed.
It was the boys turn. We did a number of jumps and then turns. The sweat was pouring down my face. I did everything I could to keep the water out

of my eyes. With every turn, I could feel the sweat spin off my face like a salad spinner.

"Across the floor. Girls, then boys," the assistant demanded. She quickly rattled off a combination by name. Everyone around me seem to understand the terms. Although, I was slow on the uptake, I watched as the words were expressed through movement. Once I set my fear a side, I understood the steps and just went for it. The music was fast. The ballet master kept time with his cane in the corner, carefully watching every step. I got the translation and moved across the diagonal. It was the fastest hour I had ever experienced.

Rebekah Harkness was the fortunate widow of Standard Oil tycoon, William Hale Harkness. With his fortune, she bought her way into the ballet world. She sponsored the entire Joffrey Ballet company, sending them on world tours, buying up real estate for ballet, and investing in her own theatre. Rebekah bought a mansion on the Upper East Side and transformed this French-Renaissance masterpiece into a breathtaking school for dancers she called Harkness House.

The Harkness School of Ballet was at 4 East 75th street. She filled the 20,000 square foot mansion with precious antiques, fine linen curtains, and every amenity a dancer would need. The school had five large rehearsal studios, immense dressing rooms, a kitchen/dining canteen, and music library housing all the classics. She set up a full scholarship fund for dancers to make sure those who loved to dance would be given a golden opportunity. I was one of those lucky students. I made the cut. I was chosen to be a part of this incredible scholarship. The hard work was paying off.

She brought in top choreographers like Jerome Robbins, David Howard, and Lee Theodore to teach. Our dance curriculum included classical ballet, as well as modern dance, jazz, and even Spanish dance. It was one of the most coveted scholarships a dancer could get.

A large chandelier dripping in crystals would greet you as you entered through the front French doors. We would ascend the grand marble staircase up to the dressing rooms each morning. The scent of lilies and roses filling the grand foyer from the four-foot-high flower arrangement on a table, half its size.

Although, Rebekah Harkness had passed away a year before I got there, her wishes were carried out by those she put in place to ensure its success. Her portrait hung along the marble staircase in the foyer, greeting her students each morning we would arrive.

The dancers were very competitive here. In New Paltz, it was a very friendly, helpful atmosphere, but here, everyone was cautious. You could smell the fear and attitude welding into a scent of sweat and ambivalence. I had contrasting styles of dance with teachers who were of equal stature. Lee Theodore was a Broadway dancer who now made it her mission to preserve and archive all the dance from the Great White Way so that it would never be forgotten. Her Broadway show and later her company, The American Dance Machine would teach us the dances from her vast repertoire.

Natalia Makarova would occasionally teach ballet when David Howard was not able. Makarova was a National Treasure. She was one of the finest ballerinas of her generation. She was a tough Russian who defected in order to live her life free as a dancer in the dance capital of the world. "You have neck like giraffe and strong legs like gazelle," she would say to me. "Perfect for dance. Feet like bricks. Work on those." Typical response from Makarova. A backhanded compliment.

David Howard was my greatest ballet teacher in New York City. A master teacher for some of the most renowned ballerinas of our time, he had been one of Rebekah Harkness' favorites and one of the board members for the school. Mr. Howard taught by example. He rarely gave compliments, yet there was something in his teachings that wanted you to do better. I believed it was my desire to "please the master" or show him that I understood what he was trying to convey. His method of the ballet was easy on the body. His teaching technique took the natural approach to working with the strengths you had and not forcing your weak points. He taught how to disguise these weaknesses by not bringing too much attention to them. My strength as a dancer was through my expression from the waist up. I was not so much a technical dancer with a perfect turn out, so therefore he would help me to disguise the fact that my feet were not perfect and helped me to bring people's attention to my persona or how I would relate to the audience. He was the one who introduced me to Jocelyn.

Jocelyn was a principal ballerina with the Joffrey Ballet. She was not the typical waif-like prima donna, but exhibited more of a Botticelli fullness. But when she went up on point shoes, she seemed to transform into a sylph-like entity with ethereal qualities. She would float through her ballet with the effort of a feather in a gentle wind, while her footwork was agile and precise.

She would come into Harkness with David Howard, along with a few other ballerinas he would bring to morning barre class. Obsessive, compulsive, moody, she was a walking contradiction. Yet I fell for her, regardless. She would coyly flirt with me and then get lost in her art again. Jocelyn expressed this passive-aggressive behavior daily. One minute coming on strong and the next, practically ignoring me. I found it to be a challenge. One I wanted to pursue.

We fell in love in Central Park. We would take long walks through the Meadows and picnic on the Great Lawn or hangout at the Bethesda Fountain and swoon over one another, with the bronze angel looking down upon us.

We moved into a five-story walkup on Elizabeth St. The landlord was Chinese and had a laundromat on the street level, which was a big convenience. Especially for dancers who constantly needed clean rehearsal clothes. The building hadn't been painted in years and the old lime green paint was now showing under the newer beige paint that was marred and already peeling off the sides of the walls. It had a wide staircase going up to the top floor of our apartment, with extremely large windows that opened up to the fire escape. We had a view from the front of the building facing West. It was summer and we had no air conditioning but the breeze coming in from the open windows was exceptional. The place was a dump. The plumbing barely worked, the closets were non-existent, and there was an occasional cockroach scampering about, but it was my Manhattan apartment. A rental, of course, but at least we weren't shacking up in the boroughs, commuting every morning. I'd been there, and done that.

The neighborhood bordered Little Italy and Chinatown. In the mornings, it was nice walking through the streets and buying fresh fruits and vegetables from the numerous Chinese stands, carts, and make-shift tables. The Chinese were early risers and knew how to take advantage of the cool summer mornings. The seafood stands would be packed with huge, ice-covered racks of crab, fish, and lobsters, with shoppers clamoring for copious amounts of shrimp and squid.

By, late afternoon, the Italians were out hawking their pastries and cappuccino, while the delis were lined up with elderly Italian women waiting to buy prosciutto and olive oil. There was always a faint scent of basil wafting in through the window by midday. It was a fascinating mix of cultures and smells all clashing beautifully together.

I loved this neighborhood. I lived right around the corner on Mott St. when I was on scholarship with Martha Graham. It had a sense of familiarity and comfort. I felt right at home on the Lower East Side.

Jocelyn seemed to love it here too. The interesting thing I discovered about myself and other dancers was our ability to accept change easier than most people. Maybe it was the surfing that taught me the ability to adapt to any situation, but it was certainly dance that solidified this behavior. If you weren't flexible and able to quickly adapt to change, you were out of the ballet, out of the company, or out on the street. No choreographer had the time to put up with someone who could not be molded into their vision. They would simply find someone else, as there was always someone waiting in the wings, ready to go on in your place. But not Jocelyn. She was combative and questioned everything. I was not sure how she got as far as she had gotten in this business. Although, artistic behavior would sometimes trump all sense of reason.

By 10 am each morning, Jocelyn and I hopped on the #6 train to East 75 St. Jocelyn would take morning class with David and then head to the Joffrey Ballet school downtown in the Village. My classes were rigorous. They shuttled us from dance class to dance class with an hour break for lunch. The ballerinas would barely eat, while the boys would eat enough for both sexes. It was really our main meal, because once we got home at the end of the day, you were exhausted and would hardly have energy to take a shower and pour ourselves into bed.

I worked out with the restaurant, a schedule that was agreeable with them in order for me to be on scholarship at Harkness and work my shifts at Windows. This usually meant, I would finish class at 4 pm, hop the train downtown to the World Trade Center, and work the dinner shift. It made for a long day.

There were always auditions to go to. Backstage would come out every Thursday on newsstands all over the city. It was the newspaper for the actor-dancer-singer who was looking for work in the industry. The auditions listed in Backstage were usually cattle calls with hundreds of dancers showing up for a job that might have eight positions. Knowing how to sing was an important skill to have, which often got me closer to a particular job. Still, there was a lot of rejection.

I was no longer a big fish in a little pond as I was in New Paltz. In New York, I was one out of hundreds of guys auditioning for a role. That made me a little fish in a huge ocean!

"Next! We'll call. Leave your resume. Try us next year. No messages." Every audition was a reassessment of who I was. What did they want this time? What were they looking for? Did I get this job? Why didn't I get this job? Was I too tall, too short, too white, too blond, too weak, too strong, not talented? Self-doubt and self-loathing were a performer's albatross.

Rejection was a way of life. At first, it was a hard pill to swallow. But, in reality you were rejected far more times in life than you were accepted, and this was a lesson that everyone should learn. Of course, it's even more so for performers, because we put ourselves out on a limb every time we go to an audition. But the lesson here was not to take rejection personally. If you accepted rejection as a challenge to learn from, or to help improve your strategy, you could learn a valuable lesson and therefore, increase the likelihood that you would get what you were after next time.

When I just couldn't take the rejection or the stress from constantly being judged, pressured, and analyzed, I would take the train to Long Island and ride the waters off Long Beach. Here, I could escape the madness in the waves. Jocelyn didn't understand my surfing addiction. She would always try and do something to sabotage me from going out to surf. I guess that was probably not a good sign. She thought it was childish.

That was probably why I needed to escape even more. Knowing that she could not accept something that was such a part of my life, was stressful in itself. There were times when I couldn't wait to make my way out to Long Beach, one of the pristine beaches on Long Island, to surf from June to October.

During some of the hot August days, Michael and Kimberly would meet me at the beach and we would hang out. I would teach Kimberly how to ride my surfboard or the three of us would body surf. Jocelyn never wanted to go. She didn't like sand everywhere.

In September, there was a cattle call audition for 42nd Street, the big, splashy tap-dancing musical on Broadway. They were looking for 3 replacements for the chorus and were holding open auditions at the Minskoff Theatre. 1515 Broadway in Times Square, was the place for many major auditions that were reputable and the Minskoff theatre and rehearsal halls could hold large numbers of people.

Male dancer call was 9 am. I got there at 8 am. The line was wrapped around the building with guys of all shapes and sizes. I was number 209.
It was already 80 degrees and you could see the eager desperation on so many guy's faces. The usual, loud show-offs were tap dancing in the street or singing at the tops of their lungs. I was pulled back and reserved. Otherwise, I would easily psych myself out before I even got through the door.

Two hours later I was on stage with 19 other guys. Dancers were already grouped in the wings practicing the routine. This was the quick elimination phase to weed out 70 percent of every Tom, Dick, and Harry who came in from Scarsdale, Middle Village, or the Grand Concourse to take a shot at Broadway.

It was a rather easy tap routine. Double time step, quick shuffle, turn, turn, shuffle, ball, change, into a riff walk with three beats, double cramp roll, traveling time step that ended in a series of paddle rolls and a double turn.

I had Brenda Bufalino to thank for her wisdom. It came in handy now. My nerves were now frenzied as the large theatre seemed claustrophobic with so much testosterone in one place. In two hours, I was called back on stage in the final group of 10. They needed two guys and one girl. We had one finale routine that was from the opening number of the show. The assistant choreographer taught the routine, while a few of the current cast members demonstrated on the side. We were each sent to the piano player for a vocal audition. The boys and girls that were now remaining, were brought together. The competitiveness was nerve wracking. After singing for the producers, we repeated the routine once more and were sent home with, "We'll call if we're interested." I walked down Broadway feeling completely exhausted. I could feel the twisting tension crawling up the back of my neck. I had a splitting headache. The rest was up to fate.

In the days to follow, I headed to Harkness for my classes. I would call into my answering machine every few hours to see if the theatre called. After class I would run down to the restaurant for the evening shift. By midnight, I would get home, fling off my clothes and stretch on the floor for 20 minutes before taking a cold shower and pouring myself into bed. Jocelyn could sleep through anything.

Day five, I got the phone call. "We want you for 42nd Street," the production manager exclaimed. I was in shock. I hung up the phone, beaming from ear to ear. My first professional job and it was on Broadway. There are no odds for that!

"Well, what are you going to do about Harkness?" Jocelyn had overheard the phone call. "And what about the restaurant?" she persisted.

"That's the first thoughts in your mind?" I asked. "How about…congratulations! That's incredible! Jocelyn, I will give notice at the restaurant and I will let Harkness know I have a professional job. They have both been a means to an end."

"What about us?" she said biting her lip.

"What about us? Jocelyn, I am working in town. It's not like I'm leaving to go on the road." I could sense her fear and insecurity writhing through the room. If change affected someone else around her, she felt uncomfortable. It made her surroundings unstable and she was not good with that.

"Well, that's great," she sarcastically spouted as she grabbed her dance bag and left for class.

Unsure as to what just happened, I sat in the big window inhaling the warm morning air, allowing the late summer morning of Manhattan to calm me down. I felt let down by the one person I thought had my back. I felt sadly disappointed that the girl I loved, couldn't share in my happiness because her own issues clouded her view. "It's our moments of struggle that define us," I could hear Big Steena say. "What's going to be your defining move?" I grabbed the phone and started calling everyone with the good news.

My life changed over the next few weeks. I gave notice at Windows on the World and my handler at Harkness was very pleased I booked a Broadway show. "Whenever you wish to come back, the door is always open."

I was now a part of an elite crowd. I had my Equity card. This was clout for any performer to have their Equity card. This meant that you were now a member of the professional union for actors. I was brought into the theatre to sign a six-month contract and get fitted for costumes. The producers had caught wind of the fact that I was a surfer. In my contract, it had a list of activities I could not do while under contract with the show. "Surfing" was listed at the very end of my hazard clause. *We'll see how long that lasts,* I thought to myself.

Kimberly and Michael invited Jocelyn and me to Sardis to celebrate my big gig. Jocelyn begrudgingly came, but was a wet blanket the entire night. The next day, Kimberly called to congratulate me again. "She's not for you, my friend," Kimberly stated. "Just sayin'"

I guess I didn't want to admit it, but I knew in my heart it was true. It was a hard pill to swallow, because I loved this girl. Quirks and all. But, constantly battling her resistance was difficult.

My opening night was spectacular. My parents and brother came to the show, while Bill and the guys even sent opening night flowers from LA. The huge cast quickly became family. After the shows, we would go out to the Starlight diner or go dancing at Roseland to unwind from the crazy performance and rehearsal schedule. This was the life of a Broadway hoofer. I would often get in at 4am, unwound from the kinetic energy post performance. By the time I'd wake in the mornings, Jocelyn was gone. When I'd return, she was asleep. It was getting harder and harder to spend quality time with her.

My life's ambition was to tread the boards in the city that never sleeps. Here I was. But, the magic of Broadway on stage was juxtaposed with the gritty life just off the boards.

Outside the stage door, life loomed large and it loomed fast. What was popular a minute ago was now passé and what was old, a heartbeat ago, was now so new. Fickle, deviant, breathtaking, Manhattan would always have a connection for me, as I learned to grow up hard in these streets. New York stripped me of my innocence, allowing me to emerge like a polished butterfly from its cocoon.

Its panache was only a subway token away. Who could resist the charcoal roasted chestnuts sold side by side with "dirty water" hot dogs and day-old pretzels? New York was a feast for the senses.

The lavish perfumes at Bloomingdales were offset with the smell of urine just outside its doors. The gleaming, towers of steel shadowed over its inhabitants while the lavish nature of Central Park gave tired New Yorkers respite from the driving tempo of its pace. You had to be a special breed of person to live and make it here. If not, you'd be swallowed up whole.

It was now early Fall; I missed the water. I would get up the nerve to take the tedious, two-hour train ride on the Long Island Railroad all the way out to Montauk. Situated on the South Fork peninsula, Montauk was known to have the most formidable surf culture on the Island.

After surfing Cali for some six years, it was hard for me to get used to the "East Coast" vibe. The indigo water of the Atlantic seemed unfamiliar. Consistently frigid, even the swells seemed different. I could always hear Big Steena in my head saying "water is water, learn how it behaves," but I guess I just missed the sunny, laid-back energy of the Cali-life. The East Coast surfer seemed more serious about their waves, more cautious, and even more guarded. Whenever I was out there, I was the outsider.

Probably known as the most popular surf spot on the Fork, Ditch Plains was a beautiful beach. There was no disputing its great expanse and inviting appeal. Moss laden stones were juxtaposed against grassy cliffs to the West while high drifting sand dunes would greet you as you made your entrance to this last spot of sand before you crossed the Atlantic.

Although it's the one beach I've heard compared to Lowers, it was not as magical. I would often get caught up on the reefy bottom, or lose my board to swells that would shift and shut me down. But compared to anywhere on the East Coast, it was one of the best surf destinations with well-formed A-frame waves and good consistency.

The board of choice out here? The longboard. Just like San Onofre, the waves at Ditch Plains were constantly picking up swell from three directions making it the best for long, even waves that worked well for those in the 9-footer club. Although, swells from the South seemed to be the best for shredding, on a longboard, any wave looked effortless. I was always attracted to the longboard. It reminded me of images I would see in Hawaii of the original surf culture posing in black and white photos with these enormous boards. In many ways I associated them with the 50s and 60s nostalgia in a beautiful way. I guess because I started out on a shorter, medium size board, it was what I was used to.

The original "Malibu longboard," nicknamed after its namesake beach, was seen everywhere North and East of the Malibu pier. Their characteristic round nose and wide width made them great for beginners (although there was an entire clan of pros who only used longboards). Here in Long Island, they were the staple.

I befriended a laid-back dude who loved surfing Turtle's Cove. "One day, I'll get you out there," he'd often say to me.

Phillip was a little younger than me, but seemed to be worldly beyond his years. Nothing seemed to shake him and everything was matter-of-fact. He at first reminded me of Big Steena, but the more I got to know this guy the more it seemed like he always had a hidden agenda.

"Dude, can I borrow your wax? Dude, do you have $10 bucks for gas? Dude, I don't know where I put my wallet, could you spot me a $20?" The pattern was becoming obvious.

Covered in body tattoos from the nape of his neck to the crease in his ankles, he would bravely (or stupidly) trunk it even in the coldest of seasons. I was constantly in my back zip and could not imagine facing that cold Atlantic water in November, but he always did, seemingly avoiding hypothermia, by surfing shorter sets.

"Today's the day we hit Turtles," Phillip insisted. "We'll be beyond the light stick today, brother." The Montauk light house was a dominant towering white and red structure located on the top of a rocky outcrop called Turtle Hill at the Easternmost tip of Long Island.

Below it, was Turtle's Cove, the best place to surf late Fall into December. Nicknamed "The End," Turtles, along with the other surf spots, were as far out on this jagged piece of New York State as possible, jutting into the ocean. Phillip showed me how to maneuver my way across the jagged rock jetty and drop down into the cold black sea. Dotted with huge Lions Mane jellyfish that offered a very painful sting if you tangled with them or sharks chumming off the large fishing boats trolling nearby, the sea was an obstacle course in awareness. By this point in the year all the tourists were gone and only the serious of wave riders were here, lined up, perched to hit the next big face that rolled their way.

Thanks to Phillip, no one seemed to question who I was or gave me any flack. As an outsider to this beach break, I was with a local, so there were no questions. We took turns, like good little surfers, catching our waves and cutting through the four-foot swells with ten second breaks. This is where hollow, crumbling barrels would find their way from across the open waters at this time of year.

The crisp air and infinite blue sky of late November was a breathtaking backdrop for the stoic lighthouse that silently stood watch for over two centuries. On my board, from the sea's vantage point, it posed as a testament to its life-saving powers and a symbol of strength and security.

By early March, I was given the option to extend my contract for another six months for 42nd Street. Job security in the city sounded great, but I was itching for more. Jocelyn was offered a prima ballerina position with the Boston Ballet, which meant she would have to move to Boston.
"You have to come with me," she insisted. "I just don't do long distance relationships."

"Wow, an ultimatum," I thought. I didn't answer her. Now I was faced with another decision. Another path to go down. What do I do? I really loved this girl. She could be thoughtful and caring when she wanted to be. She had a work ethic I admired, and she enjoyed many of the same things I loved about New York, but there were so many signs that made me instinctually hesitate. "Your intuition is your best guide." I would hear Big Steena in my head. "All you have to do is pay attention," he would preach.

A fellow surfer and former dancer friend of mine was out on the road with a huge review show as the stage manager. Jose called me to tell me the show was auditioning for three replacement dancers for a world tour through Asia. "If you get the job, you can bring your board and we can surf the waters of the Far East," Jose teased. "Come, audition," he said. "The producer likes blonds."

I started fantasizing about the possibility of riding waves around the world. Hopefully, there would not be a "no surfing" clause in my contract. Well, I didn't even have the job yet. But it was nice to dream.

After the audition, I got the phone call from The Fantasy Factory, that I was chosen to join the rest of the cast, who were already in Malaysia. The producer, Errol Manoff called me himself from Japan to explain his vision of the show and how happy he was to have me on board.

South African producer Errol Manoff, was a famous puppeteer, costume designer, and the mastermind behind, The Fantasy Factory, a large scale blacklight puppetry and magic show. This extravaganza featured huge foam puppets of some of Hollywood's most famous celebrities including Liza Minnelli, Joan Crawford, Betty Davis, Dolly Parton, and so many more. The show took its viewers on a magical journey around the world.

The production featured 25 dancers and 10 puppeteers who worked seamlessly together with 10 different sets and 15 costume changes. This huge production had been on the road for years and this Asian leg of the tour would cover Malaysia, Singapore, India, and Thailand over a year's time.

The timing was perfect. The Universe was giving me all the cues. All I had to do was act. I gave everyone notice. The show, my girlfriend, the landlord, they were all on the list. It was painful saying goodbye to Jocelyn. I struggled with heartbreak and a sense of letting go. But after she was gone, there was almost a sense of relief that I seemed ok with. Maybe because I had a new adventure on the horizon.

I had to get a passport and suspend my Manhattan life while I prepared to travel the world for a year. It sounded surreal. I even had a surf buddy who I could relate to and surf the waves of the Far East with. It was a bonus. I was going to travel the world on someone else's dime, get paid, and surf.

Chapter 14

The Mystical Far East

As it turned out, Jose couldn't go. He was hired as a stage manager for a show in Manhattan and decided he was tired of touring and living out of a suitcase.

Another suckerpunch. Of course, he waited until the morning I was leaving to tell me. There I was, standing in the middle of JFK airport with my suitcase and surfboard. Maybe I shouldn't go? What was I getting myself into? "It's going to be ok," I told myself. I checked my gear and headed to the gate. There I met Suzanne and Tommy; the other two dancers hired for the gig. We instantly hit it off. My anxiety decreased the more we talked to each other. I realized we all shared the same trepidations and that it was going to be alright.

The Gentian Highlands Resort was a spectacular hotel property perched on the rocky peak of Mount Ulu Kali giving its visitors an unparallel view of Malaysia's rich, green highlands. Nicknamed the "Hotel in the Clouds," Gentian had a 5-star reputation with exceptional service and large spacious rooms, each with breathtaking views. From my suite I could see the hotel's towering logo on this castle-like building. The mountain was at such a high elevation, the resort always appeared draped in layers of white, puffy, billowing clouds.

The show had a three-month contract in Malaysia, which gave us time to settle in, enjoy, and learn more about the country. Suzanne, Tommy, and I got settled and had a cast meeting in one of the beautiful restaurants in the lobby of the hotel. We got to meet the entire cast and for the following two weeks, we went through rigorous rehearsals until we were fully integrated into the show.

The show was a non-stop, fast-paced romp around the world with dance, magic, and puppetry. The lead couple and cast of dancers took the audience on a journey with celebrity puppets, singing ostriches, moving sets, props, and fantastic costumes. My mom always said I came out of the womb dancing. I bet she never imaged in a million years that it would become a career that would take me around the world.

Performing was like sharing a bit of magic with audiences. It gave me a golden opportunity to make people feel good about themselves or to laugh, cry, sing-a-long, or just bring a smile to their face. Dancing was the most rewarding job I ever experienced. Helping others to forget about their problems for an hour or so, was an honor and a joy. If you could help someone find a little more wonder in their lives, your heart would always be rewarded.

We were each assigned a dresser who would help us with quick costume changes and keep us on schedule through the grueling 2-hour show. We would often do two shows a night, so the dressers would pick up after us, iron or mend costumes that needed assistance, and make sure all of our props were in the right place for each entrance we made on stage.

Ramain was the dresser assigned to me. He was a local boy who lived in Kuala Lumpur with his wife, who was a seamstress for the show. They would drive up the mountain in the late afternoon to work in the theatre. The dressers were fluent in English and very excited to be a part of a big American production. Ramain had a polite and respectful manner and was always so intrigued by the way we would stretch and warm up for the show. It was a ritual that dancers did, essentially to avoid injury during working hours. Suzanne, Tommy, and I seemed to hang around together the most, as we were the newbies, but most everyone was willing to help with cultural explanations, directions, or how to manage a particular costume change.

I shared a room with another dancer, named Vince. He was a tall lean performer with incredible ballet technique. He was a sweet guy from Pennsylvania and knew the city my cousin Bill grew up in. We got along well. He loved to talk and ponder the curiosities of life, which often lulled me to sleep at night. I don't know how many conversations I fell asleep in the middle of, but I would often apologize and explained how it must be the jet lag. I was guarded. I was in a faraway country, living and working with people I didn't know, and joining a show that had already been traveling together for a year. I felt like the foreigner.

We finally had a week with four days off and Ramain was willing to take us on a "seaside trip" he called it. Cherating was on the other side of the Malaysian peninsula about three hours from Kuala Lumpur. Frank and Lori were the adventurous married couple in the show who wanted to go anywhere that was new and different, as they were always up for squeezing every ounce of adventure out of life. Tommy and Vince wanted to join us, so off we went.

Ramain suggested we leave early morning from the hotel. The driver took us down the mountain and through town to the local bus station, Chow Kit's Putra Bus Terminal. Ramain quickly negotiated six bus tickets to Kemaman. From here we were able to get another bus that would drop us off along the side of the road. It was then a 10-minute walk to the tranquil seaside town of Cherating. It was situated on a precious little cove that arched into the lush green jungle side. It was now late November and according to Ramain, it was the best time of year to surf as it was the beginning of monsoon season. The morning started out with a light mist that cleared to a blazing blue sky. The 4-foot waves were great for gently surfing and teaching my new, curious friends about a surfer's life. I spent more time showing them how to pop up and ride the white water than I did riding swells, but it made for a perfect day.

Ramain found a sweet elderly couple who rented rooms along the beach for pennies on the dollar and who were thrilled to accommodate all of us. The couple set up a grill spit they fashioned out of beach wood and stones and grilled fish they had caught in the morning. They wrapped them in big green leaves from the nearby banana trees and let them bake in the embers while we talked with our host and hostess. The elderly couple was so curious about surfing and how was it possible to stand on a board in water? Ramain would translate a local dialect of Malay as we talked about the day's experiences. They fed us fish and rice as we sat around the fire and watched the golden sunset dissipate below the horizon.

I woke early to see what the water was like. Ramain woke to see me leaving and quickly got up and followed about 15 paces behind me. "Ramain, you don't have to wake up and go with me," I said.

"It's always better for two," he smiled. His comprehension of English and his manner of speaking made his presence that much more appreciated. He had learned the Queen's English in school and because of this, was able to get better paying jobs that kept him and his wife earning a good living. He silently walked behind me, seemingly giving me space and privacy. I wanted to walk with him and have a conversation, but he wished for me to enjoy the moments as if I were alone in nature.

This morning, the tide was very low which made the beach almost unrecognizable. The distance from the tree line to the water was now three times wider exposing a beautiful sandy stretch of sugary white sand. Not a soul in sight, we had the entire beach to ourselves. It wasn't exactly a surf morning, but definitely a time to swim. Ramain couldn't swim so he sat on a rock from a distance and watched over me as I enjoyed the warm, still waters.

The next day, the conditions were incredible. I could not believe I was halfway around the world surfing in an ocean that was unfamiliar to me. Yet, all I had learned about the water so far, gave me a sense of familiarity, even in a strange land. The extended point break waves were rolling in longer than a football field, with smooth breaking water that reminded me of Lowers. I could ride the face of a wave for minutes, coasting along the pristine water.

I surfed for hours, catching wave after wave, as if I was on a revolving carnival ride. Later in the day, I saw two other surfers, both with long boards enjoying the amazing surf. They both gave me a thumbs up from a distance.

Frank and Lori were relaxing under a big palm tree, Vince and Tommy were swimming and Ramain stayed on shore all day, close by, crafting fans and little dolls out of green palm leaves as gifts to us. "Mementos of your trip," he said.

The show's contract was coming to an end for the Genting Resort, which meant we would do our last show days before Christmas and head to our new destination, Singapore. It was hard to say goodbye to Ramain. We had been through several "firsts" together. Traveling through a foreign country, showing me Malaysia's surf culture, and getting me through my shows each night, he had become a valued friend. We said we would write to each other. Sadly, that never happened.

In Singapore, we were given accommodations at Raffle's Hotel. This landmark was one of the crowning jewels in Singapore's history and was a property steeped in time and tradition.

I was assigned a dresser who was a very book-smart girl named Jana. She was studying law in Singapore's most reputable University. She spoke perfect English, was devoted to the independent state of Singapore, and couldn't wait to show me the city on our off days from the show.

"You live in the home of the "Singapore Sling," Jana told me. This gin-based feast for the eyes included a dash of Angostura bitters, fresh lime, garnished with pineapple and a cocktail cherry, which her and I enjoyed quite often after the shows finished in the evening. Singapore did not have a reputation as a surfer's paradise, but 2 hours and 40 minutes away, was the magical island of Bali.

Bali was a lush green island in the Indonesian archipelago. Known for its beautiful temples, beaches, and rain forests, it had a reputation for surfing, diving, and nightlife.

By February in Asia, the Lunar New Year was the biggest holiday tradition of all. People would travel hundreds of miles to return home from which ever part of the world they were in to share the New Year with family and friends. Universities would close, business would go on break for 10 days, and the entire Far East would shut down in honor of Lunar celebrations.

With the show on hiatus, it was our golden opportunity to go to Bali to celebrate the Year of the Ox. The word was out backstage that we were going to Bali, and 10 of us were on a plane to Kuta Beach, Bali's biggest and most energetic spot on the island.

Also known as the Isle of the Gods, Bali's untrodden forests and pristine water seemed already threatened by the hand of man. In no time, this fantasy island would surely become a major tourist trap, overdeveloped and polluted. Its patchwork of rice paddies and black sandy beaches were its unique trademarks.

Surfing Bali was a dream come true. Katu had a wide, sandy white beach that most of the island life centered around. Just like Malibu in California, the beach produced long stretches of waves that would roll in, one after the other.

At dawn patrol you would find 10 or 15 surfers in the water. By 10 am the number would double. By mid-afternoon, the surf crowd tripled. I would meet surfers from all over the world. They were all drawn to Bali, one way or another. The rituals of the California surfer seemed to mirror the same love and respect for nature I would see in every surfer I encountered in these faraway lands. It's as if the mental appreciation was an ingrained calling with the love for the sea as a common thread.

This beach had a sandy bottom, with no coral, making it the perfect hang 10 spot for surfers to relish. You would see locals come to the beach early morning to do blessing rituals, placing flowers, candles, or incense afloat in the beautiful water. The town, although a tourist haven, had a strong spiritual sense to it. Just looking around and admiring the tropical paradise gave the impression that God was present through his gift of nature.

I would spend most of the days surfing, while my cast mates spent their time swimming, shopping, or eating. I was grateful that there was not a "no surfing" clause in my contract. It gave me the freedom to really enjoy the moments without the fear of knowing I was going behind the producer's back. The nightlife in Bali was an imaginative side show of tenacious drunks, party girls looking for the next club to take over, or the endless stream of crazies flowing down the main strip. Although it was fun to be a part of, it really wasn't much different than the parade of tourist clamoring through Venice Beach on a Saturday.

I would often take my board to the beach and find a rock to sit on, watching the moon play on the constant rotation of waves coming in from the swells that were being pushed across the Indian Ocean. I wondered what the guys were doing back in California? I wished I could share these waves with my cousin and the gang. They would love it here.

Balinese Hinduism was a form of Hinduism practiced by the majority of Bali's population. Partial to the island people who made their home here, the indigenous rituals and practices became woven into their Hindu beliefs.

They recognized that every element in nature truly reflected an omnipresence within it. Spirit lived in every rock and tree, wind and water, earth and mountain. Their reverence and respect for the whole of nature was awe-inspiring.

Aside from the majority of Balinese Hindus, there was a large population of Chinese immigrants whose rituals and traditions seemed to become incorporated into that of the locals. This Sino-Balinese blend of faiths embraced their original beliefs yet honored the mixture of Hinduism, Buddhism, Christianity, Taoism, and Confucianism, harmonizing it with the other spiritual practices. This panoply was a far cry from the one-track mind of the Catholic diocese I grew up in.

Vihara Dharmayana, was a Buddhist temple where you could find peace and serenity from the mayhem and party revelers not that far beyond the main strip. The open-air temple was a series of red archways leading into altars of worship to Buddha, stacked high with plates of oranges and flowers as offerings. The air was ladened with fragrant incense. This hidden gem was engulfed in red paper lanterns and leis of fresh flowers in preparation for the day's New Year celebration.

"Gong Xi Fa Chai," a monk greeted me with Happy New Year, bowing his head with humility. I quickly repeated the phrase back, mirroring his actions. He handed me four golden pieces of paper and asked, "Is this enough for your family?" It registered in my brain that these were like blessings or wishes. One for each member of those most dear in your life. He extended his hand out towards a large, red furnace where I saw others tossing their golden papers into the flames. He offered me to do the same. Even though I did not really know or understand the tradition, it felt wonderful to partake in the ritual.

The Year of the Ox was upon us. The quiet temple, usually at peace among the jungle setting, was starting to fill with spiritual revelers hoping to start their New Year off right. Soon after, four boys set up drums that were three times their size. Beating a rhythmic pattern, they tempted the lion out from its lair to dance the dance of celebration. Out of one of the temple rooms pounced a large yellow and red lion's head, helmed by two boys. One commandeering the front of the giant head and mouth while the other boy, maneuvered the back of the massive mask, dressed in the feet of the lion. The Chinese New Year Festival had begun!

Behind them slithered ten men manipulating a 50-foot dragon that would precisely weave up and down, mimicking the movement of the great serpent as he frolicked and danced for the now, massive crowd, that had assembled. Children, dressed all in red, stared in absolute wonder as their parents pushed them forwards in order to catch sight of the rollicking dragon. This little island in the middle of the Bali Sea, at the tip of the Indonesian archipelago was exploding with the celebration of a New Year. It was one of the most meaningful observances of new beginnings I had ever experienced.

Canggu beach was located North West of Kuta beach. The rays from the morning sun stretched the length of the coast obscured by low hanging palm trees to the North and a long line of clouds, dotting the blue sky, Eastward. I was joined New Year's morning by two guys from down under and a dude from Malta. We bonded over boards and brews the night before and vowed we would surf Canggu in the morning.

We meet at the narrow entrance to the beach in the South and walked along the reef to greet the glistening, black sand. I waded into the water. The undertow was strong. I could feel the tug on my board as I stood waist deep in the refreshing morning sea. The waves were rolling in on a hard left, thanks to the stone reef jetty that lay just under the surface, perpendicular to the coast line. Even at low tide, the waves were tugging me back into the water as the white foam would recede. The two guys from Australia were anxious to do a hang 10, together on their boards, by walking forward to the nose and curling all ten toes over the board's front edge. The waves were 3 - 4 footers and would make this very possible. Malta seemed less experienced, as I watched him make some of the same mistakes I did, years before. I gave him a lot of credit for trying. We had all been there and like Big Steena would say, "he had all ten toes in play."

I should not have ignored the line of debris that caught my eye earlier or the deep, dark pockets of water. I should have paid attention to the break in wave patterns and the unusual tug I felt in my morning ritual. But, I didn't. We paddled out and made attempts to ride a wave, but before we knew it, we were caught in a riptide, being pulled out to sea. These narrow, unpredictable but extremely powerful currents could sweep even the most experienced surfers far from shore. There's no way to outswim a riptide; you're literally fighting the ocean. That's not a fight you are going to win. I looked to my right to see Malta floundering. His board five feet out to sea behind him dragging him further away from the shore by the leash. On my left, the Australians were in trouble. One seemed to be drowning, while the other one was on his board being pulled further out. I was in the water holding on to my board fighting the pull underneath me and the water hitting me in the face above.

As young kids, my mom, the Ester Williams devotee, made sure my brother and I had swimming lessons before we ever went to the beach. I would never forget her words. "If you are ever caught in a rip current, swim parallel to the shore." She and her girlfriends went through a similar fate off the shores of Atlantic City when she was only eighteen.

"Malta, pull your board to you," I yelled to the panic-stricken surfer. "Stay calm! Try and follow me."

I slide my board underneath me and started paddling furiously. I knew rip currents were thin channels of energy underneath the water. By swimming parallel to the shore, you could swim through these channels to break free. A problem may arise when there were several channels next to each other.

I looked up from my own personal chaos to see that both Aussies were on one board paddling towards the nearest wave. The wave rolled underneath them and pushed them further to the shore.

I looked back over my shoulder to see Malta paddling, then giving up. His arm strength was not yet there and he would start and stop, ending up back in the same position he started from. "Get to the wave," I yelled. He barely looked up from his fatigued spirit, and scanned the water around him for the incoming wave.

The wave hit my board and lifted me upwards, two feet closer to the shore. This would have to be a game of endurance. I dug into the deepest part of my soul to find my survival mode, buried somewhere between my insecurities and my common sense. I was now in the wave pattern. I turned the nose of my board and paddled harder, my arms feeling like cinder blocks hanging off my shoulders.

The Aussies were nearly to shore and Malta was now following my lead. I could sense he found his courage and was now driven by determination. His "fight" kicked in. What felt like an hours' struggle was perhaps twenty minutes, but the back and forth, the starting and stopping, and the falling off the board and recovering, made me feel as if I had just run a marathon.

The four of us collapsed on the beach, minus one board. Several tourists, who were watching our struggles in horror, now slid blankets under our head, offered us water, and words of encouragement. One guy came running over to us with the lost board, now beached on the reef. Needless to say, we didn't go back into the water that day. Instead, we commiserated over Nasi Goreng and beers at the Muddled Mermaid. We had just shared a near death experience. Four complete strangers brought together by an unforeseen circumstance. The terror quickly bonded us together like brothers who had been through a war together. It was an experience I would long remember.

Bali offered an incredible place to surf perfect waves, which seemed to be created from its unique location and geographical setting. Bali showed us how many beliefs could live and function in harmony with love and respect. Bali also offered the lesson of respect for the water and not to ignore our instincts. Finally, no matter where we came from and no matter our experiences, we all shared the same sense of wonder and ultimately, the human experience.

Chapter 15

Namaste

Bombay, India was a sprawling, bustling city. Known as the financial, commercial, and entertainment capital of India, it was alive with culture, history, and for a farm boy from central New York - intrigue!

The Taj Mahal Palace Hotel was a sprawling, luxury hotel designed in the Saracenic Revival style. Also known as Indo-Gothic, the stylistic and decorative elements were dripping in detail and eroticism. Every room was on a grand scale, with pristine colonial furnishings, marble bathrooms, and over-the-top embellishments. In a word, breathtaking! Vince and I were given a room in the front of the hotel overlooking The Gateway of India. This was a commemorative arching monument built in the early 20th century to honor the arrival of King George V, the first British monarch to visit India. Situated in front of the Arabian Sea, it became a symbol of pride and a gathering place for all of Bombay to enjoy. It was bustling with tourists who clamored after the hundreds of vendors offering India's greatest silks, spices, and the occasional Taj Mahal t-shirts. It was also a meeting place for locals to enjoy tea, relax along the sea, or find respite from the searing sun, in the shadow of the great monument.

Our show moved into the Tata Theatre, India's first theatre designed with exceptional acoustics and visual enhancements. This 1010-seat premier facility was constructed specifically for music, dance and drama at The National Centre for the Performing Arts complex. With a revolving stage, brilliant acoustics, and a foyer with a beautiful view of the sea, the Tata Theatre was the shining star of Bombay.

After two weeks of rehearsal and an exceptional opening night, we were ready to explore the city. Bombay was filled with things to do. Top of my list was finding the surfer's life. But Lori insisted I go with her to a yoga teacher she had heard about. Since she couldn't talk Frank into going, she wanted me along as her escort. I was very curious about yoga. I also felt obligated to escort her for security reasons. So, I agreed.

We managed our way through the beguiling streets of Bombay, constantly avoiding cars splashing through large puddles of rain water, vendors hawking everything from dates to snakeskin shoes, and the occasional spice or carpet sellers roaming the streets with products balanced on their heads.

Lori managed to find the address she scribbled on a little piece of paper. The gothic structure looked like an abandon temple, complete with gold and aqua tiles depicting ancient Gods and warriors. We followed the music we heard meandering through the hallways, until we came upon a room with over 25 students facing their guru. He peered over his broken wire-rimmed glasses, and smiled.

"Namaste," he bowed, palms pressed together. "We have two new life students today, my children," he beamed to the others in the class.

He quickly sized us up, looking us up and down from head to toe. The silence was uncomfortable. He looked at Lori. "You have an unquenched curiosity for life. I sense much fire in you. But you have issues with trusting others, yes? he questioned.

Lori shook her head in disbelief, knowing he was right. He turned to me.

"I sense much air in you. You wander freely through life, like a nomad, this is true, yes?" Before I could answer...

"You have a very strong Vata dosha," he informed me. "But you are ruled by your heart and it's emotions. The heart is fire, and when fire is out of balance with air, you are now chained by the one thing which keeps you from flowing. You must find balance between the two," he advised. "Balance comes from the realigning of priorities."

I knew balance was rooted in trust. Trust was knowing that your body would respond to the training it endured to keep it aligned over its center axis, regardless of which direction you pushed or pulled. A ballerina found herself teetering on a point shoe that was the size of a matchbox while trusting that her own body would find its way despite what gravity was doing to her.

I knew balance was believing that your body would find its way through a barrage of commands and demands while teetering on a board in the middle of the ocean. Balance meant finding that familiar spot on your surfboard where, you just knew, was the spot that would keep you upright. But finding balance between my heart and my emotions seemed like a much harder task. I didn't even know where to start.

He motioned to Lori to join the class on the right side of the room and me at the opposite side. He went on to instruct the class. "Developed from the ancient text of The Vedas, Ayurveda views the human body as a homunculus of our cosmic Universe, regulated by the balance between three primordial humours, we call dosha," he smiled.

"Your dosha are your Ayurvedic mind and body type. There are three doshas in Ayurveda: Vata, Pitta, and Kapha. We each have all three of the doshas in our physiology, just in different proportions. Hence, your dosha are unique and personal, just like your fingerprints," he said raising his hands skyward. "Let's awaken all these elements with Sun Salutation."

Sun Salutation was a series of poses or asanas done to not only wake up the body, but to encourage the soul. Sun Salutation was the greeting of the day as you embraced the power of all things, which would rise before you.

By the end of class, I emerged from it in bewilderment. A shift in my Universe had taken place, opening a new door to my curiosity. Lori and I didn't speak the entire way back to the hotel. For professional dancers, the class wasn't physically challenging, but the emotional impact was another thing altogether. We seemed to be processing what just happened. But once we walked through the door, we filled Frank's ear with the amazing experience we both shared. We couldn't stop talking. The class seemed to spark Lori's desire for spiritual enlightenment as much as mine. And here, we thought we were going for a bit of exercise.

For the next six weeks, Lori and I would go every day. We would occasionally take one of our cast members from the show along with us, but none of them seemed as blown away as the two of us.

The yoga poses were challenging. With a different vernacular and philosophy of movement, yoga was not mind over body, but harmony between them. The incredible thing about yoga was that you would be shown a very simple pose but yet you could find within that posture a level of difficulty that perhaps, the person next to you would not discover. Yoga was a very personal experience. Even though you were in a room full of people, doing the same pose, the degree to which you could take that pose was up to you.

Like surfing, it was an intimate relationship between you and it. The time you offered it helped to build a connection between you and your body, as well as, you and your mind. Yoga helped to broaden my spirituality and made me more and more comfortable with myself.

We finally had time off from the show, due to a schedule change in our show's venue. Errol suggested we go to the beach or travel upland to see other sights along the peninsula. I had already done my research with my dresser, Terrin and he arranged for us to go to Arambol Beach.

Arambol Beach was known as one of the best beach breaks to surf in Northern Goa. The break featured some moderate swells of up to 6 or 7 feet with winds that blew in from the Northeast making for a great surfing experience. With the approaching monsoon, we knew the waves should be exceptional. We just had to time it right.

We flew from Bombay to Belgaum and then commandeered a taxi for a two-hour road trip to Arambol Beach. The beach had a hippie backpacking vibe with a relaxed lifestyle that was perfect for the surfer or those seeking a mellow atmosphere. Known for their sweet water lagoon and many beaches stretching along the Arabian Sea, it was the perfect getaway from nervous Bombay.

Terrin found an inexpensive hotel along the beach and Lori and Frank were going to hang back and do some shopping before heading down to the beach. Our taxi driver tagged along hoping to surf also. He pulled a small wooden board out of the back of his trunk and was ready to ride. "The more the merrier," I told him, not sure he really understood what that meant.

We met two surfers who had come from Australia to surf the coast of North and South Goa. The minute they heard a monsoon was heading for the coast, they knew they would find great waves to skim in Arambol. They were the "ambitious twins," Terrin called the two blond foreigners. "Unbridled eagerness with child-like wonder," he described them in a nut shell. They showed us where we could rent a board for Terrin and we were all off to the beach. We jumped in the car and drove down a dirt road that took us a little further down the beach.

Terrin had a good command of his board, even though he had not surfed in a few years. He was eager to get back to the water and his love and reverence for surfing had shown in his face. Our taxi driver on the other hand, was just happy to be in the water. The waves were not as fantastic as I was anticipating due to the shifting winds. You could feel something had changed since we arrived and there was almost a scent of foreboding in the air as a coastal haze started rolling in.

Sitting on our boards in the large swells, you could see the dark clouds gathering in the distance. The heavy odor of rain now lingered in the air like the scent of smoke from a fire. From a far, lightning could be spotted along the fringes of the incoming storm, expressing its path - forming an opinion.

Thunderous clouds reached high into the sky as the potency of nature's fury started to back build behind them. Lightning, often referred to as the finger of God, expressed a natural charge that was unleashed prior to thunder's rumble, which could be seen and felt from a distance and it was coming closer.

It was time to paddle in. We were now being lashed by bands of rain that would swing in sideways and catch us off guard. At the opportune moment, I latched on to a raucous wave that escorted me half way to shore before crumbling apart. Between the wind pushing in and the sea pulling away, we were now in a back-and-forth tug of war, between two elements vying for takeover.

A bolt of lightning found a huge metal buoy about 200 yards out from our position and cracked into its heavy facade. The lightning's path seemed like the decisive choice to go after this specific target that it was attracted to. Its intense heat and pinpoint accuracy would appear to be the outstretched finger of reason, being pulled to its obvious conclusion. Sparks ricocheted from this once buoyant marker as it sank in two pieces to the depths below.

The sound was deafening and the electrical charge seemed to give us all a jolt to the heart as our brain immediately sensed the danger. We scrambled in the opposite direction as on impulse, trying to avoid being the next target. My heart was thumbing in my chest as I discovered superhuman strength, making it to shore on pure adrenaline.

My board buddies were right behind me, making a mad dash to the tree line. As we gathered our senses, we were on the lookout for our two Australian friends who we spotted about 300 yards off shore still trying to catch a wave. By this point, the surge of wind and water were breaking waves apart, closing down every option. Yet, these guys were determined... or stupid. It was too late to be concerned about them now.

We made a beeline for the car and stuffed our boards inside. The road we came in on was now a muddy paste that slowed the wheels of our getaway car. It felt as if we were in slow motion inside the car as the now raging monsoon thrashed about in double time outside. The old jalopy managed to get through the mud but now had to contend with huge palm fronds snapping in the wind and accosting our windshield.

Terrin knew of a large cement structure we could seek shelter in and we were almost there. The car hit a large stone hidden in the mud, jacking it upward, into the air. Just like that, the car came to a jolting halt. The taxi driver repeatedly tried to turn the engine over, but it was dead. "We must make a run for it, my friends," he said. The car doors flung open as we grabbed our boards and gear. The wind would hit the surfboards steering each of us in a different direction. The mud was now mixed with the water, which was up to our calves. The ground was already saturated with slop and it had nowhere to go but up.

We reached a building, not the one we'd hoped for, and found shelter with about eight other people who were forced inside from the deluge. The rain was pummeling the makeshift roof and all we could do was pray it would hold.

The water rose. We moved to the second floor. Crouched down and huddled together, I was shivering from the combination of cold rain and whipping wind that found its way through the building. Was this going to be my end? The rain and wind pelted the cement structure and tin roof for what seemed like hours. All we could do was wait it out.

It seemed like days we were barricaded in this little cement structure along the coast of India. In reality, the torment lasted a few hours and by now the rain and wind had died down. The sky was grey and overcast, making it difficult to tell what time it was. I then realized I had lost the watch Jocelyn had given me. As we looked around, there was destruction everywhere. The water level seemed to be receding and was now about ankle deep. Garbage and plastic were floating down the streets, chickens perched on car hoods, and thatched roof tops were strewn across the landscape. The heat was oppressive and far off in the distance, the tree line was beaten back to revel the relatively calm sea intruding into the shakes, restaurants, and make-shift tee-shirt shops who were all caught off guard by the encroaching storm.

The wooden structures along the beach were tattered and beaten down. Motor scooters that were washed down the street were meet with piles of tin roofs and people's personal belongings hanging all over the place. The young boy's house we took shelter in was now disheveled by the wind and water that blew in through the tin roof and three corners of the structure where windows once stood.

"But mamaji, why are you smiling?" The young boy asked his mother. "Our home is destroyed and everything we own is gone!"

The mother turned and looked at her son. Calmly she explained, "my son, you and your brother are before me here, my greatest jewels. Everything else I can replace. You two are my greatest treasures." The boy grabbed his brother by the hand and started picking up the place, shaking his head. My mind had just been rearranged by her words. All her material possessions were gone and yet she valued the only things that gave her pure joy - her two sons. Like a lotus flower in the mud, her inner beauty had shown through and it was palpable.

My heart went out to them. I was again reminded of so many blessings we had been given as Americans. Many of the cultures and people I had experienced so far on my trip were dealing with such grave poverty. It was hard to believe that there was still joy left in the world. If someone could be happy with nearly nothing, what did that say about the rest of us? I was truly humbled.

We all pitched in and helped the woman and boys clean up their house. We washed down the walls and floor with buckets of rain water and picked up what little furnishings they had left. We went with the boys to find them enough food that could last a few days.

My thoughts were with Lori and Frank. I had hoped they found a safe place to secure themselves from the storm and that they were alright. Terrin, our driver, and I went back to the spot where we abandoned the car carrying our surfboards overhead. A few guys, who were walking down the road, helped us to get the car out of the mud and recommended a mechanic in town who could help us.

The grey clouds had cleared out by now and the sun was about an hour from setting as we made our way back to the hotel that Terrin had found for us earlier. Luckily, the building was intact. Lori and Frank were gone, so we quickly cleaned up and headed out again to see if we could find our friends. Stepping outside, we could hear drums coming from the beach. "It's the drum circle," Terrin explained.

The Arambol Drum Circle was a sunset ritual along with its nightly beach market, that would occur just before sunset to honor the passing of the day. Apparently, even a monsoon rain could not stop the community from hosting the party-like atmosphere on the beach. It brought people together, especially, after a devastating storm, to assure the community that life was going to continue and that resources were being offered for all those who needed them. It was one of the most heartwarming spectacles I'd ever seen.

People brought their drums, hand-flutes, and gourds in order to offer music for the disappearing sun to enjoy. The music filled the air, as if it were a call to the Universe. There was no sheet music or familiar songs that people knew, yet rhythms embraced the wind, calling to everyone within earshot. The receding water opened up the spacious beach for vendors to sell handmade clothes, hot food, hand-crafted jewelry, and hand-blown glass pipes. Community and tourists alike, came to the beach with juggling balls, colorful kites, hula hoops, and hacky sack balls. It became a music festival on the beach and best of all, there were Lori and Frank, dancing cheek to cheek in the middle of it all!

Chapter 16

The Space Between

We decided not to stay and headed back to Bombay the following day. Although the accosting city beat was intrusive and abrupt, it was almost a relief to come back to.

Our Guruji mentioned a change of venues for the next yoga class. We all meet at the studio and then he summoned cars which took us from the water's edge about twenty minutes deeper into the center of Bombay. The Dharavi was the poorest, most underdeveloped neighborhood in Bombay. The cars pulled up to an abandoned lot. We got out and Guruji had us quickly form a circle.

"Yoga's origins can be traced back to the town of Rishikesh in northern India over 5,000 years ago," he started. "The word yoga was first mentioned in the ancient, Sacred texts called the Rig Veda." He went on to speak about yoga as a matter of philosophy, psychology, and self-improvement.

We unrolled our yoga mats on the uneven ground and started with Tadasana, the Mountain Pose. With eyes closed, feet together, and hands in prayer position, I could feel a sense of oppression around me. It was discernible from the ground up. I couldn't figure out why.

"Tadasana demonstrates stillness," Guruji explained. "Stand tall and lengthen out of the sacrum, stretching each vertebra away from the vertebra below it. Lift the chest. As your neck stretches upward keep the throat, and jaw relaxed. The chin is parallel to the floor. Visualize a straight line running from your chin, to your sternum, to your pubic bone. Soften your gaze; quiet your hearing; relax your jaw. Breathe evenly and comfortably through your nose. Imagine the top of the head continually lifting upwards, while the soles of the feet are grounding downward. You are literally pulling in two directions."

He looked around at each of us, as we struggled with the simplest of poses. "Repeat after me," he suggested. "I am a mountain. I endure through every situation. I stand solid and strong as a testament to my will and focus. I am not persuaded or distracted. I am still. Like a mountain I am a symbol of surmounting and overcoming obstacles."

As we started class in the middle of the poorest neighborhood in Bombay, a crowd of onlookers began to gather. From my peripheral view, I could see a group of men walking towards the group. Lori noticed this too, and shot me a look as if to ask, "do we run, or stand and fight?"

The tension was now noticeable from other students who were aware of the gang of men approaching. What was even more unnerving was that our Guruji's back was turned so that he could not see what was coming. Lori stopped and came out of her pose. As she pointed to the group of men, Guruji turned around, elated to see them. In an instant they sat on the ground and began to play music for the class. My body melted into my mat with a sigh of relief…and embarrassment. Before too long, many of the onlookers started doing the yoga poses Guruji was showing us. The crowd got bigger and bigger and now we were all in sync with the music. It's as if the town's people were waiting for this day to happen. The music traveled through the barrio, lifting the spirit of the crowd that had gathered. This was the second time in days that we experienced the power of music. From celebrations and ceremonies to proclamations and processions, music marked the empirical reference we associated with time and place. I had seen firsthand how music was that magical medium that seemed to be a metaphor for our spirit.

"You are accepting of your surroundings?" Guruji asked me after class.

"It was amazing," I quickly responded. "But my heart goes out to those suffering around us," I hesitantly replied.

"My dear boy," he peered down through the tops of his broken wire-rimmed glasses, "we are born equal, and we leave equal. What makes you think they are unhappy?"

I looked up to him with confusion on my face, yet did not speak.

"The enlightened are more aware, yet the 'not knowing' may be just as blissful." He pushed his spectacles further up his nose. "One of life's fundamental truths, which we all have to experience, is arriving on this earth and leaving it one day. With that said, we bring nothing when we are born and we leave with nothing when we die."

It seemed to make sense. If you didn't know what you were missing, how could you miss it?

"Those who are resourceful enough to get the basic food, water, and shelter, may then find their interests increase. Perhaps life works this way to teach us all how to survive. Once we have mastered basic survival, it's up to us to make the most out of our lives. Education comes to us as life changes and we either learn to adapt or not. It just depends on how much you are willing to stretch."

I lowered my head, as if I had offended him.

"Most of these souls have never left The Dharavi. Even the poorest soul can find happiness where they are. Or they can find their way out of their current situation and improve their life. It is a matter of education, ambition, and resolve," he said to me as he brushed the dirt off his tunic.

"How much are you willing to exercise your free will to improve your life and follow your dreams?" he asked. "The plight of many is made less overwhelming when we focus on the mastery of the self."

I listened intently. He had a point to make and he wanted to make sure I was paying attention.

"Your trajectory is the single most important journey in your life. This acts as a blueprint which outlines how your life will play out. Opportunities and challenges faced along the way are heavily influenced by our choices. This is peppered with your general character and the course of action we take along this journey. Based off the choices we make; our life represents our whole being and will change as your path changes. Don't' be afraid to follow where it leads."

I bowed my head and thanked him greatly for the lessons.

"You got an earful," Lori pulled me aside. "What did he say?" I tried to repeat everything he told me.

"I'm so glad we came here," she smiled.

India was a marvelous place full of wondrous experiences and spiritual truths, but it was also an exercise in mastering patience. Some nights, the show would have to close because of rolling blackouts the city would impose in order to keep the power grid from overloading.

Our patience was challenged every time we tried to get from one place to another, as nothing seemed reliable. The trains would stop working, public spaces would be closed all of a sudden, for no apparent reason. If you made plans, the itinerary could change due to the unpredictable weather.

We would occasionally get to yoga class late because of the frustrating circumstances that would constantly try our patience. Yet, Guruji was never mad or upset with anyone coming to class late. "Your patience is a reflection of your inner peace. This virtue is something most do not possess," he pointed out. "When situations are out of your control, berating yourself or cursing the cause of your tardiness will never serve you."

That is exactly what I do to myself, I thought.

"Do you think your life is a series of random events or the consequence of cause and effect? What are the series of events that led you to this place?" Guruji asked his room full of students.

He would lead us through a series of poses to bring about balance. "The hardest process is what lies between. The transition. The key to creating balance and coordination is by mastering transitions and developing your strength. For what are transitions but the moving between one situation to another," he emphasized.

Guruji moved from Tadasana (mountain pose) to Utkatasana (chair pose) to Vrksasana (tree pose) with excessive ease. "This applies to your lives as well," he smiled. "Master the in between, with strength and patience and you shall forever be virtuous," he bowed.

"This may be a yoga class, but I feel as if I'm living through my philosophy class all over again," Lori said sincerely. "Only this, I understand!"

Overall, the shows in India were a great success. The theatre was overbooked for every show each month and the theatre management were so pleased, they invited us back again next year. We had one show left and Lori and I vowed we would go to yoga class one more time before we left India. We got to class very early the following day.

Guruji was in the class room, setting the yoga mats and directing the musicians as to the day's program. "It will be a great void once you two leave India," he said craning his head to the side.

He handed us Japa mala beads made from Tulsa wood, the sacred prayer beads of the Hindu culture. "I want you to pay attention," he said to Lori and I. We looked him in the eyes, once more through his little dirty spectacles.

"These beads consist of a strand of 108 beads plus a "guru" bead at the end," he smiled. "They are traditionally used for meditation and prayer. Why 108 beads?" he asked rhetorically, "8, which has long been considered a sacred number in Hinduism, stands for infinity and timelessness. This combined with the number 1 stands for God, the Universe or your own highest truth. 0 stands for emptiness and humility in a spiritual practice. You will notice, between infinity and God, is the space between. Now we do Surya Namaskar," he said. He led Lori and I through a series of four Sun Salutations together. "Now go," he said raising two hands. "We will be friends forever."

Once Lori and I got back to the states, our experiences with yoga were much different. The fitness craze in New York had become very interested in the ancient art of yoga. But many times, in a quest for exercise and a hard body, yoga classes became a workout and not yoga. The spirituality was filtered out. Much of the yoga we experienced after India was a series of poses designed to help you sweat and melt pounds away. It was void of any connection between the mind or Ayurveda.

It was time for our next transition: Thailand.

Bangkok was a frenetic assault to the senses. Gleaming temples and opulent palaces poised amidst the squalor of the chaotic streets. Smog from daily traffic jams lay low in the air as tuk-tuks darted in and out between the mash of merchants and shoppers, animals and trucks, school children and monks - each trying to reach their separate destinations.

The smell of diesel fuel mixed with the pungent scent of curry, cardamom, and exotic spices. Colorful flowers peeked through the mounds of trash discarded along the streets, while an occasional monkey swooped down and stole dates from an elderly woman trying to make enough baht to buy a bowl of sweet mango rice to eat.

Five Star hotels lined the boulevard while the poorest of poor begged for something to eat yards from the door. For the next six months the Hilton would be our home. The bus pulled into the grand lobby with gleaming chandelier overhead. A host from the hotel greeted us with a convoy of beautifully dressed men and woman in colorful Thai silk uniforms offering exotic fruits and garlands of flowers in an attempt to distract us from the sheer poverty just beyond the hotel grounds.

The hotel property had a huge 500 seat theatre adjacent to the main hotel which would be our playground for half a year. We were shown to our suites and within the hour we were backstage being matched with our dressers and the 20-person crew it took to run the inner sanctum, which the audience would never see.

My dresser was a short Thai man in his mid-30's named Kamnam. He had a very pleasant vibe about him, something peaceful in his eyes. When he saw my surfboard, I brought down to store in my dressing room, his eyes lit up!

In his delightful broken English, he asked, "This is you...kradāntôkhlụ̄n?" Although we learned some very basic Thai terms and greetings before we got here, I didn't know this word, but I knew what he was trying to say.

"Yes, this is my surfboard," I gestured, tapping the board. He smiled and made the international gesture of "you and I" and then of him surfing, as I shook my head yes. "Excellent, I found my local guide," I smiled to myself.

We had two weeks of rehearsal in order to set the show to the largest theatre we had played yet. The distance to cover from one end of the stage was enormous. Doing this in full costume, puppetry gear, or just dancing the routines within this space was like running the length of a football field. Errol made the executive decision to hire ten more dancers to fill the space. His Australian version of this show had just closed so he quickly flew ten additional dancers to Bangkok. We spent another two weeks adding these dancers into the show.

As a professional dancer, something always seemed to hurt. Pain was a part of your career as were the joys from accomplishing feats of super human strength. Getting your body to do things most people could not imagine possible, also came with the illusion of ease. Your tool of protection was the smile you learned to put on while your body was expressing just the opposite. The audiences were in awe. The show quickly became a huge hit in Bangkok. With two shows a night, the pace was rigorous and our bodies were struggling. We had two days off in a row which would vary, according to the hotel schedule and other headliners they would book into the theatre. But this week, they were in succession.

We finally got a chance to see the city at night. Several of our dressers were our tour guides for the evening. The hotel sent around three taxis and twelve of us were out for a night on the town.

Patpong was the premier nightlife area in Bangkok and considered the red-light district. The taxis wouldn't go through the teeming streets of sailors, foreign tourists, and expiates milling about, so they dropped us off at the end of the street. Bright neon lights shimmered in the steamy night air, while hordes of people mingled about, staring at each other as if the crowds themselves were the entertainment. It was the opportune time of the night for young mothers to solicit their even younger, underaged daughters out for sex.

"Looky looky, very pretty girl. She virgin. You like?" a desperate Thai mother whined, grabbing my arm.

Little Thai children who should have been in bed by now, were playing stick ball in between traffic, while smoking cigarettes. The sights and sounds of laughter and drunken businessmen singing at the top of their lungs was met by very young "lady-boys" waving handkerchiefs or spinning colorful umbrellas in an attempt to get your attention. Trying to promote their shows inside the nightclubs, these beautiful boys, who were either transvestites or boys who had now transitioned into females, were the main attraction.

Famous for its sexually explicit shows, Patpong looked like Mardi Gras on steroids. The shows consisted of lovely Thai girls popping ping pong balls from their private parts into glasses of champagne or lady-boys lip syncing to the latest pop star's hit song, while doing a strip tease with a boa constrictor. Not only entertaining to watch but it was to the point where you couldn't take your eyes off them because you didn't know what they would do next.

Our dressers introduced us to Fant-Asia, a tall Eurasian boy who came to Bangkok at sixteen to make his fortune in the "entertainment industry" he called it. Now the host of his own variety show in Patpong, he would gather "talented" boys and girls for one of the biggest shows on the strip.

Fant-Asia, dressed in full wig and make-up, wore a revealing sequin gown, showing just a hint of scandal with enough intrigue to make you want to keep looking. Smart and funny, he spoke four languages and hosted his review show, making jokes and innuendos in several languages keeping the disco crowd completely engaged. Apparently, his show was the hit of

Patpong and people came from all over to see it. Fant-Asia would start every show with the pop anthem from the musical *Chess*, describing Bangkok and its nightlife in the context of a chess match.

"One night in Bangkok makes a hard man humble
Not much between despair and ecstasy
One night in Bangkok and the tough guys tumble
Can't be too careful with your company
I can feel the devil walking next to me." **

Weeks later, we invited Fant-Asia, with four of his entertainers, to come and see our show at the Hilton. After the show, my dresser, Kamnam brought them backstage to see the inner workings and meet us for a drink.

Fant-Asia, whose real name was Quan, "it means warrior in Vietnamese," he said, was now dressed in a handsome, Thai linen suit with skinny tie and spats on his shoes. His short black hair was slicked back to reveal a handsome young man with a porcelain complexion and masculine mannerisms. Almost shy in his demeanor, you would never know that this was the infamous Fant-Asia of Patpong.

His colleagues, too, looked like young, urban professional men, in suits and ties who lived a double life. The transition was unbelievable. They were amazed by our show and promised, “we are going to swipe a production number or two from your show,” Fant-Asia vowed. “That was spectacular!”

The following week, three tour vans pulled up in front of our hotel in the early morning, helmed by Fant-Asia and his bevy of boys. They had promised to take us to the floating market, just outside of the city. We were off to Damnoen Saduak.

Thailand's best-known floating market, about an hour away from the inner city, was entirely afloat along the banks of three river canals. The maze of narrow canals hosted traders, mostly in traditional farmer apparel with blue shirts and large wide-brimmed straw hats, using sampans to sell their goods. These small wooden boats were often brimming with fresh, colorful produce such as vegetables and local fruits. We boarded sampans that would float along the canals drifting past a bevy of other boats with merchants hawking caged animals and reptiles, souvenir tee shirts, and Thai silk. There would sometimes be traffic jams as there were so many boats going in every direction in a race to connect tourist's boats with farmer's boats. If you saw something you liked, the two boats would pull up next to each other and make the transaction.

Banking on its popularity from its use in a scene from the 1974 James Bond movie, *The Man with the Golden Gun*, boats would float by with James Bond tee shirts and toy guns, spray-painted gold. It was a feast for the eyes. The floating market would only go until noon, and then the canals would clear for other boat traffic shuttling goods between different parts of Thailand.

Fant-Asia wanted us to get a better feel for some of the local flavors so he paid the boats to travel up stream to a traditional Thai Tea House in the country, along the banks of the canal. There, we enjoyed tea and sticky mango rice, seared chicken, and delicious lemongrass soup.

We walked along the river bank admiring the tiers of rice paddies. "We've come at a very auspicious time," Fant-Asia clapped, "they are releasing the ducks." To rid the rice paddies of pests and rice husks, farmers would release thousands of "field chasing ducks" throughout the paddies after the harvest. This long-standing tradition was famous among Thai farmers making their job twice as easy and feeding the ducks at the same time. It was a sight to behold.

As we sat there under a huge tree watching the ducks work their way through their smorgasbord, four Thai girls from the Tea House arrived with iced tea and mango juice accented with fresh mint. The refreshing drink was a welcomed relief from the hot Thai sun.

By late afternoon we walked back to the Tea House following the gentle river alongside of us. As we turned the corner there was a boy, no more than 12 years old, walking down the path hanging on to the trunk of an elephant. It looked as if the boy was leading him, but in fact the boy was blind.

Being led by this enormous creature, they sauntered along, as the elephant seemed to guide the boy past obstacles in the road. I could hear the boy having a conversation with the elephant in Thai. There was something so endearing and mystical about the boy and his elephant.

"Elephants are social animals," Fant-Asia said. "They are regarded as a symbol of luck, loyalty, and companionship. They are also very wise creatures."

"What is the boy saying to him?" I asked Fant-Asia.

"He's simply telling the elephant about his day."

This blind boy's greatest friend and companion was a mighty beast. The elephant seemed to understand what the boy needed, almost as if he was this pachyderm's child. The boy found his companion easy to talk to, and what appeared to be a level of trust and understanding.

My heart sank.

Chapter 17

The Path of Dharma

Thailand was intoxicating. It was such a pleasure to meet locals who could show us places other than the typical tourist traps. Although, some of those places were exciting to see, as well. For a twenty-something farm boy, every experience was like receiving gold nuggets. I was literally on the opposite side of the world living a life, that was hard to imagine from my early childhood days.

One of the greatest tourist attractions was The Grand Palace, a complex of towering gold temples and palatial buildings gleaming off the Chao Phraya River. It ran through the center of Bangkok. Home to the King of Siam for centuries, He, the Royal family, and government officials were officially housed there until the abolition of absolute monarchy in 1932, when even the last of the government agencies moved out. Now, the most popular tourist attraction in Bangkok, The Grand Palace was a must-see on our list. Of course, most of my cast members were not early risers after a long evening of performing. Most of them didn't wake up until noon.

My dresser, Kamnam, Tommy, and I set out early morning to see the spectacular sunrise and beat the crowds to the Grand Palace. The streets were already overflowing with traffic, vendors, and children making their way to school. "It would be easier to complete our journey on foot," Kamnam suggested as our taxi crept along, starting and stopping for more than 20 minutes.

Walking through the streets of Bangkok was a particular challenge for me because I was blond, but when Tommy and I were together, we would literally stop traffic. In 1985, blond Westerners were a rare sight in Asia. These people honestly considered blond hair as a good luck omen. To a dark-haired population, blond hair was as shocking as seeing spun gold. The school girls would want to touch your hair and the boys would want their picture taken with you. When we first got to Thailand, it was a real novelty. Tommy and I always felt like celebrities. It would happen to both of us separately, but when we were seen together, our two-shining, tow-headed coifs of hair would always bring havoc to our surroundings. The shock factor was something we became use to. Although people were very respectful and mostly just rubbernecking, we would often have a crowd around us, who wanted a photo or to rub our heads for good luck. "I guess we should have stayed in the cab," Kamnam sighed.

The Grand Palace was a city within a city. As monarchs would come and go, they would each add their own design to the sprawling grounds. Constructed in layers to resemble the order of commoners to royalty, there would be an outer court, middle court, and inner court. The palace housed the country's administrative staff and was its religious center. Each monarch had their own government staff with thousands of inhabitants including princesses, ministers, guards, servants, concubines, and courtiers. Each court had to accommodate the amount of people for each group. Kamnam lead us through large, impressive palace rooms, intimate little meditation spaces, and even through secret passages the Royal family might have slipped through to escape an unwanted guest or to meet with a discreet encounter. We meandered through spectacular gardens and cavernous ballrooms gilded in gold with colorful lacquered walls, stone buddhas, and precious artifacts.

We would come around a corner to find breathtaking temples, with the scent of Nag Champa drifting, languidly through the warm morning air. Groups of monks would scurry from one end of the court yard to another, either practicing their vow of silence or hastily performing chores. Tommy and I stopped to take in the glinting reflection of gold, shimmering off a reclining brass buddha, sparkling before us. The sun seemed to make it dance.

“Pssst, Ji Bong,” Kamnam whispered as someone he knew scuttled by. He said several things to the monk in Thai and the monk approached us. Dressed in an orange robe with brown sandals, his shaved head and pearl-like skin emanated a sense of purity.

“This is my childhood friend, Ji Bong,” Kamnam introduced us. “We were friends as youngsters even though we were from a different caste and background. Ji Bong’s family had a path set for him at birth, promised to the order by the age of 16.”

“Did he want to go?” Tommy smirked.

“It was his lot in life,” Kamnam said, matter of fact.

Ji Bong, who was not supposed to speak to anyone, was on his way to meditation, but knew that sometimes his longtime friend would come to the Grand Palace to give him news from the outside world. Kamnam would share some rice cakes, bring him a message from his family, or sneak him his favorite sugar candies. It was evident that the bond between them was strong and child-like. The sincerity was a beautiful demonstration of unconditional love.

"Come sit with us and share some new found wisdom," Kamnam encouraged the monk. He looked over his shoulder to make sure he was not in view of his elders or other monks. He sat down on the steps with us. "What did you learn recently?" Kamnam asked his dear friend.

Ji Bong, closed his eyes, as if to find his center. He took a moment to gather his thoughts, as his gentle breathing seemed as calming as his silence. He turned to Kamnam and spoke quietly in phrases. Kamnam would then turn to us and translate…

"Your Dharma stands for the ultimate moral balance in life. Dharma belongs to the Universe, as well as to the individual."

Kamnam listened once more. "Just as there is divine order of the natural and cosmic realms, there is the same order within us. However, each one has the responsibility to balance his own Dharma."

Tommy and I looked at each other. We listened more intently.

"Your Dharma unfolds in all areas of your life including your family, social life, and religious devotion. If a person makes a promise, the promise must be kept." I could feel the tension run up the back of my neck, as this was not my strong suit. After this lesson, I would never make a promise I couldn't keep!

Ji Bong leaned into Kamnam as his voice became softer and quieter.

"When these responsibilities are not met, the outcome is equal to your lack of commitment towards it." Kamnam translated, "Reaping what you sow, is the result of your actions. This is your Dharma. If an individual is following their Dharma, they are pursuing their truest calling and serving all other beings in the Universe by playing their true role."

"This becomes our Karma" Ji Bong said in Thai. Kamnam repeated in English.

"Karma stands for the belief that a person experiences the effects of his actions and that every act or thought has consequences. Living in a balanced Universe is important." Ji Bong stopped to wipe the sweat off his brow. "If an individual disturbs this order, he will suffer proportionately. So, a life lead with undisturbed Dharma, will lead to happiness."

Kamnam smiled at Ji Bong, in a manner that expressed he was proud of his translation from Thai to English.

A deep resonating, singular gong rang out through the garden. Its' comforting tone seemed to align with the most tranquil part of my heart. JiBong lifted his eyes upward. It was time to go. He smiled for the first time, as if he was proud, he could share one of his many life teachings with us.

"Sawa di cup", we bowed in gratitude, thanking them both for the rare experience. As Ji Bong stood up to leave, he whispered something into Kamnam's ear.

Kamnam turned to us and asked, "Ji Bong respectfully asked if he could touch your hair."

Tommy and I turned to each other and smiled. Without a word, we bowed our heads so the little monk could reach the tops of our heads. He gave our hair a soft brush with his hands. By the time we raised our heads, he was gone.

Several months into our contract and the show had become grueling. Having one day off a week barely gave our bodies time to recover. We had heard a rumor that Peter Graves, the American TV actor from *Mission Impossible* was coming to town to host a show at our theatre. The talk among the ranks was finally confirmed, which meant we would have an entire five days off, while Peter Grave's show would occupy our theatre.

I was itching to surf some of the beaches I had researched and this was now my opportunity. Half of the show's cast just wanted to stay at the hotel and enjoy their days, resting by the pool. My "clique" was eager to meet up and head to the beach.

Phuket was an island south of Bangkok along the coast of the peninsula of Thailand. Situated between the Adaman Sea and the Malalacca Strait, this island paradise was home to spectacular views.

The West coast of Phuket was dotted with great surf breaks exposed to Westerly swells, which made it a great place to ride the waves, especially between April and November. This was the wet season aka "surf season." Kata Beach was the most famous surfing beach among all of Phuket's beaches.

Tucked away in a private cove, Kata was the picture-perfect spot, complete with swaying palm trees and emerald green water. The cloudless sky looked like a pool of blue drawn to meet the sea. The mellow, listless air offered a sense of calm that immediately put your mind and body at ease.

Several long fishing boats sat a few feet off shore ready for the journey out for the day's catch. The viridescent tree line gently sloped along the shore defining the borders between the two worlds. It was one of the most beautiful places I'd seen so far on my travels through Asia.

The waves moved with determination to reach their destination. Coming in at about waist high, the water was already dotted with eager surfers ready to catch a swell. There was no territorial clashes or localism. Everyone surfing this island was a visitor. The few locals that did surf here, were happy to see other wave riders who shared their interests. The friendly line up was filled with guys from this side of the Universe. I was clearly the only American, which made me the novelty. Later, on shore, I was asked all kinds of questions.

"Have you surfed pipeline?"

"Did you grow up in Malibu?"

"Is surfing as popular as it looks in America?"

The questions were naive and innocent and it was nice talking with guys who were not crass and jaded. Their pure intentions were genuine and their sincere conviction was refreshing.

We spent the entire day surfing. In between sets, we would grab food at one of the local huts offering fresh seafood and Singha beer. This was truly the epicenter of the nomad and backpacking culture. Phuket was considered "the great escape."

The group of guys I was surfing with talked about another surf break, North of Kata that had even more challenging waves. A friendly local told us that surfing there was best at high tide. About twenty-five minutes away, Surin beach was much more isolated.

The following day, we decided to meet and go North. We wanted to be sure we got to the beach by high tide, but realized we had missed the first one, which was at 3am, so we knew the next high tide would be in approximately twelve hours. It was late in the afternoon when we arrived for the next high tide and it was worth the wait. These waves were overhead.

This beach had long rolling waves that broke forward into a frothy foam. In the middle of the beach there was an out cropping of rocks, just hidden under the high surf, but at the North end of this spectacular spot were tall lefts, feeding in, one after the other. These waves were fast and they were some of the biggest I had surfed in all of Asia. The waves would bank off a huge rock and allow us to ride them right into shore.

Mastering the power of the sea seemed to be an innate goal of the surfer. Although an impossible task, the lessons to take away were how you'd master your own self-control. Reaction time, decisions made in an instant, or being able to anticipate your next moves, were just as powerful as being the son of Poseidon.

Out of the corner of my eye I would catch the sun as it sank closer and closer to the horizon. I didn't want the day to end. We were each surfing our own waves, yet we were still somehow, bound together. No one got tired. No one wanted to call it quits and everyone seemed to be enjoying themselves. It was only due to the diminishing light that we finally realized; the advancing twilight would mean an end to our reign.

We decided to watch the majestic display of sun's final act from the beach. It was as silent as vespers or an evening prayer as we observed the end to one of the most satisfying days of my trip.

After living the dream in paradise, we were back in Bangkok entrenched in our busy show schedule. It was a wet and very damp week. The rains deterred much of our day's activities, keeping us indoors. Yet, the crowds were not discouraged. We had full houses every night. I had finally gotten a new pair of dance shoes and was late to show call, waiting for the bell man to bring them up to my room. I got to the theatre with about 30 minutes to spare. I did a very quick warm-up, checked my costumes, check-in with my dresser Kamnam, and I was out on stage.

Between the wet, damp weather and the new shoes, I could feel my muscles struggling on the kicks. My turns were late, or I would keep slipping when coming off stage. I could feel the tension in my neck and shoulders during the quick costume changes, before running back out on stage. The finale had a series of high kicks that ran in succession down a long line of the entire cast standing across the stage.

I suddenly felt the tear in the back of my hamstring as my leg went up and my standing leg came out from underneath me, falling to the stage in a half split. Tommy was standing next to me and I could see the mortified look across his face as I went down. I couldn't get up. The cast managed to dance around me, as I crawled off stage. It was a good thing I was close to stage right, so the distance from on stage to backstage was very close. As I pulled myself along the hardwood floor, I could see our stage manager calling an ambulance.

I think my ego was more bruised than my leg, but I definitely heard the hamstring rip as I kicked. The cast did their final bows and curtain calls, as they came running over to me to check on my condition. With everyone circled around me, I just wanted to crawl under the floor boards. Two medics showed up backstage in a matter of minutes. My dresser ran up to them to translate.

Once they determined that nothing was broken and I didn't appear to have a concussion, Kamnam explained that the medics wanted to take me to a doctor. Errol, the show's producer wanted to go with me and Kamnam. All parties agreed it was the right decision to go to a doctor.

The ambulance took us several city blocks with the sirens wailing as they sped down the street, dashing through the midnight traffic. You'd think I had a heart attack, instead of a torn hamstring. The ambulance pulled up in front of a white medical building. The medics helped me to walk into the building with Kamnam and Errol following close behind.

Looking around, the building did not look like a hospital. It was oddly dark and there seemed to be no staff on duty. The medics took me into a room with a very plush gurney and laid me back on the table. Kamnam translated what the medics said to him. "They calling doctor now," he said in his broken English.

We all assumed he was in the next room. It turned out that the doctor was actually at home in his own bed, and it took him nearly a half hour to arrive, rushing to the hospital after being awakened. An elderly Thai gentleman, about 5' 4", with grey temples, and a starched white doctor's coat entered the room. "Good evening! Is this our celebrity?" he said in perfect English.

"Doctor, thank you for coming," I said gratefully. "But I am no celebrity."

"You are from the big show at the Hilton, no?" he questioned.

Before I could answer he asked me to stick out my tongue. He looked very closely for almost a minute. "Ah, very damp," he said. He used three fingers at my wrist to take my pulse on the left hand, then on the right. "Clearly you're in pain, particularly in your lower body," he surmised. "So, what did we do, pull or tear something?"

I explained to him what happened. He stood me up and had me put pressure on the leg. "Walk from here to the door," he said directly giving me a little push across the floor. "Stop," he commanded. "That's all I need to see. Come sit down."

I limped back to the table, looking inquisitively at Errol. He had his typical showbiz smile on, not letting anyone around him know what he was thinking.

"We can start tonight. I would like to see you every day for two weeks. Then every other day for two weeks. You will be back on stage in four weeks' time," the doctor said assuredly.

Errol immediately smiled bigger, probably hoping he wouldn't have to get the understudy to fill my position on stage for the remaining length of the tour.

"We can start what, tonight?" I asked the doctor, rather confused. "Physical therapy?"

"No sir, acupuncture."

"I'm sorry, I thought I was seeing a doctor," I said shaking my head.

"Ahh yes," he nodded, "I am a doctor. The medics determined many factors. No concussion. No broken bones. You have torn your hamstring at the insertion of the gluteus maximus. Western doctors can do nothing but give you pain killers. That is the solution with Western medicine. So, these fine men brought you to me," he smiled proudly.

"Well, that's fine," Errol interrupted. "Do we have insurance forms to fill out? Can you tell me the cost?"

"My good man, we do not charge celebrities or skeptics," he said bowing his head. "The pleasure is mine."

Did I look skeptical? How did he know I was unsure or unclear as to his methods? How did he know I would be back on stage in four weeks?
The doctor rolled me over gently so that I was face down. He opened the drawer closest to my face and pulled out individually wrapped needles ranging from an inch to three inches in length.

"Don't worry," he smiled. "The long needles are for deep spots or areas where there is much muscle to get through."

Be brave, I told myself. You're in good hands. The doctor sprayed me down with alcohol. He unwrapped a needle which was in a guide tube. He placed the tube on a point on my skin and tapped the end of the needle so that the tip would gently insert into my skin. He would then pull the tube off the needle and push the needle deeper into the acupuncture point.

"May I ask questions, doctor?"

"Of course," he said as he continued to insert a series of needles down my spine, into my legs and ankles, and several into my arms.

"Why put needles into my neck and shoulders, if I tore my hamstring?"

"The action involved in tearing your hamstring, also involved many other muscles. Your neck and mid-shoulders are out of alignment, probably from the fall."

I looked at Errol. Then asked the doctor, "how did you know I fell?"

"I don't know. Your contorted muscles told me this."

He proceeded to insert about 15 needles. I felt no pain throughout his needling technique. At certain points I could feel what could best be described as a little electric shock when the needle was inserted deeper.

"Ah… that's the reaction I needed," he would say, when I reacted slightly to the electric shock. He covered me with a silver, lightweight blanket that seemed to retain my body heat.

"Let us leave him for about 20 minutes," he told everyone in the room.

I woke from a deep sleep, sensing the doctor pulling the needles out of my body. The shock of the cold room slowly made its presence known as he peeled down the silver blanket, removing the needles underneath.

"You were out like a light," Errol told me.

"It was the adrenaline. The minute we inserted the needles, they started to work on your central nervous system, calming your spirit," the doctor explained.

It was the deepest, most refreshing nap I had ever taken. I sat up slowly. The doctor took my pulse again and thanked me.

"It is I who should be thanking you," I insisted. "I will see you tomorrow." I got up from the table, feeling like I could run around the block. *It's amazing,* I thought to myself.

I was furloughed from the show for a month. The swing dancer, Devin from Australia had a chance to go into the show in my role. I was happy to see that he got to perform in front of a live audience. Understudies would be brought into the show to learn all the male and female dancer roles in case a dancer had a sick day or there was an injury, as in my case.

I went every day to see the acupuncturist for the first two weeks. He would do the same ritual of taking my pulse and looking at my tongue. He would then do a somewhat similar treatment as the first, or vary it slightly based on my tongue and pulse readings. He would stretch me in the beginning of the session and then he would follow this with acupuncture.

Each day, I felt better and better. I was amazed by the results. From sticking little needles into my skin, the doctor was able to speed up the healing process of my torn hamstring. He gave me an herbal tea decoction he would brew up and I would drink it twice a day. "To nourish your spirit," he would tell me.

By the third week, the doctor would insert the needles and then hook up two electrodes to the head of the pins. He would then send an electric pulse through the needles. The sessions were intense. He insisted that the pulsation should be just on the border of uncomfortable. As my body got used to the sensation, the doctor would raise the intensity of the vibration. I could feel the tremors of electricity raise my consciousness with each turn of the dial. At points, it would be unbearable, yet in exactly four weeks, I was back on stage performing again.

Our contract was up a week before Christmas, but the hotel asked us if the show could stay on until the 26th of December. With an added bonus and the promise that we would be stateside by the New Year, our cast unanimously agreed to the contract extension. With the tour over, our producer asked where each of us was heading? As part of our contract, he would pay our ticket home. "Where's home these days?" Errol asked me.

"You can send me to LA," I smiled. “There's no snow in Los Angeles.”

I flew into LA on New Year's Eve December 31, 1986 When I got to LAX I called Bill to let him know I just got into town. My aunt Martha picked up the phone. "Oh, my goodness," my aunt exclaimed. "Happy New Year! Your cousin is on his way to a party at Stella's? Stencil? Ohhh, that big kahuna guy," she muddled.

"Steena's," I laughed. "Happy New Year to you aunt Martha, Ok, I'll head over to Venice."

With my pockets full of cash and a sense of complete awe being back in the states, I decided to jump in a cab to Venice Beach. The sun had already set, as winter always seemed to have the darkest of nights with the shortest of days. Yet, the Los Angeles landmarks were glowing like beacons in the cool chill of night, welcoming me home.

The cab dropped me off at Dell Avenue and I walked through the canals dragging my luggage and surf board behind me. I was feeling so grateful to be back on the beach I called home and better yet, back in this magical town.

I crossed the foot bridge and knocked on the familiar blue door. Big Steena answered the door with a big smile, as if he were expecting me. "How’s my favorite gypsy? You're just in time," he said. "Grab a broom and sweep behind me. It's a New Year and we are sweeping all the dirt and evil out the front door."

I thought that was an interesting combination of words. "It must be a cultural thing," I thought. We swept every room moving from the back of the house to the front door and together we swept all the "dirt and evil" past the threshold.

He walked over to his altar and picked up his partially burnt sage bundle. "Here, light this," he said handing me a lighter. I stood holding the flame to the tip of the pungent herb as the smoke wafted upwards. He blew out the flame on the end of the sage and the smoke doubled. I followed him through the house as he mumbled a prayer in Spanish, swirling the smoke above his head. He paid much attention to the corners of each room, as well as the windows and doors. He then went back to the altar and extinguished the few fragments of sage he had left in a vase of sand.

He then dipped a cup into the large goblet of water, reached two fingers into the cup then blessed himself. He repeated the action over me and then passed through every room in the house doing the same gesture.

"Ok, we are good for another year," he said, relieved. "Now let's hear all about those hot surf spots in Thailand!"

Chapter 18

What's Next

Dancing in foreign countries for over a year was exhausting. Now I knew what my friend Jose meant by being tired after living on the road for so long. Living out of a suitcase, moving around between hotels, and performing for thousands of people was the most incredible experience of my life. It would probably take me years to catalog all these experiences in my head, but my body was tired and beat up. My mind was even more so. Just being back in the States took a few weeks to get used to again. No more tuk tuks, odd smells in the air, or elephants in the streets. It was back to my new reality.

I was able to save about $25,000 from the tour after all my side trips and adventures. I never felt richer in my life. Now, all I had to do was be thrifty and I could lay low for a while and surf! Aunt Martha insisted I stay with her and Bill. Both of the girls had moved out. "On to bigger and better things," Aunt Martha surmised.

My cousin, Martha-Jayne was spearheading a new campaign to make Los Angelenos more aware of how campfires and fireworks could be a major cause of LA's massive wildfires that would burn out of control for weeks at a time. She moved to Silver Lake to be closer to the organizers. Libby had met a new boyfriend and was living in Seal Beach.

"Ahh a suburb of Long Beach," I said. Bill knew what I was thinking.

"Consistent surf break, North side of the pier," Bill read my thoughts. "We'll have to go visit my sister."

Like old times, Bill and I maneuvered around LA. for the next few weeks. "This week, JackO had inventory at the Surf Shake. Big Steena was in Redondo beach giving surf lessons to rich kids. Canter was on life guard duty training new recruits, and here's Sting Ray." We were now in Venice Beach. Bill pointed down the boardwalk.

Sting Ray was acting strange. He was very fidgety and behaving erratically. He was even more obsessive about working out, according to Bill. He was off to the gym twice a day. He'd lost his job at Gold's gym and had lost his job working on the docks at the marina. Now he was selling t-shirts and beach bracelets to tourists for Buddy Mac, the T-shirt king of Venice.

"Millions of tourists visit Venice Beach every year, not for the sun and the surf but for the people. They come to see the artists, the freaks, the skate boarders, the bodybuilders, and street performers and even the junkies. Why it's a massive stage, and I'm its ring leader!" Sting Ray exclaimed.

"And with delusions of grandeur to boot," I wanted to add, keeping my mouth shut.

"Hey, ring leader?" Bill jumped in. "I need a t-shirt for my sister's boyfriend."

Bill and I headed towards Pete's for lunch. "What's up with this guy?" I questioned Bill.

"He jumps from job to job, or gets fired from them. He has these fits of anger that spin out of control and his employers don't take to kindly to it, so then they fire him and he's off to the next meaningless job."

"We have to keep an eye on him," I suggested. Bill changed the subject.

"So now you're Mr. Broadway and a world traveler. What's next?" Bill joked.

"I need to take a breath and find my rhythm again," I explained. "I need some discipline back in my life. Let's go surfing. The water will show me the way."

The surf, in the Winter months in LA. was an entirely different experience. This was prime time. This was when waves grew in size, thanks to the North and West swells that crossed down from the North Pacific to break onto the shorelines of Los Angeles. I called this the "Siberian Surf" because the water would be so cold, I needed to wear my full wet suit to stay warm. The frigid water, brought a chill to my bones so deep, that I needed coffee and layers of warm clothes ready when I got out of the water. It took time for me to get used to this penetrating cold. Every time I went out in the winter months, the water temperature was daunting. Usually though, the winter months would offer less crowds and bigger waves, but there was always a tradeoff.

Seal Beach was a suburb of Long Beach in Orange County and had a suburban feel mixed with beachside vibes. It was the perfect seaside town which made it a great place for retired and even active military to live. Since the Seal Beach Naval Weapons Station was close by, it was very appealing to incoming Navy men and woman who wanted to find a beach town to call home. Many Navy guys would be assigned here for weapons duty or Navy SEALs training.

The beach was graced with a beautiful wooden boardwalk with quaint seaside shops and homes. Like Bill said, it had great surfing. The North side of the pier attracted every professional and wannabe from here to LA county.

Bill and I strolled past the pier, observing the snappy peaks on the waves being formed by the famous “wind tunnel” effect that was made possible due to its location below the Palos Verdes peninsula. The South facing coastline and many jetties made the location perfect for pairing down the huge swells from Huntington pier and forming the ideal “Pier Bowls.” These steep, round shaped waves would form when the winds blew in from the West-Northwest. It was almost reminiscent of Hawaii. Bill and I spent several hours riding the glossy faces that rolled into the beach, making for a great day on the water.

I was literally frozen and wiped out. I peeled my wetsuit off and collapsed on the beach piling layers of sweaters and sweatpants on my shivering body. My legs ached from the jumping up on the board and pumping it over the surface. My sides were sore from twisting and over extending my arms. It had been a while since I tackled waves this big.

“Hey I think that’s Libby waving from the pier,” Bill said.

I turned to see my cousin’s bleached white hair reflecting off the nearby satellites. She was a vision in her signature wedge shoes and hot pants. On her arm was a tall guy in a Navy uniform.

“Must be my sister’s boyfriend. She has a thing for guys in uniform. Navy, Army, gas jockeys, construction workers…”

I laughed, as I gathered my stuff and we made our way towards the entrance of the pier. As we got closer and closer, the guy’s silhouette looked familiar. It was that same lanky, awkward sway I remembered from another place and time. My cousin Libby walked up and gave me a big squeeze and kiss on the cheek. All the while I was staring at her new “beau.”

"McCreedy! What are you doing here?" It was the big Irish guy who had made my life difficult in high school, thousands of miles away and years in the past. I was in utter shock.

"Of all the piers in the world," he smiled.

Libby looked at me. "You two know each other?" She was just as surprised as I was.

"Sure, high school," McCreedy mugged.

"You're in the Navy?" I asked.

"Of course, he is," Libby answered. "Can't you see the uniform."

"Oh, you guys were friends in high school?" Bill asked.

I could feel the bile rise up in my throat waiting to see who would answer first. I wasn't going to answer that question.

"Oh sure," McCreedy confirmed.

I wanted to jump off the pier.

Bill handed McCreedy the t-shirt Libby asked him to pick up from Venice.

"Nice," was his only response.

As we strolled down the beach, the three of them talked about Southern California, and surfing, and the Navy. I remained silent. Still trying to process what was happening, I almost felt as if I was back in that horrific state of limbo from high school. The feeling of not knowing what the next move would be, coupled with my own insecurities about being an odd ball-outsider-stand-out, was unnerving.

"I didn't know you surfed bud?" McCreedy said to me over his shoulder.

I quickly tried to think of a smart-ass retort, but all I could say was, "surprise."

"How did the two of you meet?" Bill asked Libby. McCreedy answered.

"Your sister picked me up at the Glide'er Inn Restaurant. A lot of us hang out there on our down time."

"Picked you up?" Libby retorted, "huh!"

I couldn't wait to get off that beach. I could sense both anger and disdain crawling up the back of my neck.

It was surreal. How was it possible that out of all the places in the world, that my past would catch up with me like this? And with my cousin, no less? It just seemed like the Universe was playing a cruel trick on me. But, why? How?

I kept playing Big Steena's words over in my head. "There are no accidents." Was there still a lesson I had to learn here? I couldn't sleep that night.

Or the next night.

Or the next night after that.

I had to channel my energy somewhere else, other than the thought that McCreedy seemed to be tailing me through life. I headed for Venice Beach to say hi to Pete. Tally roller skated over to me, "Hey Broadway," she called out. "Welcome back to La La!"

We shared a couple of laughs and stories before Pete was barking at her to get coffee to table 12. "Gotta roll," she tweeted. "There's Sting Ray in the corner booth," she pointed as she skated by me with three coffees and three of the same ketchup-stained menus I remembered from my very first day at Pete's.

Sting Ray was in the corner booth, talking to himself, with a table full of food. He looked up from his conversation. "Hey Golden Boy," what's doin?" He motioned for me to sit down. I slid over in the booth and asked if he was waiting for someone?

"No, just eating lots of protein, protein, protein!" he jerked.

I was not in the business of getting in someone else's business, but I was concerned for Sting Ray. He always seemed like a lost boy to me and I didn't want him to head down a path that was not going to make his life better.

"I'm working out a lot now. Can you tell?" he asked, flexing his biceps.

"Dude, you're massive. What's going on?" I asked him just as a tall bodybuilder walked up to the table.

Sting Ray got nervous, his eyes darting between me and the bodybuilder. "Hey Serge," Sting Ray said uncomfortably with his crooked smile even now more pronounced. "This is my surf bud," Sting Ray introduced me.

"Got my stuff?" Serge asked directly to Sting Ray, practically ignoring the introduction.

"Sure, ya, sure," was his answer. "Be right back," Sting Ray said to me. He darted out of the booth. Serge followed him out the back door of the restaurant.

He returned in about five minutes time. "What's going on?" I repeated to him.

"Ya, ya, doing good, doing good! You?" he smirked.

"Bill told me; you aren't working at the marina any longer. Do you need some money? Did you have enough for the rent?"

He smiled like a Cheshire cat, hiding his uncertainties behind his crooked grin. "Nah, I'm shackin' up with my old lady. I'm workin' for Buddy Mac plus I got my own thing goin' on," he assured me.

"Hey, it's JackO," Sting Ray changed the subject. He motioned to JackO to come in. I knew JackO saw us, but it seemed like he pretended not to and kept walking. "He must have not seen us," Sting Ray suggested.

"OK, cool," I said, "I have to dash."

It was disorienting, coming back from Asia, being away for so long. Being in LA in the winter was also unsettling, even though I thought it would be a better transition into the States and a bit more familiar.

Now, tossing and turning in bed, I was somewhere between reality and a dream state. I was not sure where I was or what was happening. I seemed to be floundering beneath the water, not being able to come up for air. The fact that an old wound from my past had reopened, and in my own back yard, so to speak, was unfathomable. My arch enemy as a kid, the one person who came into my adolescent life and upended it, was now dating my cousin and we were together in the same city on the other side of the United States.

My friend Sting Ray, who I had known since I was 16 years old, was drifting away from the group, wrapped up in some downward spiral that seemed very fishy to me. This was now weighing around my neck like an anchor.

I was also struggling with the next move I should take in my career. I was drained from my year's commitment in Asia, returning to roots that seemed unstable and not as familiar.

I felt as if I was shipwrecked, and lost without a compass. I shot up in bed, sweating profusely. Then I thought, I needed to talk to the one person who could give me insight. The one person who just seemed to get it. That person who understood all of us. I called Big Steena.

I left a rather vague message on his answering machine in the early morning hours. He called me back at my cousin Bill's house and recommended I stopped by his house in the late afternoon.

I got to Venice a little earlier than expected and walked through the canals sensing a welcoming vibe, once more, as I crossed over one of the decaying bridges. I knocked on the familiar blue door. I thought I heard Big Steena say, come in, but I wasn't sure. I opened the door to the ever-present scent of patchouli and candles.

My eyes caught a beautiful brunette coming out of Big Steena's bedroom. She looked to be half his age with a beautiful tan. The subtle scent of her jasmine perfume preceded her into the room. The fragrance clung to me as if it were nectar to a flower. She flashed me a big, pearly white smile as she buttoned up the last button on her blouse.

Big Steena came out of the room behind her, shirtless. "Ahhh Drew," it was the only time I remember him calling me Drew. "Thanks for coming over. Say hi to Randi."

She smiled again, gave Big Steena a little peck on the cheek, and snuck out the backdoor.

"Sorry about that," he turned to me, "board meeting."

He invited me into the living room after bringing me a beer. He dipped three fingers in the cup of water on his altar and then shook his dripping digits over his head as if to cleanse himself. He smiled and faced me as he slowly took a seat next to the gleaming crystals that caught the afternoon light.

"You seemed confused in your voice message to me."

I quickly explained how I was feeling about the events of the last few days. Running into McCreedy made me feel like I was right back in that drama of high school. I was concerned about Sting Ray; and I didn't know what to do next in my life. There was a part of me I couldn't let go of and that was my past.

"Did you learn anything from that traumatic first experience in high school?" Big Steena asked me.

I quietly thought about his question for several minutes. "I guess I learned that no matter how I tried, I couldn't control what people thought of me or how I was perceived."

"What could you do?" he asked.

"I would say… just be myself?" I inquisitively asked.

"If you ponder the questions of the Universe and beyond, just stop and take a good look around you. You just might see the answers." Big Steena suggested.

My mind was racing. He loved this phrase. He was trying to tell me that the answers were within my own microcosm.

"Did it ever occur to you that McCreedy was just trying to fit in himself? A foreign kid, in a different environment, using every tool he knew how, to feel accepted? In some way, he found you to be the one who challenged him. The one he needed to win over?

"Me?" I scoffed.

"So, if you're feeling different, you are not alone. We all have feelings of inadequacies. You took him down three times, if I recall your story. He felt, he needed to feel important again, and he thought by humiliating you, like you did him, he would feel better about himself. Why do you think he went into the Navy? To feel better about himself!"

"But he is now here! How could that happen?"

“There's a rhythm to the Universe,” Big Steena suggested. "We are constantly trying to measure the unmeasurable? Defining the human spirit is like trying to bottle smoke. There is a lesson here that still needs your attention.”

He was right. As humans we were constantly trying to define things, compartmentalize situations, or fit people into categories. We put people in class, race, orientation, and would see life as one way or the other. This couldn't be further from the truth. It is just our way of trying to understand something that we just can't put our finger on.

“Therefore,” Big Steena added, “we give something a section or category to be a part of. It's easier to put things into column A or B then really try to understand the subtle differences. That is the beauty of life - that which stands beyond reason.”

“I had a lot to learn,” I mumbled.

“As for our friend, Sting Ray, all we can do is be there for him, when he needs us. He must forge his own path and currently, this is the one he is on.” Big Steena shook his head. “He has lost much of his humility. Be it from his relationship or his work, his head is held in a place that doesn’t allow him to remember how down to earth he needs to be again.”

“And for your next career move? Why don’t you allow yourself some recovery time and allow the Universe to present its next offering to you?” Big Steena could see the stress behind my eyes. “You just worked for a year straight. You can allow yourself some healing time.”

“Healing time?” I questioned myself. Once again, he was right. My drive and ambition were constantly firing, while my body was just trying to keep up. It was time to harmonize them.

Sure enough, in a few months, I got a dance agent in LA and a commercial agent who was now sending me out on auditions constantly. Since the drive from the Valley into downtown LA and Hollywood was getting to be a rigorous commute, I took some of my savings from my Far East gig and rented an apartment on Hollywood and La Cienega. I bought my first car. Of course, it was used, but this 1985 Silver Chevy Camaro Berlinetta Coupe had a 5.0L V-8 engine with automatic transmission, power steering, brakes, windows with power locks, and was my own personal beauty.

Now that I was no longer staying with my Aunt Martha and Bill, it seemed harder to carve out time to go out to see them or even get to the beach to see the guys. It's as if life got in the way. Between auditions and dance classes I would pick up here and there, I would make my pilgrimage to Venice beach to stay grounded and see if I could run into the guys. I would usually see Sting Ray, holding court in his corner booth at Pete's, with a bevy of guys stopping by his table. He was often loud and aggressive and confessed he hadn't seen the guys in months. "Don't you surf any longer," I asked him.

"Don't you? I don't see your board," he snapped back.

It didn't seem to warrant an answer.

The following week, I got a call from Bill. "Hey Drew, whacha doin?" I knew my cousin so well. Whenever he asked me what I was doing, it meant he wanted to go somewhere specific.

"Where are we going? I asked.

"Well, Libby called me, hysterical. She's in Seal Beach. She says her boyfriend called… you know, your friend from high school."

I cringed.

"He says there is a big protest forming at the main entrance of the Seal Beach Naval Weapons Station and that he saw MJ leading the protest. He said he's afraid for her because the Seal Beach police and Naval police are everywhere."

"OK, can you get to Pete's? I'll pick you up there!"

The hours' drive to Seal Beach put us right in the middle of one of the largest protests I'd ever seen. We pulled up to the Southwest corner of the complex and found Libby and McCreedy yelling across the group of protestors to get MJ's attention.

"What's going on? What is MJ all riled up for?" I asked.

McCreedy quickly responded. "They are protesting the U.S. military presence in Central America," he yelled over the noise of the crowd.

There was my cousin MJ, waving a sign "America, mind your own business." Her fire engine red hair and military style outfit made her stand out in the crowd. Not only that, her arms were linked with a blind man waving his cane on one side and a man old enough to be her grandfather on the other side.

The confrontation lasted almost an hour before the Seal Beach authorities moved in and started arresting over 60 people. That included MJ and her two male companions. We had a front row seat and couldn't do anything about it. They were cited for trespassing on government property and released.

This made me realize that sometimes there's nothing to be done and people need to follow their own paths – even if those paths involve getting arrested for what they believe in.

Chapter 19

A Change in Times

Big Steena thought it was a good idea for all of us to commune with the sea when the offshore Santa Ana winds were coming over from the East. "So, we can head to Upper Haggarty's. Let's meet in the parking lot of the Neighborhood Church."

Once the luxurious seaside beach house of garmento, JJ Haggarty, this Mediterranean villa-style coastal castle was now the property of the massive Neighborhood Church community, perched on the high bluffs in Palos Verdes.

We weren't at the beach for more than 15 minutes and already the boys were confrontational. JackO and Sting Ray were always getting into it. JackO also tended to be the instigator. "Hermano, que es eso? What is that?" JackO was pointing to Sting Ray's body. "If you get any bigger, your gonna sink to the bottom and explode."

"Dude, why don't you get a new board already? That thing is falling apart. You work in a surf shop!" Sting Ray barked back.

"And you're stilling riding waves on that Kook box," JackO retorted.

Although, short in stature Sting Ray would always stand up to JackO. "Kook box? Bro, this is a twin fin fish," Sting Ray defended his choice. "You know who shaped this surfboard? Rod Sorensen."

"I like the swallow tail," Canter added.

"I'm diggin' the blue and red stripes, Big Steena called out.

"Well, I like my old board. It's a great board," JackO defended. "She and I go way back!"

"I'm not taking sides," Bill smirked, grabbing my arm and walking away. "If you get in the middle of these guys arguing it could go on for hours. To the point where no one even remembers what the real issue was in the first place."

We edged our way down the steep bluffs catching a glimpse of all the reckless surfers in the water as we walked along the beach. JackO and Canter were calling out to the young and the restless, snaking over each other, dropping in on the kooks, and making fools of themselves. We stopped to watch the show, as these crazy, disrespectful surfers found the unsuspecting rocks below, ripping a few of the bottoms of their boards to shreds. “Serves you right,” JackO yelled.

“Surf etiquette, boys, surf etiquette,” Canter yelled on deaf ears. “Someone should teach these guys respect.”

“Looks like 7-foot swells. We should get over the reef with no problem,” Big Steena observed, changing the subject. “Hey Zip, do you think Golden Boy is ready for this?”

I could feel the apprehension creep up.

Bill shouted back, “He’s been ready!” Bill turned to me and explained how the perfect left-handed waves rolling into shore, had a reef below. The best strategy was to paddle out, jump and dash on the board, staying low so that speed was on your side. “That will get you over the reef with this size swell. We don’t have to paddle out too far on the shoulder to catch the wave, because if we start out too far, the reef will shred your board.”

I had a new sense of confidence. A week ago, I was a mess, but now, in the water, I felt assured and knowledgeable, as if I had done this hundreds of times before. Then I realized…. I had. The waves were large curling barrels that I found my way in and out of, with stellar technique. I just needed to get back in the water to find my rhythm again. Bill kept applauding me, as I hit one sweet wave after another.

Sting Ray, on the other hand was becoming reckless, impatient, and aggressive. He cut Big Steena off at one point, not paying attention, causing Big Steena to dive off his board to avoid being hit. Bill and I were the only ones to see this. Had JackO witnessed it, there would have been a full-blown battle, as JackO was a fierce defender of Big Steena. It seemed even more so, now.

Bill and I saw Big Steena collect his board and paddle in. He was visibly shaken, just missing the reef by inches. He never said anything to Sting Ray, but Bill knew that Sting Ray’s aggression, intensified frequencies to the gym, and excessive welts forming over his back were signs of steroid abuse. The explanation seemed to make sense to me.

The inevitable was setting in. Like all athletes, those moments of mortality start to rear their ugly head. Your reactions become slower, your turns may not be as sharp, or your bold approach to something wanes. I was now seeing this with Big Steena. Still a vibrant light, he seemed a different man than when I meet him five years before. Of course, the changes were subtle, yet I could sense in him a slight hesitation when it came to certain moves, or even quick decisions he would think twice about.

There was also a melancholy that would show on his face when he thought no one was watching. Coping with a transition like aging could not be an easy pill to swallow. Getting extremely winded after a usual sprint you've recovered from quickly in the past or not seeming to be able to push yourself one extra set, could play psychological head games on your psyche. I was now seeing the effects in Big Steena.

I mentioned it to Bill. "Ahh, he's just having an off day," Bill brushed it off. But as a dancer, and someone who was not always around, I could see the distinct differences. I knew there would come a day, when I would go through this too. How would I handle it? Would I take it gracefully, or struggle against nature and my ego, not believing it was possible?

Relationships were now strained. Sting Ray's change in behavior was driving a wedge between him and the rest of us. Big Steena seemed to want to distance himself from Sting Ray because his efforts to bring us all together seemed futile.

Sting Ray and Canter, life-long buddies since grade school, appeared stilted. Canter would try to make an effort, but he was constantly being shut down by one of Sting Ray's sarcastic remarks.

Bill avoided conflict. He was never one to confront or defy someone. He would make a joke and then walk away. He just avoided talking to Sting Ray, which made it easier for him to handle his odd behavior.

JackO and Sting Ray were always at odds but their words now seemed more than sarcastic, bordering on hostile.

I was willing to help Sting Ray, but I wasn't sure how. Talking to him did not seem to penetrate that thick shell of denial and indifference. The last time I saw Sting Ray, I thought I'd ask him if he wanted to go surfing with me. Perhaps I would be able to get him to open up. I knew I could usually find him in Venice selling t-shirts in front of Pete's.

Sure enough, a few weeks later, I spotted him and he was having words with JackO…again. I could visibly see that they were arguing. JackO threw his hands up in the air and walked away. As he stormed off, he noticed me coming towards them. JackO ignored me and walked right by, not responding to my greeting.

As I approached Sting Ray, I asked him what the argument was about.

"He was being his usual abusive self," Sting Ray howled. "Thank God I have a surplus of self-esteem," he boasted.

"Thank God," I confirmed, sarcastically.

"I gotta go to Muscle Beach and do legs, Sting Ray proclaimed. "I got friends waiting for me."

"How about we hit some waves?" I asked.

"Dude, the waves are wonky right now, I'm not hittin' that glass," Sting Ray huffed.

I got in my car and headed back to Hollywood.

It was nice to have a set of wheels to get around in. I loved Woodhill Hills because it was quiet and more relaxed, but living in the middle of Hollywood was a dream. I learned when and how to take the freeways to avoid the ridiculous rush hour traffic. I found back streets easier to get to my favorite shops, restaurants, and dance studios. It was a study in patience. Still, I preferred the laid back, warm, sunny days of LA to the dirty, crowded streets of New York. Los Angeles had a different pace and rhythm of doing things, that were unique. Just like New York.

After about six months of this routine, I missed the New York edge. Living in Los Angeles was different than being on "summer vacation" here. Now, I was paying rent and utilities, car payments and insurance, food shopping and cleaning. I had dance classes and auditions, commercial casting calls and callbacks… No wonder I wasn't finding anytime to surf! When I decided to settle down here, I thought I'd be surfing every day, seeing the guys more often, and slowing down my pace. I was wrong.

The following afternoon, I got a frantic phone call from Sting Ray. "Hey Golden Boy, I need your help." He sounded desperate.

"What's up Sting Ray?"

"Can you pick me up?" his breathing was heavy and labored. I could sense the stress in his voice.

"Where are you?" I asked, not sure what he was into now.

"Long Beach."

"Long Beach? What are you doing out there?"

"I'm stranded," was his answer.

The hours' drive to Long Beach was fraught with traffic jams. We agreed to meet at the Eagle Marine dock, which was perched far out into the Port of Long Beach. Once I got there, it was a serious of wrong turns on streets I wasn't familiar with along dilapidated docks I didn't feel comfortable by. The area was dark and vacant and I started to get an overwhelming sense of dread. "What was this guy into?"

As I turned onto the last street before the water, I spotted Sting Ray sitting on a dock dangling his feet over the side. I beeped the horn to let him know I was here. No response. I beeped again. He didn't look up. Despite my better judgement, I pulled the car over and walked down the pier to meet him.

Before I knew it, I saw a large, dark-haired guy get into my car. Another guy, who was an obvious steroid-abusing freak, came out from around a shack that was teetering on the edge of the pier next to Sting Ray. "What's going on?" I yelled. Sting Ray slowly seemed to come out of his fog and sluggishly looked up at me.

"Wow… you're here. Guys, he's here. I told you my… my… my supplier would show up," he slurred.

"Dude, what is wrong with you? What's going on? Who are these guys?" I questioned. My heart was racing. I wasn't sure what Sting Ray had gotten me mixed up in, but my adrenaline was pumping as I help him stand up.

"This guy gave us bum 'roids," the guy on the dock mumbled to me. "He said you'd bring the real stuff."

My mind was quickly trying to process what they were telling me. I hesitated to answer, but knew my words needed to salvage what could either be another chance to get out of here, unscathed…or not. These guys were holding Sting Ray hostage. And now, they had my car as well. After a long pause….

"Sting Ray, didn't fully explain the situation to me over the phone. Probably because you've drugged him and he's not thinking straight," I surmised.

"We gave this moron, five hundred bucks for favors and he thought he could scam us," the guy in my car yelled.

"Ya," the guy on the dock barked back. "So, we made sure we'd slow him down so he wouldn't go anywhere. Either we get our 'roids or we get our cash. It's up to you."

"Ok, well, I was unaware of any of this," I confessed. "No problem. We can make this right."

"So? Give us the cash or the 'juice'."

Sting Ray slowly looked up at me, as if to listen to what my response would be. He could barely stand and was now drooling out of the corner of his crooked half-smile.

"Well, right now, I don't have either."

The guy in my car turned the key, that I stupidly left in the ignition, and revved the engine.

The guy on the dock hauled off and punched Sting Ray in the chin. His body slipped from my grip and fell into a heap on the dock. "So were gonna take your car as collateral until we get the cash or the 'juice'."

"Wait, wait, wait! You can't strand us here," I yelled back, as both guys jumped into my car.

"You got exactly three days," the dark-haired guy warned. "Meet at the back of Pete's at 6pm or we're keeping the car and your friend will have to learn how to walk again."

Just like that, they sped off with my car, leaving Sting Ray passed out on the pier and me in disbelief. We were stranded in Long Beach.

It was hours before Sting Ray came to and I was able to walk with him to the nearest bus stop. Three busses later, we were back in my apartment in Hollywood. It took Sting Ray a day to recover from whatever they gave him.

I frantically paced back and forth, trying to come up with another way in which I could have handled the situation we had just gotten pulled into. There was no sense in trying to figure out what I could have done. Now, I had to figure out what we had to do to fix this mess.

Sting Ray later confessed to me that he had been selling illegal steroids to body builders all over Venice. He started branching out his business after word spread that he was the "go to guy." He was supplying key guys in Long Beach, Huntington, and Hermosa Beach. His supply was now smaller than his demand, so he would improvise by buying counterfeit, black market steroids for half the price and charging twice as much.

The problem was, now he was not only selling illegal and counterfeit steroids, but he didn't have any idea how much they were harming his clients as well as himself. He was in over his head.

"We should call Big Steena," I told Sting Ray.

"Are you kidding? We can't let anybody know about this."

"Dude, these guys have my car! This is all your fault," I yelled.

"I know, I know. I'll get them their stash."

"I don't think that's a good idea. Don't you still have their cash?"

"Spent."

My blood was boiling. Not only was I mad at Sting Ray, but I was mad at myself for getting into this mess. “Everyone told me I should mind my own business. Bill told me not to get involved.”

“Well, you’re a caring guy…”

“Don’t patronize me, Sting Ray.”

“Well, you are,” he said sincerely.

I half believed him. But, my blind naiveite did not protect me from getting neck deep into trouble.

The event haunted me. I would wake in the middle of the night recalling the dank smell of the rotting wood from the docks. I kept seeing the grotesque bodies of the two thugs in my mind. Obviously steroid abusers, their gravelly voice and menacing actions brought up a fear in me that took me right back to those abusive guys in high school.

The following three days I kept running solutions in my head. I was so deeply entrenched; I was too ashamed to go to Big Steena for advice or talk to Bill about it. No, I got myself into this mess, I had to find a way out myself.

Since getting the money or the steroids were out of my control, I was left with no alternative but to go with Sting Ray's plan. Since he didn't have the five hundred dollars thé guys gave him, he would have to show up with the drugs. If he didn't show up with one or the other, I wouldn't get my car back and I believed they could really harm Sting Ray and possibly me.

Sting Ray insisted he could get his hands on more steroids. "Don't worry," he reassured me. "But I don't have my driver's license, so I need you to take the car back," he insisted after I suggested he meet them on his own and get my car. "Plus, these guys now think you're my supplier."

"Yeah, thanks to you. What were you thinking?"

"Dude, they drugged me. I wasn't in my right mind."

His lame excuse didn't work. My face was red with anger again. The fact was, this guy would lie to smooth over any situation. It became his survival technique. He was still just a boy with an addiction, unable to take responsibility. Unfortunately, I felt as if I didn't have a choice. Being the eternal optimist, I still thought, after knowing this guy for years, that there was still a glimmer of hope. That maybe, this time, he'd change.

The day came. I was a nervous wreck. This could go wrong in so many ways. Sting Ray had left my apartment the day before and I didn't see him until we were to meet in the back alley behind Pete's. This whole situation felt like the wrong decision. I took the bus from Hollywood to Venice. I met Sting Ray in his usual booth at Pete's. Out of the corner of my eye, I thought I caught a glimpse of JackO's red Firebird parked along the side of Pete's.

Sting Ray was nervous. I could see the sweat running down his face. "Did you get the money or the stuff?" I asked.

"What do you think?" he said sarcastically.

"Was that JackO's car I saw out front?"

Sting Ray froze. "What? Why would he be here? We got to go. Let's go."

We walked out the back door of Pete's into the alley. Not soon after, I saw my car turn the corner and slowly idle down the back street. The same two thugs in the front seat.

"Where's our stuff?" The guys lumbered out of the car wielding baseball bats and an attitude.

Sting Ray swung a backpack off his shoulders and put it on the ground, slowly opening the zipper.

"Hang tight guys, I got it right here." Sting Ray was shaking as if he were a junkie that didn't have a fix for days. I nervously just stood there, looking around, praying to myself that this was going to go right.

Sting Ray reached into his bag and pulled out a package in clear cellophane that looked like small vials all tightly wrapped together. He handed it to the guy closest to him.

"This is real?" the thug questioned.

"You wanna try it right here?" Sting Ray snapped back.

Just as the other guy was about to hand me my car keys, we heard the one thing that my nightmares were filled with. A screeching siren from the Venice Police turned into the alley behind us. In an instant, the guy snatched my keys back and jumped into my car. His buddy darted down the alley with the package of steroids, while Sting Ray grabbed his bag and dashed back through the restaurant. I stood there, in shock. My car sped down the alley with the police chasing it. Another police car pulled into the entrance of the alley and two officers jumped out of the car. One chased the guy with the drugs over the fence. The other officer ran up to me. In an instant, two other officers walked through the back door with Sting Ray, already in cuffs.

"What's going on here?" the officer addressed me. I stood there calmly; almost happy this was over. I knew it did not look good for me, but I was going to stick to the truth. It was all I had. The officer cuffed me and took Sting Ray and I to the police station.

The police interrogated us separately. I explained to him over and over again what had happened. I had no idea what they would charge me with, but it was one of the most compromising positions I'd ever been in. After four hours of cross-examination, they seemed to comprehend that I was just a pawn in all of this, caught in the middle. They were sympathetic to my side of the story and released me. Sting Ray was not so lucky.

I swore I would never put myself in that kind of situation again. Now, with no car and no idea what happened to Sting Ray, I slithered home from Venice.

Chapter 20

Escape from LA

Devastated, I ran from LA with my tail between my legs. I had betrayed my cousin's trust, I pushed away Canter, and was angry with JackO. Sting Ray had no reservations throwing me under the bus, driving an earthquake-like crevasse between everyone who cared for him. I knew somehow, everyone would find out.

I was hurting inside, because the one person I cherished, I felt I hurt the most. Bill was a stoic enigma. He kept his emotions close to his vest, rarely revealing how he was feeling. With Bill, life was always copacetic. He seemed to see every situation as a balancing act that was out of his control. If things would go wrong, he appeared to know that the Universe would right itself. He was just an observer through it all. It took me half our life time to see this, but the more I got to observe my cousin, the more I realized how much of a centered human being he was. I believe surfing taught him this.

He approached surfing as he did life. With a cool ease that showed he just knew it would all be alright in the end, no matter what the current conditions expressed. The outcome would always be the correct one. Another words, he didn't have to work so hard for it, "it" simply came to him. If not in the moment, then eventually. He was my mentor in many ways and he didn't even realize how much knowledge he gave to me. I let him down.

Coming back to New York was like riding a bike. It took no time to reacclimate myself with the gritty vibrant, resilient Big Apple. New York was the place I could still call home.

I had an actor friend who was looking for a roommate in a large, top floor apartment on the corner of 13st and Greenwich Ave. This quaint little corner of the village was quiet and devoid of traffic because of the angles of the streets between Eighth avenue and Seventh avenues. Top floor apartments seemed to be my inherent luck. I was grateful for that.

Every time a job finished; it was the same as starting all over again. Find a place to live, find a place to study, and find a job.

Reeling from my near incarceration in LA, I needed to get my head back in the game and find my focus again. Harkness House had closed by this time, but I heard my previous dance teacher, David Howard, had opened his own school on Broadway across from Lincoln Center.

I strolled uptown, midday to see if I could catch him in class. The open space had a huge ballet studio that could easily hold 30 dancers. The space was separated by a seating area with comfy chairs and little changing rooms in the back.

I paid for class and quickly changed into dance clothes. There had to be 25 students waiting in the small seating area for the class before us to finish. Madame Eglevsky, one of my ballet teachers from Harkness was now teaching at David's new school. As she finished her class, her students clapped fervently, which was the tradition after every dance class. Applauding your masterful teacher was like giving them your adoration and love for who they were.

Immediately dancers from my class spilled into the room scrambling to find their best place at the barre. We patiently waited the arrival of David Howard. He soon appeared in his signature white linen pants and white t-shirt. "Ok, let's begin," he instructed.

David spoke gently and seemed to choose his words wisely. Not expressing too much, but at the same time, he could get his point across over the slightly off-key banging of the class piano player.

He would softly walk up behind students as they would be concentrating through a specific exercise at the barre. He would give corrections or adjust a dancer's hips over the center of their movement.

"Where have you been?" I heard his voice in my ear as I struggled to get my leg higher and higher. It was a rhetorical question, of course. He didn't care about the answer. He just wanted me to know he was watching.

After class, I sat again, once more on the floor, drained of every ounce of energy, my mind wandering. It's funny, I was not competitive in high school. I put up with the fact that I had to compete to get somewhere in either sports or in music classes. I exerted only as much physical exercise as was minimally required of me. Now, here, I was, a professional dancer, competing in the dance capital of the world, as a stealth athlete. I'm not sure where that came from but it seemed to be for the passion and the love of what dance gave me. I was glad to be back.

I strained to stand up. My hamstrings screaming for a hot bath. My feet were bloodied and bruised from new dance shoes and sliding along the linoleum floors during class. I bent down to pull the tape off my big toe, which I put there to protect it before class. Now removing it, I would only pull off more skin with a rip of the bandage.

"You need to come around more, young man." I looked up to see David standing over me. "We need to further work on your turn out and your upper back needs more strength." he said. "Have you been lifting weights?" Again, another rhetorical question.

All I could do was smile. "I can tell by your posture. Come see me four times a week. Nancy will arrange it." He walked away.

That was David's way of offering me a scholarship to his school. As I was leaving, his administrator, Nancy ran over to me to get my information and officially offer me the scholarship. "Are you currently working? she asked.

"I'm between jobs," I replied.

"Ok, David will see you at his 2pm class or 6pm class, four days a week. No weekends," she said laying down the ground rules. "If you get a job, let us know as soon as possible."

I thanked her so much and headed straight to the Actor's Equity building.
I maneuvered through the rush hour streets like a sprinter. I jumped on the 1 train downtown to 50th street and zipped down four blocks to the building my union was in.

It was like old home week. I ran into familiar faces I'd known for years, sometimes not sure what segment of my life they were from, but knowing that they were still around was somehow, a comfort. It was as if time stood still.

A call board in the back of the lounge listed equity approved auditions that were coming up. So many job listings were for out-of-town gigs. I didn't feel ready to go on the road again right away. I wrote down a few possible auditions that I seemed right for.

Back on the audition trail, I went through the rigorous routine of finding a job. David's scholarship had me returning to my "fighting weight" and my technique felt strong. My head was back in the game, which is probably what got me the six-month contract for a new show in Atlantic City for Caesar's Palace. I wasn't crazy about leaving New York City again, but this was a good job with the perk of being able to surf.

Atlantic City had a beach, perched along the Jersey shore. I was more excited about surfing the Atlantic than working at Caesars. But it was a well-paying gig and several of my friends from the Asian tour were dancing in the show with me, so it was a win-win.

The cast was put up in a large two-story house in Margate. This quaint little beach town was about a 20-minute drive to Caesars. Each night a van would pick up the cast and bring us back after the show. The days were free for us to do what we wanted.

There were a few good surf breaks in Atlantic City. There seemed to be no central hub or apparent surf culture that I found on the Jersey shore. I would meander along the open beaches with the towering casinos and famous boardwalk looming in the background, searching for waves. Somedays, a good swell would roll in producing some decent, waist-high breakers. The bitter cold March waters were dark and disheartening, but nothing a back zip couldn't fix.

There would be an occasional pod of surf brothers who I'd see adrift on the churning, brown water. Localism seemed much more territorial here. Perhaps it was due to the fact that good waves were far and few between and they didn't want to share what little they had, with an outsider. At this point in my life, it just seemed childish, but that was the nature of the sport.

I would get cat calls to move further down the beach, or "try surfing off the pier," would be some of the love-calls I'd get. One day, a local told me to check out the East side of the pier. "Nice obstacles there," he said. What I realized after attempting to find a wave there, was the buried re-bar, cement slabs, and the absolute dump, that lay just under the surface of the water. I actually thought the guy meant, good wave obstacles. It was a tragic look at Atlantic City's past and just how the city dealt with progress. Burying it under the water where no one could see it. Of course, at that point I realized the surfer who recommended this spot was sending me into a mine field. Just another case of "friendly localism."

Surfing ice cold, brown waves were not a thrill to me. So, I hung up my board until June. The average ocean temperature by June was about 70 degrees and from July until the end of September, the waters warmed to an average temperature of 75 degrees. The beach and boardwalk were now a huge carnival of color and sound. Besides the lure of gambling at the casinos, the beach was the next biggest draw to Atlantic City.

At the most Northern end of Atlantic City was Crystals. This was a good beach, dedicated to the summer surfers who came from inland to find solace in the water. Situated in a poor and broken-down neighborhood, the beach itself was the cleanest and beach goers and swimmers alike seemed to respect the surfers here. Unlike other areas around the boardwalk where, even the city didn't want surfers in the water. To the city, the beaches were their other gold mine, catering strictly to the tourist trade. Yet, anything off the glittering boardwalk was a neglected and disheveled town, wracked with years of decay.

"You've missed the super rad waves, sir. That was in March."

I had befriended a brother and sister who were locals at Crystals. Half my age, they were the most conscious and respectful kids I'd met in a very long time.

"Please, call me Drew."

"What my brother is trying to say is that when winter swells come in from the Northeast, they can be practically overhead," Emily said with such passion. I could relate to her child-like exuberance.

Twins Emily and Jason, seemed untarnished by their less than stellar surroundings. Growing up on the Jersey shore their entire lives, they had graduated from high school and were now working in different jobs on the beach. Jason worked as a waiter in one of the big casinos, while Emily helped her mom in the convenience store in town. They discovered surfing through their dad, who was killed in a car accident coming home from work one night.

"Ya, we surf for our dad," Jason smiled, his golden heart just beaming. "It was his life. It's all he wanted to do. He worked to support us and pay the bills, but all he really wanted to do was have his feet in the water 24/7."

"So, he taught you and your sister how to surf?" I asked.

"Oh ya," Emily interrupted. "He taught us everything," she beamed with pride. For all their hardship and pain, they seemed angelic and unscathed. I couldn't imagine the inner scars they bore. Youth seemed so invincible.

Summer surfing in Atlantic City was an education. The waves would not always be surfable, due to crosswind sheers or prevailing onshore winds that would cause the waves to fall apart or blowout before they'd start. But, that small percentage of time when Crystals would fire, my younger co-horts and their friends were all over it. Emily and Jason's surf skills were "East coast" and different from my approach. They were more determined and aggressive which, at first, made sense. They were trying to make something out of waves they didn't have.

Yet, when a good set would roll through, they were smooth and easy on their approach. They respected the lineup and made sure I was a part of their session. Now, I was the adult in the room.

Jason was more of a show off. He often seemed to want to impress me with his moves. "Oh, watch this," Emily leaned over to inform me as we sat on shore watching Jason do a complete aerial out of the water on his board.

Jason would glide in the pocket of the wave, bottom turn, climbing perpendicular back up the wave to lift off, doing "airs" above the lip of the water.

"That's called boosting," Emily giggled.

"Did your dad teach you that?" I asked, surprised.

"Well, it's really skate board moves, but Jason translated it to the water."

I smiled.

By Labor Day, my contract at Caesar's was over and the last show finished that evening. I invited Emily and Jason to see the show. They were so excited to come back stage and meet the cast. It was a pleasure sharing waves with the most unlikely of friends. I saw how passion, dedication, and love for something was passed on. Surfing was given to these kids as a gift from their dad, who would now live on in their memories for a lifetime. I prayed he would always be their guardian angel through life.

I went home to visit my parents after six months in Atlantic City. My parents picked me up from the airport. As we made our way through the back roads, traversing the green countryside, I began reminiscing about my childhood. The rolling hills of central New York were beautiful, verdant, and lush. Dotted with hedgerows, these natural borders divided huge fields of corn, hay, or cow pastures. The scent of manure that was always offensive to me as a kid, now offered a scent of familiarity.

We pulled into the pebble stone driveway leading to my family home. The long ranch-style clapboard structure glowed a bright white against the row of tall pine trees towering behind. I stepped out of the car inhaling the relaxing aroma of freshly cut grass I loved so much as a kid. I exhaled an elongated breath that seemed to be trapped in my ribcage from years before. After decades of trying to escape this same farm, I finally seemed to come to terms with my surroundings.

Sitting in the backyard, I contemplated why I had such disdain for this picturesque land as a kid. The more I thought about it, the more I understood that it wasn't the farm I was trying to run away from, but it was the mentality that enveloped it. It was really my own fear of being stuck here or not growing. It was my own insecurity that I would never make anything of myself. I guess everyone goes through those emotions, especially when we're young. As twilight slowly ascended, I was here again, back in my yard after almost half a lifetime, staring up at the stars, now without my little book. The Universe was undeniably filled with wonder, waiting for our conscious minds to catch up. My discoveries in life came from my own self-realizations. Why did it take so long?

Even though I was more worldly now, I still seemed effected by the delicate opposing forces that would tilt again. The stars I reached for as a kid, still seemed as far away as before, even though I had so much more stardust in my pockets. So, what was it that we kept searching for? As wars would shift the balance of power, or economic upswing would send markets into a frenzy, the sun would rise and set each day oblivious to our minutia. Our petty differences would be forgotten in a flash of time, while the things that were earth shattering to us, were nothing more than an afterthought in the cosmos.

I spent the next few weeks retracing my childhood steps through the fields and hedgerows, around the gardens and woods, and barefoot through the lawn and grass I had mowed a million times as a kid. I had a brand-new outlook on the beauty of the land I grew up on. Ultimately, I was able to come to terms with my own ambivalence. I did not regret my choices or feelings I had about my home as a kid. On the contrary, it was that motivation which led me to an incredible dance career and helped me to find the one, true equalizer in my life, surfing. That desire to leave, was the impetus which took me all around the world! I finally understood.

I had traveled from one part of the world to the other. No matter where I went, people had the same fears and joys about money, love, and happiness. No matter what the race, creed, or socioeconomic status, we all shared these feelings. Each day was a series of solving problems and finding solutions.

Each location I ended up in seemed like a smaller subset that was generally considered to be a representative of the whole. Everything I faced in that little microcosm was a reflection of who I was and how I would behave in that world. So, no matter if I was growing up on a farm, surfing in LA, attending a ceremony in Bali, or dancing in Atlantic City, I would still have to learn how to deal with fear and insecurity, earn a living and save money, and find love and happiness. We were all experiencing the priorities of life together. It was a sobering realization.

I was out in the field, one morning, in late June. I heard my mom yell out, "there's someone on the phone for you."

The Venice Beach police were making a courtesy call to let me know they found pieces of my car in a chop shop in Huntington Beach. They'd hoped I had insurance.

I hung up the phone, letting my mom know what the police had told me.

When the phone, rang again with an LA number, I thought the police had forgotten a particular detail they wanted to tell me.

It was my cousin Bill.

Chapter 21

The Paddle Out

I arrived in LA. on the morning flight. I went out to the curb and saw the ever-familiar station wagon with the engine running, black smoke now meandering out of its tail pipe from age and abuse. Bill jumped out of the car and gave me a big hug. It was reminiscent of my first time I arrived in LA. at the age of sixteen. We didn't speak until we got in the car.

"It was very sudden," Bill leaned into me to make sure I heard what he said. "He is being cremated. It was his final wish."

My heart was actually aching from the loss. When someone you know and love passes away, we seem to go through a denial process that is hard to fathom. But, when it is sudden, it is like a punch in the gut. "The guys must be taking Big Steena's death very hard."

"They are all devastated, but JackO is destroyed. Big Steena was his father." Bill shook his head.

With a perplexed look on my face, Bill explained. "Many years earlier, Big Steena had discovered a very young JackO breaking into his house one night. JackO had broken in through the back door looking for food and anything he could sell to make money."

"Why would JackO do that?" I was still unclear as to where this story was going.

"JackO had migrated across the Mexican border with his mother when he was only 10 years old. They lived mostly in the streets of San Diego until making their way through off-road migrant camps reaching Los Angeles three year later. That's when JackO's mother contracted pneumonia and died trying to reach Santa Monica," Bill said shaking his head.

I stood there, silent, trying to imagine the complete fear JackO must have felt.

"JackO was now 13 years old and was left to fend for his own survival. He did everything he could, living in the streets of LA, stealing food from markets, or clothes hanging on clothes lines. When Big Steena caught him rummaging through his refrigerator, he knew he could relate to JackO in Spanish, and JackO could understand. Big Steena knew the plight of the unwanted and downtrodden. He had a special place in his heart for kids who had suffered or who were not accepted."

"What did he do," I asked Bill, now totally engaged in the story.

"Big Steena gave JackO an ultimatum. Either he'd report him to the police or he would help Big Steena when he needed and he would give JackO a place to sleep and food to eat. Of course, JackO was untrusting and extremely cautious, yet he must have felt some compassion from Big Steena. JackO told me he would sleep under the bridge in the canals and knocked on Big Steena's door in the morning." Bill was clearly upset by this point, remembering when JackO first told him his history.

"Eventually the bond and trust between Big Steena and JackO proved to be genuine and beneficial for both parties. JackO moved into Big Steena's house. He became the son Big Steena always wanted. 'The door is always open,' he would tell JackO. 'There is nothing keeping you here,'" Big Steena affirmed.

"The bond and mutual respect grew. Big Steena got JackO a job at the Surf Shop. JackO discovered a new found interest and real calling to the surfing life. He became a child protege of Big Steena's and grew to master the sport."

Bill's story, had me in tears. It was a painful and heartfelt past that all seemed to make sense now. It explained so much. JackO's personality was so much a result of where he came from and how he had to survive. I had a new found respect for both JackO and Big Steena.

The drive back to Woodland Hills seemed endless. After reeling from Bill's story about JackO, there was an odd silence between us. I needed to address the elephant in the car, but I didn't know how to start.

Almost intuitively, Bill said to me, with his eyes still on the road, "we are good cuz. After you went back East, Sting Ray confessed to us how he deliberately dragged you into his plans, when he knew, you were only trying to help him. He's gonna see you today, with his head between his legs."

“You know I never meant to hurt anyone, but it ended up just the opposite,” I said with more tears in my eyes. It was a wound that I was carrying around for a year. “I had forgiven Sting Ray in my heart, but it still hurt.”

“It’s all good cuz, it’s all good.”

Aunt Martha greeted us with a hot pot of coffee and California’s best Mission Burritos. “You’re a real gypsy.” Aunt Martha pulled the cigarette out of the corner of her mouth and gave me a sloppy kiss and a bear hug. “You remind me of me.”

Her laidback disposition and carefree attitude hadn’t changed. It was like coming home again. We scarfed down the burritos and laughed over several cups of coffee. Just like old times. It was as if nothing changed. Except now we had to face the fact that one of our greatest influences was gone. I mentioned to my cousin that I brought a black suit for the funeral.

“Black suit?” Bill looked at me. “You won’t need that bro. Just your board and a pair-a-board shorts!”

We jumped in the station wagon and headed for Malibu. On the way down the PCH, I was anticipating the reunion I was about to have. I felt this uneasiness in the pit of my stomach because I was angry with the way JackO pushed Sting Ray aside. Because I was associating myself with Sting Ray at the time, JackO treated me the same way. So, my inner turmoil was warranted. Now there was an even greater reason to reunite and mend bridges.

We pulled up in front of the Malibu Surf Shake. Before Bill could turn the engine off, I see JackO jump over the wooden railing and ran over to our car. The minute we stepped out JackO had his arms around me squeezing me tight. He hugged me for what seemed like an eternity. I could sense his tears moistening my shoulder.

“I’m so, so sorry,” I whispered in his ear. He sobbed harder, as my apology had a double meaning. I didn’t know which way this was going to go when I saw him, but I am so glad it was like this.

He finally pulled away from me, his eyes red from tears. His perfectly coifed hair was now hanging down in his face. He looked gaunt and his posture was hunched over, obviously riddled with grief. “Thank you for coming,” he whispered. "It would not have been the same without you here." He managed a smile and invited us up to the shop.

JackO popped open three sodas and we walked down to the beach. Surfrider Beach hadn't changed. There were surfers edging the smooth waves rolling in past the pier. The Malibu Pier stood ever strong, watching over its little corner of paradise. Even the Bird Man of Malibu was still on the Pier communing with his feathered friends.

"He was like a father to me," JackO said as the three of us stood facing the horizon, water splashing at our feet. I didn't know if JackO knew that I just learned of their history not 30-minutes before, but I simply shook my head in agreement. "He gave me a life, when I no longer had one."

We stood silently drinking our soda, admiring the swells rolling in, and thinking about Big Steena. Although it was another perfect California day, the atmosphere seemed heavy, weighted down with an underlying sadness.

By 4pm, we headed to Pete's. We drove the station wagon, while JackO followed us in his Firebird. We parked in the alley behind Pete's. The same alley Sting Ray and I were confronted in by the cops. We walked through the popular joint, with the ever-present smell of greasy hamburgers and golden fries lingering in the air. The once vibrant energy of the place seemed dampened by the presence of melancholy.

I saw Sting Ray back in his usual booth. He stood up as we entered. He shook our hands, somewhat officially, almost as if he was asking to be back in our good graces. We ordered food and made small talk. It was obvious that although we were together again, it would take the guys much longer to ever trust Sting Ray again. After we ate, Sting Ray grabbed me by the arm and asked Bill and JackO if he could talk to me privately.

Sting Ray and I walked out to the front of the restaurant. I could sense the crowd in the street and the sea splashing onto the shore, but it was as if I was hearing it through a tin can. It wasn't the same Venice Beach surrounding me.

"The law offered me six months in prison, if I would give up my source," Sting Ray said shaking his head.

I was afraid to ask if he did give up his source, but I knew from my cousin that he only did six months and was then let out on good behavior and also because he was a first-time offender.

"I owe you an apology and I don't know where to start. I was so deep in my head, that I couldn't find a way out. I know you were only trying to help me see my wrongs, but I was blinded by my pride and ego. At least that's what Big Steena told me. I see that now," Sting Ray confessed. "I am really sorry, Golden Boy. You were the only one that tried to intervene and help me. I have learned how valuable someone like you can be in life. So not only am I sorry, but I need to say thank you."

"It's all good buddy, it's all good," I said, repeating the same words Bill said to me. I quickly changed the subject because at that point, there was nothing else to say. "Where is Canter these days?"

"On lifeguard duty in Huntington. You'll see him tomorrow," Sting Ray affirmed.

The following morning, we met at Venice beach. It was pre-dawn and the tranquil, early morning was humming as though it was offering an invocation to the dead. The tide was low and the ocean seemed as if it was ready to receive a great spirit.

Over sixty guys and gals came to the beach. These were people whose lives had been touched by Big Steena's love and generosity over the years. We all made our way in silent vigil paddling out on our boards to "the spot." Our collective strength seemed to be gathered from each other. We knowingly faced the horizon as the sun was now rising to the occasion, its light casting long shadows across the once Earthly home of a man who was adored by so many in this community.

Bill laid a beautiful wreath, woven with palms, branches, and sprigs of rosemary, into the gentle water. Bill cleared his throat and announced, "we have all been touched by this solemn saint of a man whose only desire was to ultimately fit in, somewhere. You are one with the sea, once again my friend."

Canter did everything to contain his tears. He motioned everyone to create a circle. "Can we all paddle round and pass it down." Word went down the line to paddle into a circle around the wreath.

JackO paddled up to the wreath and hesitantly opened the heavy urn that now sat on the edge of his board. He slowly and begrudgingly emptied its contents through the center of the wreath. Sobs could be heard along the line as we somberly watched the descent of our icon into the murky depths. Some friends tossed flowers in the water, while others offered mementos of love and appreciation to the ocean and spirit.

I could see Sting Ray, across from me in the circle. His head was down in despair, occasionally looking up at the wreath floating gently in the water.

"Just grains of sand," I muttered to myself, reflecting on the same words Big Steena passed on to me, years before.

We all sat there, straddling the rails of our boards, bobbing up and down in the soft waves, watching the sun stretch to the point of the wreath. Then one by one, people started splashing water into the circle, cheering on the celebration for a life that made a difference to so many. Slowly and reluctantly, friends peeled away from the circle heading back to shore.

Back at Big Steena's house, there was one more celebration for the life of a man who truly made a mark in his corner of the Universe. It just happened to be the same corner we were in. Arriving at his house, the ever-present scent of patchouli was a familiar and welcoming aroma. His modest house now seemed like a shrine to a soul, bigger than life itself.

Jeffery, Big Steena's lawyer, came up to me with a large, champagne bottle and uncorked the already opened decanter. He pulled out a rolled-up piece of paper and unraveled it in front of me. "Big Steena wanted you to have these things," he said to me walking over to the altar. He handed me the large, deep purple amethyst and clear quartz crystal point that I had admired years before. "He also said, you would know what this meant." Jeffery handed me a small, extremely smooth stone.

"Ahhh, his gratitude stone." I said to myself. "Thank you," I said to Jeffery, grinning. "I'm honored to receive them. I was surprised that Big Steena even remembered such a minute detail so many years ago. It was a beautiful gesture.

"There is something Big Steena wanted you to know," Jeffery looked me in the eyes.

"In the late 1960s, ten years after his father passed away, a lawyer contacted Big Steena to inform him that his mother had died suddenly of a heart attack. That lawyer was me," He smiled. "I came to Los Angeles with her last will and testament. After the death of his father, his mother inherited millions of dollars from the Texas ranch her husband sold a year earlier. Now, in one last attempt to reconcile with her son, Big Steena's mother passed those millions on to him."

I slowly sat down in the chair behind me. That made sense, I thought.

"Resisting at first, he thought the money should be donated to one of his mother's charities. 'If she wanted to do this, she would have stated that in her will,' I told him. So Big Steena agreed and stashed the inheritance away in an investment account. He then used a percentage of the money towards his own good causes. He loved Venice beach and helped with its progress. He invested in the surf industry and helped those in need who had nothing. His immediate life never changed. He would continue his journey in board shorts and live by the sea. He garnered a little beach house in Maui and hired Kai, his good friend of many years, to watch over, live, and care for the house. He made it very clear that he was never in this life for the money, but wanted to make a difference with his fellow man. His comfort level of being a millionaire, was uncomfortable, so he never shared his good news with others. He simply laid low and let his good deeds slip under the radar."

Now, as I slowly stood up in the middle of his quiet living room, my heart ached. He touched so many lives. He truly achieved his goal. I thanked Jeffery for the gifts and for confiding Big Steena's beautiful story to me.

"Big Steena knew you would appreciate everything and" he added, "he said he was very fond of his Golden boy." I burst out in tears, uncontrollably.

Throughout the day, friends, students, even ex-girlfriends stopped by the little house on the canal to offer a memory, bring a trinket, or have a beer. "It's that time," JackO announced standing on the picnic table.

It was a familiar parade out through the backyard with a group of Big Steena's students leading the way, surfboards overhead. The crowd had tripled in size since the morning and the mourners appeared in every shape and size, from every walk of life. Solemnly, we marched through the same sidewalks along the Venice Canals that Big Steena fought so hard to bring back and maintain. So many had tears in their eyes, including me. I can honestly say, for me, it was not tears of sadness, but tears of joy. Tears for a man who made such a difference in so many people's lives. He was probably unaware of how many of those whose lives he turned around, made whole, or just offered up words of encouragement.

The Golden Hour. That time of day that transforms daylight into a spectacular palette of red, orange and yellow light splashing across the indigo sky. The crowd now stood, silent, single file, at the ocean's edge, barefoot. It was a loving moment, facing the setting sun, remembering. The sun seemed to tell little tales to each individual reflecting back to every one of us, a memory of a larger-than-life character from humble beginnings.

Steen A. Suarez performed his duties and lived his life exactly how he wished. He cared for others, gave back to his community, and enjoyed the little pleasures that brought a smile to his face. A private man, he was always doling out words of wisdom in Buddha-like quotes that went straight to the heart. And if they didn't go there, they went to a place that really made you think about the "gift" he just offered you. From a silent, last vigil as the final rays of sun disappeared beneath the sea's embrace, a huge rousing and raucous applause could be heard all the way to Malibu.

Chapter 22

Miami Magic

I don't know how it happened, but I lost my desire to return to Los Angeles. After the death of Big Steena, I could not get myself to return. I would send cards to my cousin or call him when I knew he wouldn't be home. It was just so hard to communicate, as I knew we would end up talking about Big Steena.

On top of this, I couldn't look at my surfboard. It's as if a part of me died with him that day and that part was my passion to ride the waves. It hurt me to even think about going surfing. I wondered if that's how the guys felt too?

Was I too grown up for this now? I wasn't sure what was going on with me. I found myself longing for my past as I strolled by familiar landmarks and hot spots I knew since I moved to Manhattan in the early 80's. I meandered through the Village and obsessed over my past choices while being even more concerned about the future. Big Steena's passing was the end of an era.

I grabbed an iced coffee at my favorite deli on the corner of Bleecker and 7th. Sitting on a stoop next door was a street musician who I'd seen around the neighborhood for years. Still in the street, still strumming his guitar, today he was singing a familiar tune that was drifting towards me.

"I'm on the run
No time to sleep
I've got to ride
ride like the wind
to be free again..."

We gave each other a recognizable nod as I passed by. His lyrics drifted through the air like a message on the wind. It was the same song playing in the car on our early morning excursion to Lowers. My first trip to that beach with the train trestle path. I thought of Big Steena.

After a series of dance gigs from summer stock in the Catskills, a few MTV videos in New York, and a year's contract in a Broadway flop called *World's Fair*, I was finally in need of a break. My body was now feeling the effects of aging and a dance career into your 30's presented new challenges.

I was practically considered "over the hill" in the dance world. I already knew of several of my colleagues who were transitioning into other fields outside of show business. Then, there were those dancer friends of mine, who just kept plugging along. I gave them credit. Passion and will power were the formula for success. Maybe, I had to look at my career in a different way. I decided to stop and take a beat. I saw the pattern in my life. When everything was flowing and easy, I didn't think about the process. But, when I felt like a fish trying to swim upstream, against the current, I learned to stop, take a breath, and come back to the task at hand at a later date.

I was reintroduced to Miami Beach in the early 90s, approximately eight years after the area was saved as a cohesive Art Deco unit by Barbara Capitman and a group of activists who spearheaded the movement to place almost one square mile of South Beach on the National Register of Historic Places. The Miami Beach Architectural District was designated in 1979. This allowed for the protection of every Art Deco building to be preserved from its early days of the late 1920s to early 30s. "South Beach" was about 23 blocks south of Indian Creek to the tip of South Point.

I had a friend who just landed a job with the Miami City Ballet company. She was telling me how great Miami was to work and live in. This is when I rediscovered Miami Beach and the sanctuary it would become. Rich in vegetation, a glow with the most amazing tropical light, warm gulf waters, and mystical sand bars, this beach seemed to be perched on a precipice that was sacred ground. The tropical paradise became my most inspiring muse, a place of many metaphysical discoveries, and the place I would always come back to in my mind's eye!

Since I could not get myself to go back to LA, I decided to buy a home here. Miami was a secret paradise that was just waiting for me. It was the right time. Miami was having a resurgence among artists and those creative, free spirits who just found Key West too far to get to. Miami was only two and a half hours from New York by plane, which made it very convenient. You could spend two and a half hours, driving out to the Hamptons and the beach would never compare to Miami's pristine waters.

Sitting on the south end of Flamingo Park and overlooking the ocean to the East, my new condo had become a place for me to find solace and relaxation. I could entertain friends and family over the winter season, on holidays, and in the summer. Summer was my favorite time here. The snowbirds were gone, the ocean temperature was warm and wonderful to swim in, and the heavy midsummer air would also bring cooling rains. It became a home where I was most inspired with ideas and a place that sparked inspiration for my business.

Although still a very new and upcoming área in the mid-90s, South Beach was raw and full of amazing possibilities. You could just feel the kinetic energy surrounding this special island. It was a place not yet fully formed. It was truly a diamond in the rough again, waiting, once more, to be reinvented. After its many highs and lows from the 20s through the late 60s, Miami in the early 70s, when I came here as a kid, was already waning from the spotlight.

Lincoln Road was an abandoned strip mall with shops that had closed down years before. By the early 90s it was still completely unkept and undeveloped. The minute you would walk past Ocean Drive coming off the beach, you would see many hotels and businesses boarded up and abandoned. But yet, you could feel transformation in the air! And transform it did.

I started to spend my winters here. After years of working and saving money, I no longer had to live hand to mouth. I would spend days frolicking on the beach, swimming in the mellow waves below 5th street, eating delicious Cuban food, and renovating my condo. There was no other place I'd been to in the world where the water and the ocean environment were so perfect. I remembered coming to this beach as a kid with my parents and how it transformed my life. It gave me such a sense of peace and made me feel completely at ease. No doubt, it had to do with the rich tropical atmosphere and turquoise waters that spun its magic spell over me.

Every morning, I would find myself at the beach. Calm was a sense of peace among my inner struggles. Calm was a relative term to my own perception of my well-being. "When we perceived peace within ourselves," Big Steena would teach us, "we'd reflect it outwards." South Beach gave me this sense of tranquility.

My sunrise walks to the beach would always be met with a bevy of geckos scattering about the perimeter sensing my presence. I would greet the morning sun at its horizon and listen to the sea. I would occasionally swim and recharge in the dawn's early light.

This seemed to be a place for people who wanted to escape or for those seeking the next "hot spot." After the decline of the beach during the late 70s, the Cuban exodus, and the drug wars, this little star, wanted to be dusted off again. Miami Beach was ready to shine.

Considered the new "Nuovo Chic", Miami started attracting celebrities, the irreverent wild child of many a European socialite, and fashion icons, including the masterful Gianni Versace. They could get away to Miami Beach and not be hounded by paparazzi or crazed fans. On this little strip of beach, on an island off the tip of Florida, everyone could just....be.

Versace bought Casa Casuarina on Ocean Drive. Originally, the mansion was commissioned by Standard Oil heir Alden Freeman in 1930, and was named for the only tree situated on the property, the Casuarina tree. By the 90s it was a delipidated hotel that Versace transformed into an opulent, Mediterranean-style palazzo complete with gold-tiled pool and frescoes.

I remember meeting up with Versace many afternoons on the beach, just by happenstance. He was very receptive and happy to discuss the crazy pace of New York, his love for fabrics, and the way the light was such an inspiration for him, here, in Miami. We would talk fashion and industry, beauty and design, and his admiration for dance, surfing, and the art of the physical body...all during our many casual days of sunbathing.

My career was about to take an unexpected turn. Versace was throwing a party at Casa Casuarina to introduce several of New York's top fashion photographers, modeling agent executives, and fashion influencers to experience the beauty and magic of Miami. He also invited friends he made in Miami to mingle with his New York friends. I was honored to accept his invitation. Versace had a knack for bringing different socio-economic and culturally diverse people together in order to cross-mingle and explore an entire world of ideas from different perspectives.

Versace would proudly introduce me to several of his influential friends. "Not only is he a looker, but he's a surfer," Versace exclaimed, introducing me to Prince Egon von Fürstenberg, former husband of Diane von Fürstenberg. Egon was a fiery mix of flamboyance and kitsch. Jaded and very honest in his opinions, he would stare down his nose at me with a half-cocked smile. "Where in NY do you live, again?"

"I'm in the Village," I responded with the same matter of fact response.

"Oh, I love the Village." He brightened up. "And you keep a little pied-a-terre here?"

"Yes, Miami is my getaway spot," I smiled.

"That's the way to do it," Egon said shaking his head. "It's funny, I know a garmento with a little company in New York who is putting together a fashion show with a surfing theme. You should really talk to him. He could use your inspiration, I'm sure."

"What little company is that," I asked.

"Levi Strauss," he responded nonchalantly.

I casually choked on my drink.

"You'll come to my interior design show in New York and I'll introduce you."

If I had a nickel for every time someone told me that… But, true to his word, one month later, Prince Egon von Fürstenberg introduced me to the gentleman in charge of Levi's fashion shows. They were excited about having dancers in their show with a surfing theme. This was my introduction into the competitive, fast-paced, ready-to-wear business of fashion.

It was the 90s and the trend at the Industrial Shows and Fashion Trade Events was to have high-energy, full-scale dance productions. These shows were designed to bring attention to the companies' products. These companies would spare no expense when it came to their production budgets. The bigger the better. I went from choreographing 10-15 dancers to producing 100 dancers, Vegas acts, and specialty groups all incorporated into one show.

In two years' time, I had transitioned from dancer to choreographer/ producer with sheer will and determination. My company, *Downtown Express,* was sought after for spectacular event shows. I received a phone call from Jockey, the underwear company. They wanted to do a large production show in Los Angeles at the Biltmore Hotel for Fall Fashion Week. They wanted to hire female and male dancers in LA and asked if I could go to LA to cast and produce the show.

How do you showcase underwear with dancers that are discreet and not too revealing? I hired a design team who came up with scenes representing each period from the 20s to the 90s. We would use dance styles and props from each period to showcase different groupings of under garments.

This meant, I had to finally return to Los Angeles after eight years since leaving behind the loss of Big Steena and the alternative life and friends I had experienced there. It was now time. I was excited!

I had done this flight between New York and LA over and over since I was 16 years old. But this time, it was different. I had slept on the plane for most of the morning flight. When I woke, we were crossing over the Grand Canyon. The wide gaping hole in the earth seemed massive, even from twenty-five thousand feet above ground. I put my headphones on…

"Every thought is a dream, rushing by in a stream
Bringing life to our kingdom of doing
Take a ride in the sky, on our ship, fantasize
All your dreams will come true, miles away" **

I looked out the window and there it was. The Santa Anita Mountains coming into view with LA nestled in the basin. I got chills over my entire body, as *Earth Wind and Fire* sang their anthem of dreams through my Walkman. I was returning, now as a choreographer in charge of a huge show in the City of Angels. It's as if I was coming home. It was impossible to keep the smile to myself. I broke down in tears of joy as the music propelled me to a brand-new adventure.

** Lyrics reprinted by permission: "FANTASY" Criga Music, C/O Irving Music, EMI April Music Inc. (Maurice White, Verdine White, Eduardo Del Barrio)

Chapter 23

Accepting

I had come back to Los Angeles on completely different terms. I was seeing it now through very jaded eyes. Instead of my cousin's old station wagon meeting me outside the airport, I had a car service pick me up at LAX and drove me to my hotel in West Hollywood. Much of LA looked as if nothing had changed. The unique 1930s architecture and famous landmarks seemed like a snapshot from the past. There were some new buildings that had popped up and some familiar icons that were now, sadly gone.

The Hollywood Hills still glowed with a familiar hue, especially at sunset. When the sun would disappear behind the hills, the lights of the city would start popping on as the sun was extinguished. The friendly, intimate lights brought back beautiful memories.

Jockey set up auditions for dancers in a large dance studio off Doheny and Santa Monica Blvd. LA dancers had great technical prowess yet danced with fearless abandon. Unlike the more rigid New York dancer, LA dancers had a more unchained style that I loved watching.

As choreographer, I had two assistants and a staff to help me with casting. I instantly thought of my first New York scholarship audition I went through for Harkness Ballet with David Howard. It seemed eerily familiar, but now, I was the one holding the auditions. Two representatives of Jockey came to the studio to give my staff a better idea of who they thought would be perfect for their products.

With over 150 dancers showing up for the 12 positions, the grueling sweat session went on for four hours, as we danced, and danced, and danced again. Repeating the routine over and over, we slowly began weeding out all but 15 dancers. After all the dancers had left the studio, the producers and my staff meet to finalize the casting. After an exhausting morning and a long afternoon, my energy was spent. I went back to my hotel.

Out of habit, I had brought my surfboard to California. There it was, in its traveling bag, starring me in the face, wondering when it would see water. Should I actually do this? It had been eight years since I bagged it and left it in a corner. I would occasionally think about the personification of surfing in my life, but was now on a different path. It still hurt to think about getting back into the water on a board.

I sat on the bed starring at the board for the longest time. I could hear Big Steena's voice in my head. "You're either 10 toes in or not at all."

I changed my clothes, grabbed the board, and headed to Malibu.

Conditions were perfect. The late day sun hung low on the horizon. Waves were overhead, sky was a crisp blue, and the ocean's rollercoaster was performing at high velocity. I couldn't wait to get out there. I was high. I was high off the atmosphere that surrounded me. I kicked off my shoes to get my bare feet wet. I splashed some water on my board and waxed up. I paddled out to a group I wasn't familiar with. After a few gnarly call outs from a couple kooks, I paddled up to a sweet blond who flashed a big smile and welcomed me to the water.

A beautiful barrel was coming down the pike. The pretty blond could see the eager look on my face, like a kid at Christmas. "Go for it," she said. "This bomb is for you. Show us how it's done."

I ripped through the water in three paddles and popped up. Immediately off the lip and down the face I went into the mouth of this exceptional curl. I barreled through, admiring the overhead view of celestial blue as the water turned into white foam above me. I had the nerve to look behind me through the long circular curve of water. The wave was closing out quickly, yet my urgency was gone. I looked ahead and simply enjoyed the ride. I seemed to glide for hours when in reality it was surely just a minute or two. As I see the wave begin to break apart, I steered the nose of my board further out of the pocket to avoid the close out, shooting out of the canon into the blue sky above.

That was it. I had just spun the perfect barrel and I had accomplished what I desired, in one wave. "You can't top that," I told myself. It was like riding a bike. Once you learned how to do something, you never forget it. I paddled in and sat on the beach. Why did I wait so long to do this? Why? Life got in the way. I had a path I needed to follow and that was the journey I was meant to take. Regardless, I still ended up back where I was supposed to be. At the sea. I took Big Steena's advice. "Live life, one wave at a time."

My following weeks were occupied with the rehearsals and finally, a successful show. From that one job, I was offered three other similar events from ready-to-wear companies who wanted the same spectacular I had created for Jockey.

I finally had some time on my hands. I wanted to go to Venice. I wanted to call my cousin, but there was such apprehension behind it, it kept me from doing so. What am I going to say? What should I expect? What will we have to talk about? I felt as if I was stuck in glue. I was not willing to take the next step but desperately wanted to. After eight years, I still felt some sense of letting my friends down. Even though we made up when I came back for Big Steena's funeral. I was then gone again for a long time. My guilt and remorse were still lingering, somewhere in the back of my mind.

So, I did nothing.

It so happened that I needed a stage manager for the last production event I was about to do in Las Vegas. I immediately thought of my friend, Jose who got me the audition for the Far East tour and then, once I got it, he bailed on me for another job. I didn't know where he was, but I tracked him down through an old phone number.

"Hey, Drew, where have you been?" he asked, surprised to get my phone call. I told him about the stage-managing job in Las Vegas and he was all in. "You still surf?" he laughed.

"Like a fiend," I answered. "Bring your board."

"Never thought I'd be working in Vegas," Jose said, thanking me as a bellman showed him to his suite in the Tropicana. "Come on in, we'll have a drink."

The Tropicana was the setting for the Cotler Jeans show I'd booked in LA. This time, I was using a combination of LA dancers and Vegas show acts in the production. Jose would manage the cast and the entire flow of the show.

"Cheers," he said as we clinked our glasses. "Well, it's only been a hundred years since we worked together last. Nice digs ya got here."

"I knew you would like this gig." Jose was a tall Ecuadorian guy, who grew up in New York and went into show business for the girls. "Dude, you are the only guy I know who went into the business for reasons other than a passion for the arts."

"It was a passion for the arts," he smiled. "The long leggy arts."

Jose was divorced from his third wife. I figured he was done by now.

"I came to Vegas to marry a showgirl," he laughed. "Hey, why did you want me to bring my surfboard to the middle of a desert?"

"I figured we could go back to LA after the gig and surf Malibu or Venice or both!" I was desperate for a surfing buddy.

"That sounds great. You know, I was also thinking about going to Ecuador to see my family and then surf the coast. Why don't you come with me? In fact, I know you have some surfing buddies in LA, why don't we make it a road trip?"

I smiled, but did not answer. I took a nervous gulp of my drink instead. "OK, well, let me see who's around," I lied.

"The Trop" was one of the oldest and most established casino hotels on the Strip. It had a reputation that preceded it. It's checkered past also enhanced its prestige. It was home to the "Folies Bergère." This glittering fusion of towering feathered headdresses, worn by beautiful topless showgirls, also featured five specialty acts and 30 dancers. It was the quintessential Vegas show.

I went backstage after seeing the spectacular, to meet several of the acts I would be hiring for the fashion event.

"Drew, is that you?" There he was, my old roommate from the Far East, Vince, dressed in a glittering white tuxedo.

"Vince, you're here, dancing in the show. At the Tropicana. In Vegas." I was surprised to see this familiar face from my distant past.

"I know," he said matter of fact. "You can't tell who any of the dancers are with all these crazy costumes, make-up, masks, and plumage! I've been in this show for four years now. I've moved out here permanently."

I told Vince about the show I was doing for the jeans company. I needed a swing dancer in my show, just in case one of my cast members got sick or injured. I asked Vince if he would do it. Since, the "Follies" only had night shows and my events were during the day, he agreed. It was a small world.

I decided to call Bill the next day. Seeing Vince reminded me, just how short time really was. Bill was so happy to hear from me. We talked for an hour on the phone, catching up with life and how the guys were doing. He was going to get in touch with everyone and see if they would be interested in the surf trip.

At this point in our lives, we all had the means of our own to travel and surf wherever we wanted. I personally didn't have to depend on a show to take me where I wanted to surf. Even though I had been extremely lucky for years. Somehow, I knew the Universe had a hand in that.

After the show in Vegas, I took Jose to Pete's to meet the guys. We would discuss the trip and make our plans. I couldn't believe it when I walked in. Pete had retired to Palm Springs but his son, Pete Jr. was running the business. Tally, was still there. Pete Jr. created a new position for her as hostess. She would greet and seat customers, sans the roller skates. Pete Jr. had a new bevy of beauties on rollerblades, whom he lovingly called "Pete's Angels." They would zip about the restaurant, taking orders and busing tables in micro miniskirts and roller derby tube tops. How times had changed. It was hard to accept that life was moving on, but here we were.

Bill walked into the restaurant and JackO followed. Canter showed up minutes later, and who strolled in last minute…Sting Ray. Everyone looked a little older, a little wiser, and hopefully a little richer than when we were kids. We were ready for a surf adventure.

We landed in the coastal city of Guayaquil. This fast-paced, bustling metropolis reminded me of India. The same third world squalor, crazy rhythm, and tropical heat. We crashed in a hostel close to the airport that Jose knew of and slept till dawn.

Jose got his cousin's truck and we were off on our adventure. We piled into the back of the truck, six guys and six boards. The truck careened down the rough roads, mounting the current bumps and railing through the deep ditches that lead us from Guayaquil to San Pablo beach. The dry, arid landscape looked parched and in desperate need of any kind of nourishment it could get. Clumps of cacti, reaching 10 feet in the air, being the only green you would see for miles. Occasionally, we would pass an acre of land that looked like an oasis, nourished by a primitive tubing system. The saturated land was covered in watermelons that would be harvested and taken to the nearby cities and towns. The land next to this fertile patch would turn back into the dust bowl you could see for miles. On the hour and a half drive, we would pass groupings of shacks along the road with locals selling grapes, papaya, watermelon, and coco ice.

All roads lead to the beach. Shacks of cement and bamboo lined the narrow coastline with eager merchants waving each prospective beach goer to relax in their establishments. Signs promoting delicious corvina, crab, shrimp, and other seafood delights lined the beach road. Here, the Pacific cut a large bay in the Ecuadorian landscape starting from Salinas Beach in the South to Salonga Beach to the North. San Pablo was considered a small fishing village that produced amazing seafood from its waters, served fresh in all the roadside cabanas.

The sea was pushing out waist high waves that were a nice introduction to the tepid waters along the Equator. The spray coming off the lip of the waves indicated good off-shore winds. In between sets we would convene under one of the tented umbrellas to eat and make fun of the way each one of us would surf.

Although it was my first-time surfing with Jose, it was a pleasure. His surfing skills were on a par with mine, and the fact that he wanted to take us to his country and hang with my crew made him a real cool, standup guy. Him and JackO would share stories in Spanish about growing up in their perspective countries and compare the Mexican girls to Ecuadorian girls. Canter and Sting Ray were ready to party. The long day was waning, so we hit the road to Montañita.

Montañita was one of Ecuador's most popular beaches. Known for its ideal mix of great surfing and the perfect party destination, it was a town built for the nomad and his party lifestyle. We pulled into town after sunset. The streets were filled with locals, expats, and surfers. Everywhere you looked, grass huts lined the narrow streets with girls hawking t-shirts, guys renting surfboards to tourists, and restaurants offering seafood and beer.

A young girl spoke to me in English. "I have the perfect gift for you," she exclaimed. She held up a beautiful silver ring with six separate thin bands connected by a silver clip, which bound the six rings together.

"I really don't wear jewelry," I said dismissing the approach.

"This would look great on your tanned skin," she pushed. "It's a ring of friends."

I stopped in my tracks. I thought of the six significant friends I had made in California. One ring for each of us...Bill, Sting Ray, Canter, JackO, Big Steena, and myself.

She slipped it on my finger. It fit like a glove. That was all the encouragement I needed. She thanked me for the sale and disappeared into the night.

Dancing was extremely popular in Ecuador and especially in the coastal towns. Latin music was a way of life and its rhythms were infectious. You just had to dance. There was always a girl waiting for a guy to invite her to dance. If you didn't ask, some girls would grab you by the arm and take you right out to the dance floor. The jovial atmosphere was contagious. Everyone danced. I loved to salsa, so I would dance, non-stop, for hours. The locals were happy to see anyone willing to join the fun. The sun was up before we knew it.

La Punta was the most popular spot in town. This beach had some of the gnarliest breaks in Ecuador. Jose took us just North of the center of town. We stood on the beach watching the waves rising almost to a double-overhead. We wired the beach, scoping out the terrain as Jose pointed out the rocks below the surface. The curve of the cove was framed by a long jetty with a rocky-faced cliff beyond that. The long, smooth picture-perfect waves shaped themselves into flawless tubes.

"We have to paddle out, about 200 yards, and we'll get a longer ride, avoiding the rocks," Jose surmised.

It was time to get wet. No wetsuit required. The warm water of the Equator made it very comfortable to surf through. It was funny to see the lineup of familiar faces again. I could accept that it was a little different, but seeing us together couldn't make up for the fact that Big Steena was not there. He was with us in spirit.

These were big waves that would swell and break right, turning over a long steady distance to the shore. We would have about a twenty-minute set and then have to wait for the next swell to roll in from across the Pacific. This

Ecuadorian pipeline was comparable to a good day at Malibu or Huntington Beach.

Eat, surf, sleep, repeat. It seemed like old times again. A time when we were carefree and surfing was all we had to do. This measured slice of fun, wedged way back in my memory left me yearning for more nostalgia.

We stayed in a wonderful, two-story bamboo hotel that night. The owners knew Jose's family and were so happy to have Jose and all his American friends occupying the rooms. At night, from my window, the full moon shimmered on the gentle evening waves. The smell of the salty air and subtle hint of boiled shrimp, drift up from the restaurant downstairs. It was intoxicating. It felt like such a long time since I had smelled the sea at night. The more than comfortable temperature and stress-free days were a welcome change from the crazy schedule Jose and I had in Vegas. This was just the opposite of that. I slept like a baby.

The next morning, I woke up to a gentle rustling at my open window. A huge iguana was sitting on the sill, chewing. His mandibles crushing some plant material he had found overhead. His power breakfast was loud enough to rouse me from my blissful slumber.

Ecuadorians loved their ceviche. This dish was a blend of either mixed seafood, shrimp, or fish, marinated in cilantro and citrusy lime juice. Every restaurant in town had their own version of the "family recipe." It was usually eaten with "chifles" (thin crispy plantain chips) or popcorn. This was breakfast, prepared by our hostess. The thought of fish, first thing in the morning was a daunting task. But, not to be rude, we politely indulged. After I got past the first few mouth-puckering bites, I thoroughly enjoyed every spoonful! I chased it down with three large café con leche and was ready for the beach.

We headed to the other end of the beach to Montañita Break. There was a smooth North swell rolling in. The off shore winds made for good conditions and the waves were about six footers. These waves were breaking closer to shore but there were also fewer rocks hanging out below the surface. It was a decent trade off.

We doubled up. Bill and I were surfing together, Canter and Sting Ray were reconnecting after a long absence, and Jose and JackO had a lot in common. Bill confessed, "I could not go surfing for several years after Big Steena passed away. I wouldn't go near my surfboard."

I was relieved to hear Bill say this.

"I'm glad to know it was not just me. You don't know how many times I wanted to call and talk to you about this," I admitted.

"The memories were just too painful and surfing would only cause me more anxiety," Bill said shaking his head.

I'd never heard my cousin reveal such an emotional part of himself. Although it seemed so out of character for my cousin, I could relate.

"On the other hand, I was able to channel my energy into my lawn grooming business and it has grown to the point where it delivers a viable income now."

I was so happy for him. More and more, this trip seemed like the right move.

Sting Ray and Canter were laughing and joking with each other, just as I remembered them the very first day they came into Pete's. I recalled how they dragged their wet surfboards through the restaurant and nobody batted an eyelash. I chuckled to myself.

Jose and JackO were competing with each other, trying to see who could ride the lip of the wave the longest distance before gliding down its face. JackO seemed a little happier now. He had established himself as an angel of the Venice Canals. He led the community in a clean-up of the waterways and was now taking on all of Big Steena's students who were eager to learn the art of wave riding. They were in good hands.

We watched the sun pierce the water in a hazy eventide, as twilight transitioned into another moon-kissed night. The carpet of stars demanded your attention. It seemed like a different sky on the Equator. Just another piece of the missing map from my childhood sky-watching.

After stuffing ourselves with fish and rice at one of the local hotspots, the party town was turning on. The volume around the city just seemed to increase as the night waned. We found an open bar and dance floor right along the beach that was hopping. JackO and Bill were doing shots of rum. Sting Ray was learning Spanish from one of the local girls who just couldn't get enough of his sarcasm and Canter, Jose, and I were dominating the dance floor. DJ Rico was playing the best dance songs from the 70s and 80s. I was in heaven!

"Out on the road today
I saw a Deadhead sticker on a Cadillac
A little voice inside my head said
"Don't look back, you can never look back"
I thought I knew what love was, what did I know?
Those days are gone forever
I should just let them go." **

Don Henley's Boys of Summer was appropriately referring to aging and questioning the past. Here we were, halfway around the world again, in a different country. Did we have any answers?

Coping with hangovers was a very common morning ritual in Montañita. The hangover remedy of choice here was a pill called Finalin. It was basically a high dose of aspirin. Between that and a few cups of café con leche, we were on the road to recovery.

Jose pulled the truck around and suggested we take a ride and maybe hit the waves later. Considering everyone's condition, we were all in agreement. We drove up the coast and stopped in a little village called Ayampa. This had a sweet little beach with phallic rocks off the coastline. We sat on the beach and watched some local surfers rip a few amazing waves. It looked like a great spot to surf. I was glad we were laying low today. My body was sore from the last two days of surfing, not to mention I was recovering from my dance marathon and cerveza consumption.

We made our way up to another town called Puerto Lopez. "We are going for a sea excursion," Jose announced. "It's just about an hour or so."

Late October in Ecuador was considered their Spring season moving into Summer. Because we were on the equator, the seasons were reversed from the US, which was something I had forgotten. This time of year was migrating season for thousands of humpback whales that would make their way down from Antarctica to the coast of Ecuador to mate and give birth in the warmer Pacific waters.

Our guide took us out in a beautiful boat with two very loud out board engines. We skirted the surface of the water cutting out towards the "nursing area." The water was teaming with gigantic humpback whales who were minding their small calves. The babies would dart back and forth, trying to escape their parents who would consistently ignore their antics, until our guide would decide to move the boat around the area. That action would seem to activate the adult whales' parenting skills. The mother would wrangle the calves, while the males would make spectacular leaps out of the sea, exposing their huge, white bellies, spraying water over the entire boat as they would land, soaking us from head to toe!

This was something to see in person. I could not believe that we were here. I had to thank Jose for being the perfect host and tour guide to his amazing country. It would be a trip we would talk about for years to come. Not only was the interaction with nature and the sea so fulfilling, it felt like our spirits took a forward step.

Thanks to Jose, the rekindling of my relationships with my longtime friends, who made such an impression in my life as a kid, was now underway thanks to the initiative of an acquaintance.

All of our lives were that much more enriched, thanks to Jose.

** Lyrics reprinted by permission: "BOYS OF SUMMER" Universal Music Corp. (Don Henley, Mike Campbell)

Chapter 24

Trial by Fire

It was the end of May and New York was flourishing in Spring fever. Every place you would look, New York seemed alive. After coming out of a long winter, it always seemed like people couldn't wait to shed their coats and walk carefree in the streets.

I hadn't surfed since October in Ecuador and I had the notion to head back out to Montauk to see what the waters would be like this time of year. I had just finished looking at a dance audition space for an upcoming event I was up for. Even though I didn't have the job yet, I knew it would be a big cast and I needed more room for rehearsals. Studio space along the West Side Highway had more square footage for a much better rental price.

The rev of a large black motorcycle pulled up behind me. The guy stopped and took off his helmet. I couldn't believe it, but it was McCreedy. "What are you doing in town?" I asked, trying not to look surprised. I wanted to ask him what had happened between him and my cousin, but I didn't. Libby had filled me in immediately after they had broken off their romance. He and my cousin dated for about eight months before he was shipped off to Cuba on an assignment.

"It's "Fleet Week" in New York and the entire harbor is filled with ships from around the world," he said proudly.

"Oh, and I guess you're a part of all this?" I questioned, sarcastically. I still didn't know how to handle this guy. He desperately seemed to want to be my friend, but yet, I couldn't let him in. The scar was too deep.

"Sure, the Navy men are responsible for conducting expeditionary and amphibious operations through combined arms, implementing its own infantry, armor, artillery, aerial, and special forces. We are here for a break." He rattled off the explanation as if he was rehearsing for a "bring your dad to work" day.

I wanted to tell him that he really didn't answer my question, but I thought better of it and just smiled.

"Where are you going?" McCreedy asked me, as I gestured downtown. "Come on, I'll take you down on the bike."

"No, no, that's no problem. I was hopping on the train," I quickly answered.

"The train is blocks away and I thought you said you were in a hurry?" he pushed.

I didn't remember saying I was in a hurry. In the back of my mind, I was curious why my arch-enemy from high school was on the corner of 48 street and the West Side Highway in New York City, some 18 years later, asking me if I wanted a ride home?

Big Steena would talk a lot about being open to new ideas. "You must learn the benefits of being open-minded," he would say. "Everyone has their own belief system. Sometimes, in conversation you learn what other people's core values are. Sometimes they will relate to yours and sometimes they will be the polar opposite."

Maybe, this was McCreedy's way of offering an olive branch. Is he trying to make amends from high school? Maybe, this was his way of apologizing. Or, maybe, he had no recollection of the events in high school or carried these memories around like I had. Did he realize how much of a jerk he was then. Maybe he was now driven by guilt?

I jumped on the back of the bike as he handed me an extra helmet. The bike careened down the West Side Highway. McCreedy would speed up then slow down, following the pattern of the traffic in front of us. He seemed capable on this big motorcycle, but on some level, it seemed like he was showing off. We stopped at a red light and he yelled back "How ya doin back there?" Thumbs up I replied.

The light changed and the traffic lurched forward. MeCreedy quickly moved out forward of the cars to our left, changing lanes in order to make the left turn onto my street. In an instant, a little girl, no more than six years old attempted to cross the 4-lane highway to catch up with her mother.

The last thing I remember was seeing the little red balloon she was holding on to, as I flew through the air. I seemingly followed the escaping red gasbag with my eyes as it launched from the frightened girl's hands into the hemisphere. I hit the ground sliding through the gravel and pavement as if my thighs were steam rollers, flattening everything in its path. The searing flesh on my left arm seemed to be an afterthought as I came to land along the curbside, bruised, bloodied, and disoriented, but alive. If it weren't for that helmet, it may have been a different outcome. The jeans I had on were now pocked and shredded. The skin on my left arm seemed dark and shriveled. I smelled a faint scent of burnt flesh. I thought to myself that this did not look right. I was helped up by several bystanders as I looked around for McCreedy, the little girl, or any other casualties I was afraid to discover.

The little girl was across the street in her mother's arms, crying but seemingly ok. My eyes caught McCreedy's overturned bike in the middle of the road and yards from the bike sat McCreedy. He still had his helmet on and he was just sitting there holding his left arm. I could feel my pulsing adrenaline wearing down. I passed out.

I woke up in a bed at St. Vincent's Hospital, only blocks from my apartment. "I had to debride your arm. You're on drugs right now, so you should not be in much pain. You sustained 2nd and 3rd degree burns. But, you're in good hands. I'm a hand specialist and plastic surgeon. Hi I'm Dr. Lee."

I seemed half out of it, as I looked to my right to see a tall, pristinely dressed Asian man in his mid-40's with a brilliant smile. "I had to cut your ring off." I thought he said finger, until I saw the mangled six ring band in pieces in a cup.

"Will I live?" I slurred.

"Without a doubt," he smiled as he left the room.

What seemed like hours later, I woke to see McCreedy standing at my bedside, arm in a cast. "So, he came to finish me off?" I thought. Was this part of his grand plan? I was more coherent now. "Hey Drew."

He called me Drew.

"Drew, I am so sorry. I had no choice, I would have hit and killed that little girl if I didn't swerve the bike! I'm, so, so sorry." He was practically in tears as he pleaded for me to forgive him.

"Hey, no one died," I replied. "Is that a tear?" I was almost enjoying the moment, watching McCreedy sweat and plead for my forgiveness. It was practically something I secretly wished for, half my life.

"I have a broken arm, but I was cleared to go back to the ship," he confessed.

"What happened to your bike?" I asked curiously, knowing he didn't live in the City.

"They towed it back to my girl's place in Queens. Her dad has a garage and they are gonna spruce it up."

There was a lot of new information in those two sentences and I didn't want to process any of it in the moment. "Make sure they scrape the skin from my arm off the muffler," I retorted in my head. God, I had become a truly sarcastic New Yorker.

"The doc says you're gonna be alright. Just some recovery time."

"I'll get there." He shook my good hand and that was the last time I ever saw Timothy McCreedy.

The terrible reality had set in. Days after surgery, I was in the hospital coping with the routine of massaging a very particular salve into my new transplanted skin on my left arm and dressing it with a tight Jobst stocking. The stocking felt like a python griping my arm, but for any burn victim it was essential that this was done daily to help the new skin to "take." The new skin came from both my upper thighs.

"You can still wear your board shorts, surfer boy," Dr. Lee smiled. "And you'll be back dancing in a few months."

"A few months?" I thought. "The rent's not going to pay itself!" I'll have to worry about that another day.

Since having the skin graft, I could not move my legs. They were in excruciating pain, which made it impossible to walk. The raw, exposed skin that was left after removing the top layer from my legs had to be monitored daily for any signs of infection and to make sure it was healing properly. My right arm was the only limb unscathed from the accident. Being left-handed, I had to learn to do everything with my right, non-dominant hand.

My brother came in everyday from Connecticut and brought me home cooked meals. He was really there for me. He gave me so much support and comfort. I was lucky to have him. The LA crew got wind of my situation and sent a big care package with new trunks, a wetsuit, a box of Neptune's famous macaroons and a can of Sex Wax. The show I just finished choreographing in Vegas sent a huge arrangement of flowers. I was happy to know I was loved.

Each morning, I would wake up to nurses pinching and probing, removing bandages, and feeding me pain killers. Every afternoon I would sit up in my bed and stare out the window. At least I had a large window that looked out over the tranquil West Village. The tree lined streets looked so inviting. The World Trade Center towers stood tall in the distance framing the sunny, blue sky.

It was mid-June and I should be out surfing or working on some dance gig somewhere. Long restless days turned into even longer, painful nights and I was starting to get depressed. I could feel my spirit weakening. I would sing gospel spirituals to myself or read a book, but my self-doubt and self-pity would seep in through the fine pores of my mind and decimate my hopes. It was the lowest point in my life and I knew only time (a long time) would heal these wounds.

The day the nurses were able to bend my knees was the day I started many weeks of arduous physical therapy for all three limbs. Each day the therapist assigned to me would help with my exercises and offer me hope. Three weeks later, I was relegated to my home. My brother took weeks out of his daily schedule to be with me, but he had to work and I couldn't ask him to keep coming in. He would if I asked, but it was time for me to put on my big boy pants and try to do for myself. Eventually the cards and letters waned, the phone calls of encouragement slowed down, and even my doctor stopped following up. I eventually realized it was completely up to me now. I had to make my life happen. I had to start working on which way my healing path would go. As I lay there in my own bed, staring up at the peeling ceiling, I had to confront a new life choice. But for the moment, I had to pee.

Pain furthers our growth. Pain has one indelible truth: at some point it is inevitable. In order to overcome pain, you must find a solution for it as you allow it to pass over you like a wave. With physical pain, it is the struggling and resisting that often makes it that much worse.

With emotional pain, stuffing it further down in your mind or ignoring it, results in it manifesting as physical pain or hidden trauma within.

With both types of pain, you can find a solution by acknowledging the situation, exploring the process, and accepting its presence. The waves of hurt, grief, or sadness will pass over you in time and you will be given a new outlook. I could sense the possible, but it was still off in the distant horizon. I remembered the daily pain I endured for the love of a dance career. It was all worth it. Each day, my body was racked with pain from head to toe, yet on some superhuman level, I found a way to push through it. All for the love of what I was doing. This new Herculean task before me was no different. Now, the goal was to live.

Yet, every day when changing my bandages and redressing my arm, I was reminded of how ugly it made me feel. How broken and damaged I was, all due to… I couldn't say his name. I was angry and bitter some days, forgiving and remorseful on others. Because I knew the reason for his decision in that moment, I understood he chose to sacrifice himself and me. I didn't consent to that, but I would have made the same choice. I had to move on from these thoughts of hatred and guilt, self-loathing and despair. But how?

I was facing the fact that my accident was the final nail in the coffin of my dance career. I was disabled. How could I ever surf again? Was I ever going back to my gypsy way of life? As time passed, I realized that fear was a mirror reflecting back my insecurities. So, it was either stand up and fight (emotionally or physically) or run, flee, and avoid the situation. Fear can serve us, by keeping us aware in a dangerous situation. Other than physical harm befalling you, fear is an emotional upstaging of our common sense. This emotional response can grow like a cancer, if you allow it. You are always in control of your fear. Therefore, you cannot allow it to dampen your spirit, cloud your judgement, or prevent you from living your life.

My outlook on life depended on where I was standing. "Don't like the view?" Big Steena would always say, "change your perspective. Unhappy with where you are in your life? Find another road. Your outlook determines your path. Your path is determined by you. No one else. If you don't believe it is, then you're looking at it from the wrong vantage point.

"If you assign your happiness to external circumstances, you will never find the one thing we all deserve… joy in life." Guruji's mantra rang true. I had to be happy with myself instead of expecting others to make me happy.

These thoughts of reinforcement had become my mantra. I needed to broaden my horizons. Think bigger. Look further. My self-pep talks brought me to a realization. I had to get out of New York. The doctor cleared me to fly and by November 1st, I was on a plane to Miami. I chose to recover in the one place that brought light to my spirit. I had to change my environment to help me change my mind.

I needed to get resourceful. I heard through the grapevine that a longtime dancer friend of mine needed to sublet an apartment in New York, as he was starting a new Broadway show and had no place to live. So, my rent was covered in New York. I had a couple thousand in the bank from my last choreography gig, so that would pay my mortgage and fill my refrigerator in Miami for a few months. That was about as far as my mind would go before I mentally hit a brick wall. I only seemed capable of solving the immediate problems that popped up in front of me. My mind would become emotionally depleted when I tried to process too much life at one time. At least right now, I could only live in the moment. That moment, turned into seven months.

I woke one morning, my heart racing from a dream. Drenched in a cold sweat, I forced myself to sit up. I was now able to pull my legs off the bed by just using my abs to place my feet on the floor. My arm was still strapped in the Jobst stocking. Constantly itchy and sweaty from the Miami heat, I had to do everything I could to not rip it off. I pried the sleep from my eyes recalling the dream. Big Steena and I were on the beach in Maui. He was describing the behavior of the ocean to me.

"The soup changes every day, just like life," he said. "You never know what to expect. It's better not to expect anything and your possibilities will be endless." He nonchalantly threw the words away like tossing a coin in a fountain and off on his surfboard he went.

"No expectations, endless possibilities," I repeated his words.

We often think that when drastic occurrences happen in our lives that it is a setback. Of course, there are two sides to this coin. It comes down to how you look at it.

If you follow the positive path, it can be a real catalyst for change.

Change is the Universal wake-up call. Change is the one constant in life. When we look at our experiences from the past, we may realize that the hardest parts in our path are the transitions. Transitions are forks in the road which make us choose which direction to move in. These decisions usually force us to make a choice. Sometimes it will be the right choice and sometimes it won't. Often times though, the "wrong choice" is not really wrong at all, it's just a greater challenge than we expected. The best solution for this transition is to never expect anything. Lowering your expectations can ultimately give you endless possibilities. That must have made an impression on me when I was just 18. Now, at 36 years of age, I pulled that lesson out of the back reaches of my cranium, through a dream. Big Steena was clearly trying to tell me something in my dreams. I really missed him.

It became another "a-ha" moment for me. I had come full circle. I realized that when I was young, I discovered the majesty of the sea. Throughout my life, I had found solace from what the sea gave me. Now, in my mature years, I came back to the one place that fed my soul and allowed me to just...be.

One morning, I was rummaging through a bag I had in the closet and found the sarong Bill had given me that very first week I got to LA. I dropped my drawers and wrapped it around my waist. The bright yellow fabric felt like silk on my skin. This was great! Unlike shorts, that would rub on my tender legs, the sarong allowed me better movement and I could go free-wheeling without a care! This was my new go-to outfit around the house. The memory made me miss my cousin too.

I pulled out of the same bag, the japa mala beads Guruji gave to Lori and I in India. The memories came flooding back. "Believe in what seems impossible. This represents your inner fire. Your heart's desire shows the reasons behind your actions and what you really want in life, as well as in love. It is behind all choices we make in our lives, including our career and our relationships. Our heart's desire was based on what we really payed attention to. If you do this, you will always fulfill your dreams. Wake up and listen to your heart."

I was emotionally half asleep. I knew myself and I could sometimes be guilty of complacency, getting too comfortable in my set ways. I would see others get to a point where they let opportunities go, losing sight of goals, or give up entirely. This person was now me. Watching the days go by, I would sit on my balcony from early morning at sunrise and watch the sun set in the evening. My taut dancer's body was now a soft spongy bagel. My brain was mush. Just a cauldron of random strings of thought with no rhyme or reason. My life was literally at a standstill.

I needed to get pro-active with my healing. I had essentially given up. I had no reason to get up in the morning and was just allowing each day to saunter by. My life had become as fleeting as a wave. The comparison of life to a wave, was not that far off. Like a wave that is generated at the furthest reaches of the world, so too is life. A wave rolls thousands of miles from its creation, enduring bumps, storms, and blue skies along the way. Life swells, engages, endures, and finally comes to rest. Therefore, nothing last forever. Our trials, tribulations, joys, and success all come and go. But like a surfer, we need to find that urge to seize our wave, ride its face, and take life's journey through to its final stage.

I was not at my final stage yet. This was my second act. I was going to start working on this… first thing tomorrow.

And I did. It was a slow start, so I did a lot of contemplating. I attempted to put a workout routine together that would help me build the strength in my legs again. I had very shallow breathing, so some type of movement to get my heart rate up, make me sweat, and build up endurance was necessary. I knew my body very well. I needed to lose about 15 pounds to feel better. I started eating fruit and yogurt in the morning with an occasion scrambled egg with garlic and onions. My lunch was grilled chicken and broccoli. My dinner was a hearty beef soup that my grandmother would make us as kids to build strong bones and boost our immune system. I ate like this every day for six weeks.

In two months' time, I could pull my legs up to my chest from a standing position while keeping my balance. My breathing was stronger and deeper. I lost 21 pounds and could actually see my abdomen again. It was time to take the surfboard to the beach and get in the water.

I could walk to the beach from my apartment. It was a peaceful walk, only a few blocks and I could see the expanse of the sea come into view.
I passed a tall overly tanned man layered in sweaters and sweatpants, barefoot. He seemed to have all of his belongings in one tattered bag, flung over his shoulder. He didn't seem to notice me, his mind deep in thought. He was distracted, distant. He had that look of unsureness in his eyes, as if he just didn't know what to do. He painfully sat down on the curb. His next step would be a life altering decision. I could sense his utter despair, as he contemplated. I wondered what the series of circumstances could have been that brought him to this place in life. That could be me. Or anyone. How many decisions are we away from the end of life's rocky road?

The robust bougainvillea greeted the morning warmth, their paper-like flowers strewn across the intersection as I crossed Ocean Drive to the wide-open beach.

It was my sanctuary. The minute my bare feet stepped into the soft warm sand it seemed like my troubles simply washed away with the outgoing tide. With the sultry sun on my face, it didn't take long for me to find my deep breathing again. The gentle breeze seemed to release those mental blocks and repetitive thoughts that had kept my mind a prisoner for almost a year.

I was beach side waxing my board for probably the thousandth time in my life. About 10 feet from shore the seagulls were having a frenzied feast in the water. No doubt gorging on a school of unsuspecting fish that came too close to the sand.

The high tide splashed at my feet calling me to play. A faint smell of beached seaweed filled the air - salty, pungent. A long column of morning sun, that breached the horizon about an hour before, seemed to line up with me and my morning ritual. It glimmered on the water top like a path, inviting me to come experience her grandeur.

In a quick reaction, the seagulls took flight from their feeding spot. No doubt, a slightly larger predator wanted to feed in the same place. The birds called and screeched alarming the others to move out fast. They circled the air and descended back to earth. A spinning cyclone of white beauties came to land all around me. I stopped waxing the board to watch the knee jerk reaction of nature. I stood the board upright in the sand and observed. Within minutes, I was center circle of a mass of seagulls, now looking out towards the sun and sea, deciding their next move. That seemed to be everyone's next thought.

It reminded me again why the beach was in my DNA.

Chapter 25

Within the Dimmest Light…

I breached the azure waters in South Beach. Below 5th street was my favorite part of the beach. Quiet, reserved, and often the place where most of the surfers went. I struggled to get on my board for a few moments, as if I forgot how to mount it. "It's just like getting back on a horse after you've fallen off," I told myself in an attempted pep talk.

I practiced popping up to my feet. Maneuvering the new strength in my legs felt almost foreign. My newly skinned and dominant arm seemed stronger, yet still strapped in my python-like bandage. Being barefoot on the deck of my board felt familiar. My feet had no problem making the connection again. Being barefoot helped me maintain the appropriate range of motion in both feet and ankle joints, as well as better strength and stability within the muscles and ligaments. I needed to just focus on today.

One challenging day of recovery, I was in the surf, struggling with my board. I had not slept well the night before and everything I did seemed forced. I left my board on shore and walked out into the sea. Letting the water cradle me, I gave into the resistance between my mind and my body. I lay back in the blue-green water and let my physique float on the surface. As I lay there being held and caressed by the soothing sea, I could feel the tension in my shoulders release. Then my lower back relaxed and then my hips followed. It was literally a chain reaction. The more I let go and gave my body up to the floating sensation, the more my body simply unwound! Since that day, not a time goes by that I don't wade into the waters and float, sometimes for an hour at a time!

It was time I started to treat myself with more kindness. The berating and belittling of my situation were not helping me heal, but kept opening up the same wound. I would go back and forth blaming myself or blaming others for my situation. But no matter what circle I ran around in, mentally, I was still where I was, regardless.

So, I chose to start accepting myself as I slowly started to let go of the blame. I knew I was doing my best for the moment and that had to be good enough. My tendency to be critical of myself gave me drive and ambition when I was younger, but being over critical was now deterring me from being good to myself. The times I would give myself a break and be more kind, the more

I started to feel a difference. "Don't underestimate the power in forgiving yourself." Those words rang through me over and over. Although my time was brief with Guruji, my yoga teacher in India, his words echoed within me.

Since my path was unclear, it was necessary to begin forging a new one. I thought clearer in the water, so I needed to go back and face my thoughts.

I floundered around for months and months. Money was starting to get thin and I noticed I was becoming more and more frugal, trying to make ends meet. The only saving grace in my life was my ability to walk to the beach and surf each morning. It is how I would start each a.m. and sometimes finish each day.

I was led to the water by surfing in my formative years and had continued to be drawn back to it my whole life. It was now time to give back that same peace that surfing bestowed on me.

All I needed, was a direction to move towards. I just needed the "where," not the "how." I knew from my past experiences that once I began to walk another path, as long as I trusted the process, the answers would begin to reveal themselves to me. I was done thinking my way into a new life, I had to act my way into one.

My old buddy, Antonio, who I knew from the gym in New York, had moved to Ft Lauderdale and started a business on a newfangled contraption called the Internet. You could buy space on the Internet and call it your site, or website. You would choose a name and then set up your space. He was making money from his home computer by selling subscriptions to his website information.

I chose a website name and Antonio helped me set up the pages. I figured I could share my experiences with surfing and maybe, life in general. I bought items at the 99-cent store that were related to my stories and sold them on the website along with little "how to books" that I would compile from my storytelling.

As I was so willfully taught by Guruji, if I was being proactive about money (or anything I wished for), it would eventually come my way. He was right. I would write an article each day. I would commit to paper my heartfelt stories about how I recovered from a serious accident, how I learned how to surf, and the best ways to cope with loss. I would sell surfer key chains, shells I would find on the beach, or a healing balm I would make in my kitchen that really helped nourish the scar on my skin.

In six months, I had a following of customers who would ask for a variety of different products. I found chat rooms for surfers, and healers, and artists who needed a place to sell their creations. My website became more about a place for healing others and helping those who needed some inspiration. This all stemmed from my cathartic process to heal myself.

After getting my business degree over 15 years before, it seemed as if I was finally executing even more of its tenets. I was making money. I continued to find products to sell on the website. I would create "themed" ideas or packages that would relate to the sea or surfing, recovery and healing, or seasonal gifts. The more I brought to the website, the more I would sell, often selling out of some items in just days.

I was constantly seeking that steady frame. This game, I incorporated into my life, had somehow become a belief as a surfer. A steady frame was my stance on a surfboard and became the foundation for my business. It was how I thought as a dancer. It was how I ran my production company, and it became a dependable formula. If you created a solid foundation or steady frame, you would have more space for the creativity within. Although, at the time, I hadn't made the connection.

I worked on establishing myself as an expert. I found a class at the Learning Annex that discussed how to use the Internet to establish your credentials, experiences, and insights on topics you were familiar with. If you felt comfortable about sharing your knowledge, then you were encouraged to write a learning manual that others could purchase.

I learned very early in life about business and didn't even realize it. The teeter totter that was my surfboard was a great metaphor for business. Walk too far forward or too far back and you lose your center of gravity. If you want to turn, you pivot on your axis, but only if you are balanced beneath yourself. Making rash decisions could sink you. Keeping yourself afloat, depended on how you maneuvered your business and the direction you would take. In business, you needed to be flexible. What may have sold for months and months, could now be overdone and sales would begin to slip. Creating a similar product or an offshoot of that waning product, could empower a new uptick in sales.

I was now finding my focus and setting the stakes higher. I would sometimes reach my website sales goals or sometimes fail, but it was important to then reach them again. As I achieved my goals or certain set of rules. I would raise the stakes and challenge my previous format. This constantly kept my website growing. I had good habits and a far-sighted outlook.

Within the dimmest light, there was hope. The dimmest light meant that even though the glow seemed nearly gone, there remained a spark that could still ignite. This positive outlook strung me along like fish towards bait. I just kept pulling myself along. In a year's time, my Internet business was helping to support me.

I was now struggling with a different matter. The board that had been so perfectly suited for me in my youth was no longer right for who I'd become. I decide to put an ad out for a used board on the Internet. In days, I came home with a longboard. It was easier to maneuver in the water, more buoyant, and made more sense for my condition and the level I was struggling with.

So back to the beach I went, dragging this enormous nine-and-a-half-foot board down the street. I went below 5th street to the cove at the end of South Beach. Along the walk, the intoxicating scent of jasmine flowers stirred a memory in my head I couldn't quit put my finger on.

I waxed about half of the board, unsure as to what I was doing. Yet, I knew the wax would keep me from sliding off this gigantic plank, so I massaged the ointment where I thought my bare feet would land when I popped up on the board. I felt like a complete novice again, but I knew there would be a learning curve, so I needed to get over it. The waves were gentle as I paddled out.

In a few weeks, the longboard gave me the ease and balance I needed. Although large and cumbersome, it was light enough for me to manage on the water. As I had learned, over and over, trust and assurance would find its way back to me, like a lost puppy. I was surprised that after all these years and for every time I found my way back, that I still doubted its resurgence.

I needed the adrenaline and push of the waves. The water dictated the direction I would go in life. The sea's fluid movement would cradle my spirit and allow me to forget the stress I would accumulate. Surfing had always been the one thing that lightened the load. Dance was my career but surfing was my lifeline. It took a long time for me to make that distinction. Surfing was my connection to nature and when the water would surround me, it would engulf my soul, giving me a sense of true awareness. The smallest of things could bring hope into our lives. We just needed to be more in tune with them.

My youthful heart still held the buoyancy of promise. Even though it was scarred by the ravages of time and life's journey, there was still hope. There were still possibilities to explore.

I only needed to give myself permission. I remembered the moment I told myself that once I stopped dancing, I would pursue acupuncture as a second career. It would give me the opportunity to treat many disorders and help people talk through their problems or emotional issues.

Big Steena would remind me that "there was no perfect time to do anything." No matter what point in your life you've reached, we can always find a reason not to do something.

“I'm too old. I don't have enough money. I don't have enough time”, or any other deterrent we could find to derail life. Our life was in constant flux. The water taught me that. It changed daily, and if you kept saying you'll do something eventually, the tide changes and so does the window of opportunity.

At 37, I was going to go back to school? I needed to take a leap of faith. After looking back at all the quests I'd been given in my life, it was time to pay attention and take the risk.

I discovered, first hand, what it was like to go back to school. The first day of school was a scary prospect for me. Being an adult student, among students half my age was a special concern. I was worried I'd feel rusty. Was I technologically-savvy as my other classmates? Could I keep up? Was I sharp enough to really learn again? There were other "second career" students in school with me, which in some way, gave me comfort that I was not alone. Still, I had to prove it to myself. By this stage in life, you were more likely to have multiple responsibilities, requiring you to juggle commitments to school, family, and employers. Some of my colleagues were haunted by earlier, negative experiences when they first went to school. Previous drop-outs were anxious about being able to complete the program this time around. Of course, all of these concerns were legitimate, yet none were insurmountable.

In other ways, I had valuable experiences to offer. I thought about the significant lessons I had learned since I was last in school. No doubt, I'd learned a great deal about human relationships through a broad range of interactions over my 30-some years. I learned much about health and medicine through my life, as well as illness and injury. I learned that lessons could happen anywhere. Clearly, I didn't have to be in a classroom to learn. Not only were my life and work experiences valid, they could surely give me an advantage over many of my less experienced classmates. Making the connections between classroom studies and lifetime experiences would only enrich my practice.

I quickly had to learn how to manage my time effectively while also establishing good study habits. By being efficient, I could get ahead of myself and not fall behind. I had to learn to say "no" to my responsibility overload. I had to relearn my good study habits by mastering my learning style. I seemed to learn best by repeating what I was taught and then reciting it back either on paper or orally.

Sometimes, I would record my lectures and create my own study notes from the audio recordings. This kept me more organized. If I broke big tasks down into smaller ones, I could make my work more manageable. Instead of buying so many heavy books, I would use the textbooks in the school's library or find good Internet resources.

The school I chose was only six blocks from my apartment in New York. I did not have to be concerned about commuting a long distance. I did not have to worry about student housing in a city I didn't know. Thanks to my friend Antonio, I now had an Internet business that helped sustain me so I could concentrate on school. This also gave me the knowledge to work on and understand the Internet and computers. This proved to be a great benefit in school.

My school counselor suggested we, as students, develop a support network. Sometimes, it just helped to know that I was not alone. There were students like me, who shared similar interests and concerns. I was not the only second career student. When things would get tough, I would think of the reasons I decided to return to school and this kept my eye on the prize. My support group became four students, all whom were on their second careers.

Stacey was a fun loving, bright girl who had a positive attitude. She had an infectious smile and was always willing to learn. Stacey was practical and smart. She seemed like the kind of girl I'd known forever. Ellie was more of a detached beauty who was easy-going and matter of fact. I suspected she was shy and was just trying to get the lay of the land and the rhythm of how the school and the city worked. The more I got to know her, the more she seemed to let her guard down. Jeanne reminded me so much of a girl from my past, but I wasn't sure who. She had a career as an established and well-heeled artist with work in New York's Museum of Modern Art. She saw parallel connections between healing and making art. One day in class there was a guy sitting in front of me, covered in body tattoos from the nape of his neck to the crease in his ankles. I said to myself, "I know those tattoos." Phillip, my surf buddy from Montauk had decided to go back to school too. It was hard to believe he chose acupuncture, the same school I picked, and at the same time! The serendipity of life never seized to amaze me. I had found my support network.

Being in school this time around, I was much more mindful. When I first went to college, all I really cared about was dance. I was not even sure how I got through all my business classes. I was asleep at that wheel. Somehow, I did manage it. But this time, I was truly aware of my learning process and fully in tune with what my end goal had to be.

During one of our school breaks, Stacey, Ellie, and Jeanne, came to Miami and spent a day visiting me. We made our way to the beach to find one of the largest swells I'd seen in a very long time. Mesmerized by the giant waves, we were drawn to the water immediately. We spent hours bobbing up and down in the warm surf, body surfing the waves to shore, and laughing and sharing the day together. These were new friends who loved the water. Maybe my passion for the sea was contagious but they seemed drawn to it as much as me, perhaps with not quit as much understanding of the water's hypnotizing appeal.

Afterwards, we had lunch on my terrace before they were off to visit more friends in the Keys. These girls were my study buddies, but that day, we become so much closer and bonded in a very special way that I would never forget. Their love for the sand and surf, the effort they made to visit me in Miami, and the fact that the day was so effortless, made me reminisce about my old buddies in LA.

It seemed the older we became, the more we looked back at the memories and the moments in our lives that defined us. I remembered that little book my mother gave me at 15 years old. The little book of the Universe, expanded my mind. It would play itself out in many ways over the course of my lifetime.

Like each celestial body that occupied their place in space, we also orbited around our earthly world, sometimes passing each other in the furthest of places not ever sensing one another. Then, sometimes we moved passed those who influenced our every gesture. Maybe for years, maybe just for a moment, as we each traveled on our own particular trajectory. The influence could be strong or subtle, depending on what we were made of and what we were seeking. Their brief presence in our lives could change us forever.

On September 10, 2001, my parents, brother and his wife were all celebrating their wedding anniversary. We decided to meet in Manhattan and go to the bar at Windows on the World for drinks. It was amazing to go back up in those high-speed elevators again. This time I was showing my family where I had worked all those years earlier at the start of my career. We enjoyed a nice evening and parted ways in the late evening.

I was on my way to meet my friend Antonio for an early breakfast the following morning. He lived in the Murray Hill area in the East 20s so it was easy for me to walk over from my apartment. Crossing Fifth Avenue, I stopped for the light. I noticed dozens of people looking downtown. In an instant the first plane hit the North Tower of the World Trade Center. I immediately thought about my old friends, Kimberly and Michael. I assumed in my mind, that after 18 years, they would not still be there. At least, that's what I chose to believe. I couldn't bear to think otherwise. My heart rose into my throat.

That became a tragic day in American history. It showed the world just how vulnerable and complacent we had become. The fact that my entire family just barely missed being a casualty in one of the more spectacularly tragic catastrophes of the century, haunted me for years afterwards.

Death had a way of changing the fabric of life. For some, the fabric teared and frayed at the edges, losing its tension and purpose. For others, death was like a stain that you just couldn't get out, as it lingered onward. Yet for others, it was an opportunity to flow. It could be the permission one felt they were given, after someone passed, in order to continue to move forward. For me it was the latter. I was at the end of one career and standing on the precipice of another. In some ways, studying acupuncture and Chinese

Medicine felt like a tribute to Big Steena and what he stood for. It was a chance for me to move on from my dance career and continue my life's flow.

Sting Ray saw an opportunity to open his own Surf and Shake shop in Venice Beach after Big Steena encouraged him to have a steady business to keep money in his pocket so that he could "continue to surf and woo the girls till the end of time." Sting Ray took his advice.

JackO had a different fate. Big Steena was like a father to him. He was someone who took JackO in when his mother lost her life. He taught JackO valuable life skills, ways of coping with the emotional pain, and giving him a hand up when he needed it most. He believed in JackO and JackO was devastated over his loss. He was eventually given Big Steena's house and inherited his money. In return, JackO honored his memory by carrying on Big Steena's love and legacy for the neighborhood and for surfing.

Canter married Maria, the dance teacher from the Venice Beach Skate and Dance Studio. They had a little girl named Ariel. The three of them shared a little apartment in Malibu. By the time I saw them again, Ariel was five years old and Canter already had her jumping on a surfboard in the middle of the living room!

Bill now had a lawn and home care business. He had ten employees that he would send all over Los Angeles. Now, the bulk of his business was in the 90210-area code. He had an office and a fleet of trucks running all over the city. He had not been surfing for almost a year. That was, until I came back to Los Angeles for a visit and reintroduced my cousin to the joys of surfing on a longboard.

I smiled at my cousin. So much had changed since that shy, awkward kid from a farm in upstate New York had come to visit his relatives in California.

"Let's go," I said to Bill.

*****

The pungent taste of salt christened my tongue as I hit the sea running. I always liked to get this blessing over with so that my body could adapt more quickly. As I dove into the frigid water, I could feel the back of my neck react to the brisk attack. My back zip, although covering me from neck to ankle, did not seem to keep me from feeling the Arctic blast that consumed my soul in that moment. “God, I hate cold water,” I thought. “What we do for love.”

I dashed a little further through the soup and then hopped on my longboard for the appropriate paddle out. I loved to pushout past the wave breaks to a point in the sea, that I knew was “the spot.”

My cousin Bill was close behind me, paddling out like a stealth fighter, seen but not heard. I looked back over my shoulder to see if he was with me. He reached up and gave me a Shaka, so I knew he was alright. This is where we stood dawn patrol.

The sun was just starting to stretch and exert himself over the Eastern horizon. His fingers slowly creeping over each wave awakening the lazy seals that were lying languid on the rocks along the Northern face of the jagged mount protruding from the sea.

It was the perfect day!

Surf Terms

A-frame – a wave-shaped like a peak that breaks both left and right, equally

Air or Aerial – is a maneuver in which the board leaves the surface or the water/wave

Backdoor – going inside a tube/barrel, also known as the curl of the wave, from behind its peak

Barrel – a tube, the curl of the wave, the hollow part of a wave when it is breaking, and one of the most sought-after in surfing

Beach break – the places where the waves break over sandbars

Bottom turn – a turn that is made at the bottom of the wave

Break – when the swell of the water breaks, turning into waves and white water

Carve – a maneuver that is a sharp turn on the face of the wave

Caught inside – being caught between the shoreline and the breaking waves

Charging – aggressively going for a wave

Choppy – rough waves due to wind conditions

Closeout – when a wave breaks suddenly and all at once

Crest– the highest point of a wave, the top of the wave

Curl – the area of the wave where it is breaking

Cutback– a surf move done sharply in the shoulder or the wave or on its flats to get back on the surf line

Dawn patrol – going surfing first thing in the morning

Deck– the top surface of a surfboard

Ding – any damage done to your surfboard

Drop – the first part of a ride, when the surfer goes down the face of the wave

Drop-in – cutting off another surfer on their wave

Duck Dive – ducking under the oncoming wave in order to conserve energy

Face or Wave Face – surfers ride from the area that is breaking, toward the unbroken section of the wave called the shoulder or face

Greenroom or Inside the Greenroom– the inside of a barrel

Grey Suits – sharks

Hang Loose – the salutation that accompanies the sign of Shaka

Hang Ten – riding a surfboard with both feet placed on the nose of the board and your toes hanging over the nose

Header – to fall off a surfboard from the front, head first

Heavy – big, awesome waves that are sometimes dangerous

Hollow – barrels, tubes

Impact zone – the place where the waves are breaking the hardest and where beginners tend to get hurt

Inside – the place between the shore and the impact zone

Into the soup – inside the foam, the white water

Kneeboard– a special type of board meant for riding on knees

Kook – a rookie surfer or someone who isn't very good at surfing

Leash – the piece of material that ties the leg to the surfboard

Left – a wave that breaks on the left of the surfer, from the peak

Line up – the area in the water, away from the swell, where the surfers wait to get their turn at catching a wave

Lip– the upper-most part of a wave, right before it breaks

Localism – hostility by local surfers towards non-local surfers

Locked in – when a surfer gets caught inside a crashing wave

Longboard – a surfboard with a round nose that is at least 8 foot long

Magic Zone – the area you should catch the unbroken wave on the wave's face at a 45-degree angle in order to time your pop up

Making the drop – catching a wave and sitting on the lower part of the wave's shoulder

Maxed out –waves that are too large to break without closing out

Noodle arms – tired arms

Nose – the front and pointed part of the surfboard

Off the lip – re-entry

Offshore – winds that are blowing from the shore towards the ocean

Onshore – winds that are blowing from the ocean towards the shore

Outside – the place beyond the lineup; beyond the place where the waves break

Overhead – when a wave is higher than an average surfer

Peak– the highest point of a breaking wave that generates both left and right surfable shoulders

Peeling – when a wave breaks perfectly

Pocket – the power pocket of a barrel or powerful wave and where you want to position yourself

Pointbreak – a type of wave that is found around a point of land, a coastline with a headland

Pop up – the move surfers make to move from lying on the surfboard to standing up to surf

Pull in – turning the surfboard up to enter a barrel

Quiver – a surfer's surfboard collection

Rails– the sides of the board

Raked over – to be pounded by strong waves when paddling out to catch a wave

Re-entry – when a surfer goes through or over the lip of the wave and then goes back in

Regular footed – a surfer who surfs with their left foot forward (this means that they don't face the wave on lefts)

Right – a wave that breaks on the right of the surfer, from the peak

Riptide– a stretch of water that is particularly turbulent

Set – a series of waves that are approaching the lineup

Shaka – a sign surfers use, made from extending the thumb and the little finger

Shape– a word used to rate the quality of the breaking waves

Shore break – mostly unsurfable waves that break right on the shore

Shoulder – the part of the breaking wave that is unbroken

Soft board – a surfboard with a soft surface, meant for beginners

Soup – whitewater

Stick– a surfboard

Swell – surfable waves

Tail– the backside of the board

Tombstoning– when the surfer wipes out and the surfboard is lying on top of the water

Tube – barrel, the hollow of the wave

Turtle roll – a technique used to get the surfboard to go through a breaking wave

Twin fin – a twin fin surfboard

Washing machine – getting rolled around underwater by a breaking wave

Wax– the substance surfers use on their surfboard to help with traction

White water – a broken, foamy wave

Wipeout – falling off a wave while surfing

*** An extra-special "Shaka" and thank you to Gabe Keegan of Surfing-Waves.com for the additional surf terms.

Soundtrack to this Surfer's Life

Summer Breeze, Seals and Croft

Live Life, The Kinks

I Haven't Stop Dancing Yet, Gonzalez

Music Is My Way of Life, Patti LaBelle

Don't Stop Me Now, Queen

Beach Baby, The First Class

Ventura Highway, America

Boogie Wonderland, Earth Wind & Fire

Ride Like the Wind, Christopher Cross

Walking on Sunshine, Katrina & the Waves

Over the Rainbow, Israel Kamakawiwo'ole

Dancing in the Moonlight, King Harvest

Never Alone, Anthony Evans

Pull Up to The Bumper, Grace Jones

You're the One for Me, D Train

Dance Forever, Ashford and Simpson

Paradise, Change

Drum Circle, Arambol, Goa

One Night in Bangkok, Murray Head

Fantasy, Earth Wind & Fire

Boys of Summer, Don Henley

You Can Do Magic, America

On the Beach, Chris Rea

Pay It Forward

Thank you!

I am grateful you have taken this journey with me. It means so much.

The first way to pay it forward is by writing a review of this book (preferably on Amazon.com) to let others know of the benefits you've gained from this. It will not only help others reach their goals, but it is incredibly rewarding for me to know how much my work has benefited others, as well as learning any ways I can improve. This way you can help empower others in the way this book has empowered you.

Showing others kindness goes a long way. A smile is one of the most powerful actions we can produce. A smile breaks down barriers, eases insecurities, and gives back to you, a sense of peace.

Gratitude is the humblest of gifts to offer. When we are grateful, we are aware. When we are aware, we are more conscious. When we are more conscious, we are in tune with the positive and natural vibrations of the Universe. Say, thank you to those who offer you…anything.

Emphasize and support positivity in your life. Positivity is all around you. It is up to you to (constantly) see it and share it. It will give you the uplifting, kick-in-the-butt, wake-up call that is a great practice to implement.

Support those around you...in work and in life. None of it, some of it, or all of it may be something you do or do not believe in, but their path is their own. Your simple encouragement can lift up another to a place of empowerment. Be that person.

Volunteer some time for others or a cause that has meaning for you. Not only does this take you out of your thoughts, but the giving back to those in need, will offer your spirit a forward step.

Value your privilege. Love, honor, and respect these gifts you've been given. They can go as quickly as they came. Make sure they remain special.

In happiness,

Andrew Pacholyk, MS, L.Ac

Resources

Essential Oils

https://www.peacefulmind.com/essential-oils
Andrew's own line of organic essential oils sourced from all over the world! Angel's Mist essential oils are 100% pure therapeutic grade oils used in any aromatherapy remedy or solution.

Herbs, Incense & Teas

https://www.peacefulmind.com/herbs-and-teas
Fresh, organic herbs, teas, vitamins, supplements and specialty herbs, and highly scented hand-rolled incense sticks, cones and raw herbal resins.

Crystals and Stones

https://www.peacefulmind.com/crystals
Huge selection of high-quality crystals, stones, crystal jewelry, crystal pouches, pendulums and specialty gifts at fair market prices.

Metaphysics & Energy Medicine

https://www.peacefulmind.com/metaphysics
Healing spiritual and emotional tools including Chakra gifts, Aura Kits, themed gifts including Mermaids, Elements, Seasons, Dreams, Spirit gifts

Candle Therapy

https://www.peacefulmind.com/candle-therapy
Beautifully, hand-crafted, highly scented candles created with love. 3-in-1 candles with exceptional scents, lovely charms and educational references wrapped around these healing tools of light!

Certification Home Study Courses

https://www.peacefulmind.com/courses
Since, 1998, Andrew and Peacefulmind.com make it possible for anyone to study energy medicine at home, on your time! Endorsed by the National Association of Holistic Wellness, we have certified thousands of students and launched the careers of practitioners all over the world. We continue to lead the way in providing the best and most up-to-date information and exciting new courses!

Made in the USA
Columbia, SC
01 May 2022